THE POSTFOUNDATIONALIST
TASK OF THEOLOGY

The Postfoundationalist Task of Theology

Wolfhart Pannenberg and the New Theological Rationality

F. LeRon Shults

WILLIAM B. EERDMANS PUBLISHING COMPANY
GRAND RAPIDS, MICHIGAN / CAMBRIDGE, U.K.

Printed in the United States of America

04 03 02 01 00 99   7 6 5 4 3 2 1

Library of Congress Cataloging-in-Publication Data

Shults, F. LeRon.
The postfoundationalist task of theology:
Wolfhart Pannenberg and the new theological rationality / F. LeRon Shults.
p.   cm.
Includes bibliographical references.
ISBN 0-8028-4686-6 (pbk.)
1. Pannenberg, Wolfhart, 1928 — Contributions in theological methodology.
2. Theology — Methodology — History — 20th century. I. Title.
BR118.S525 1999
230′.044′092 — dc21   99-046840

To Elizabeth

my wife, who loves not only in word
but also in deed (1 John 3:18)

Contents

Foreword

While much of the current talk on postmodernity remains somewhat obscure, one of the real issues is the criticism of foundationalist claims as they developed in modern thought either in empiricist or intellectualist fashion. There is no a priori warrant of truth if only one bases one's argument on the proper foundation, be it sense perception or principles of reason. Even theological arguments cannot be convincingly derived from some pure source of revealed truth. It has first to be established by argument what can be considered as God's revelation. Even in the case of Scripture there is no a priori guarantee, since Scripture is also human and historical, though Christians hear the Word of God from it. Theological reconstruction itself remains tentative like the hypothetic reasoning in other disciplines, as I tried to show in several publications on the rational structure of theological thought. Professor F. LeRon Shults presents in his book *The Postfoundationalist Task of Theology* a very subtle and detailed analysis of my understanding of this issue and of its application in my own theology. He is correct in placing me neither in the foundationalist camp nor among certain forms of nonfoundationalism that surrender the rational quest for truth. I feel rather sympathetic with the position he describes as postfoundationalist. He correctly criticizes interpretations of my thought that take me to make anthropology the foundation of Christian theology. His book shows that anthropology rather gets "sublated" in the course of my argument, though I often start from anthropological data since in modern culture anthropology has been treated as the basis of religion. The importance of sublation or elevation into something else within the procedure of my argument is presented in this book with excellent clarity.

Wolfhart Pannenberg

Preface

My early childhood was spent in Pentecostal charismatic churches (which has raised the eyebrows of my more recent pastors), while my early adulthood was spent in mainline Presbyterian churches (which has furrowed the eyebrows of my earlier pastors). My sense of calling as a theologian emerged within and was nurtured by the matrix of Wesleyan-Arminian thought, yet my identity as a theologian was forged and shaped at Princeton Theological Seminary, an institution deeply rooted in the Reformed-Calvinist tradition. My initial philosophical training was in the "analytic" tradition (which subsequent teachers were to call "dry"), but I soon came into contact with and became immersed in "continental" philosophy (which earlier teachers had called "speculative"). This brief allusion to the contours of my autobiography may partially help to explain the ubiquity of the phrase "middle way" in the pages that follow!

This book is in fact shaped by my desire to bring into dialogue two traditions that historically have avoided (and often derided) each other: the analytic and continental streams of philosophical theology. Theologians influenced by the analytic tradition will be surprised that I see the problem with "foundationalism" as larger than simply deciding how to (or whether it is possible to) justify beliefs. Thinkers embedded in the continental tradition may be put off by my occasional use of the tools of analytic philosophy (which I have mostly limited to Chapter Two). Many of the misinterpretations of Pannenberg as a foundationalist, on the one side, and many of the dismissals of postmodernity as mere foolishness, on the other, are a result of the chasm between these philosophical approaches. By engaging representatives from both traditions, I hope to show how we can work together.

The last part of Chapter One offers a preview of the flow of my argument, and the first part of Chapter Five gives a summary of the main theses. The emerging "postfoundationalist" model of theological rationality outlined in this book aims to overcome the stalemate between dogmatic foundationalism and skeptical nonfoundationalism by challenging their shared assumptions about the relations between belief and experience, truth and knowledge, individual and community, and explanation and understanding. Proposing four "couplets" that link these emphases in the current dialogue about the nature and function of rationality, my goal is to illustrate how the *post*foundationalist model accommodates the positive intuitions of both foundationalism and nonfoundationalism without collapsing into either extreme. The postfoundationalist task of theology is to engage in interdisciplinary dialogue within our postmodern culture while *both* maintaining a commitment to intersubjective, transcommunal theological argumentation for the truth of Christian faith *and* recognizing the provisionality of our historically embedded understandings and culturally conditioned explanations of the Christian tradition and religious experience.

Wolfhart Pannenberg is identified as a surprising ally in this task — surprising because his work has often been viewed by North American theologians as foundationalist and modernist. I offer a new interpretation of Pannenberg's basic theological principle as understanding and explaining all things *sub ratione Dei* (under the aspect of the relation to God): this relationality is formally structured and materially filled out by the interpenetrating concepts of the true infinite and the Trinity. This reading of Pannenberg's theological method is corroborated by a careful analysis of the whole of his writings and is shown to subsume earlier popular interpretations of his key concept (reason, history, prolepsis). Using theological anthropology as a case study, I focus on Pannenberg's unique way of linking philosophical and systematic theology, demonstrating how this underlying methodological reciprocity may be carried over into the postfoundationalist's concern to link hermeneutics and epistemology in the contemporary postmodern context.

This new way of construing the task of theology develops out of a *reconstructive* interpretation of and response to "postmodernity." Most students of culture agree that "postmodernism" (whatever else it may be) includes a challenge to the Enlightenment "modernist" ideals of absolute truth, universal reason, autonomous subjectivity, and inevitable progress. Scholars differ widely, however, in the way they *respond* to this perceived challenge. We can classify these responses broadly into three types:

- *de*constructive response: fully affirm the postmodern challenge and conclude that because there is no neutral knowledge we must be content with a plurality of interpretations;
- *paleo*-constructive response: reject or ignore the challenge of postmodernity and appeal to an earlier premodern era in which truth and knowledge were allegedly unproblematic;
- *re*constructive response: attempt to distinguish the positive from the negative contributions of postmodernity and aim for a reconfiguration of the task of epistemology.

This book as a whole is driven by a desire to respond "reconstructively" at the intersection of historic Christian faith and contemporary culture. The specific conceptualization of the task of theology proposed herein is self-consciously molded by a concern to avoid the theological pitfalls of both the liberal "deconstructive" and the fundamentalist "paleo-constructive" responses to the postmodern challenge. The former sometimes renders Christian faith so diffuse that the boundaries that distinguish it from other voices in culture are nearly erased; theology loses its identity. The latter sometimes reacts so violently to the plurality of cultural forces that boundaries are reified into impermeable walls; theology becomes isolated. Neither of these approaches allows for authentic dialogue. We need a more subtle model of the relationality between theology and culture that captures their actual differentiation as well as their real coinherence. Such a model would support a praxis of authentic response that neither dissolves nor dissects and that refuses to settle for mere conflation or conjunction. I hope the efforts expended in the following chapters (especially Chapter Four) might contribute to this task as well.

Because my interest in "postmodernity" is much broader than French deconstructivism, I do not offer extensive treatments of the works of Foucault, Derrida, and company. While such analysis is important, it is beyond the scope of the current work. My focus will be instead on the *postfoundationalist* vision of the "postmodern" as a dynamic self-critical movement that shuttles back and forth between the privileging of hermeneutics and the valorizing of epistemic concerns.

While this book was in press, the journal *Kerygma und Dogma* published an issue with several helpful articles on Pannenberg's theology (45, no. 2 [April/June 1999]). Especially relevant for understanding his use of the concepts of true infinite and Trinity is Niels Henrik Gregersen's "Einheit und Vielfalt der schöpferischen Werke Gottes" (102-29). The article by Juan A. Martinez-Camino, SJ, "Aufhebung: Zur Architektur des ersten Bandes der Systematischen Theologie Wolfhart Pannenbergs" (91-101) confirms and complements my reading of the reciprocity in Pannenberg's method (Chapter Four below). At the back of the issue, Frederike Nüssel provides a Pannenberg bibliography from 1988 to 1998. The most thorough bibliography for works prior to 1988 may be found in Reginald Nnamdi's *Offenbarung und Geschichte* (1993).

I wish to express my gratitude to all of the teachers, pastors, and friends who have supported me during this project, and especially to my parents who have encouraged me in every step of the journey. Encountering Ray Anderson of Fuller Seminary was a major turning point in my career — through his influence I exchanged the goal of conclusively proving the existence of God on purely philosophical grounds for a desire to link theology and the life of the church. Encountering James Loder of Princeton Seminary marked a key transition in my spiritual life — he modeled the integration of rigorous theological analysis and wholehearted worship of God. I offer special thanks for the mentorship that became a friendship with

J. Wentzel van Huyssteen. As my Doktorvater, he not only shaped my view of rationality but continues to shape my vision of what it means to be a Christian theologian. Thanks also to the administration, faculty, and students of Bethel Seminary for providing an irrefragably committed yet irenic community of learning within which theologians are encouraged in their scholarship and nurtured in their faith.

Thanks to my beautiful children, Sara, Mischa, and Laura, for their limitless love and for their relentless theological questioning that always keeps me on my toes. Most of all, I thank my wife Elizabeth for all the delightful intimations of divine love that she continually and increasingly provides in our life together. To her this book is dedicated.

F. LeRon Shults
August 1999

Abbreviations for Works by Wolfhart Pannenberg

ATP   *Anthropology in Theological Perspective*

BQT   *Basic Questions in Theology* (2 volumes)

JGM   *Jesus — God and Man*

MIG   *Metaphysics and the Idea of God*

ST   *Systematic Theology* (3 volumes)

TKG   *Theology and the Kingdom of God*

TPS   *Theology and the Philosophy of Science*

WIM   *What Is Man?*

CHAPTER ONE

Introduction

In the last four decades of the twentieth century, the theological writings of Wolfhart Pannenberg have exerted considerable influence and elicited a wide variety of responses. With the recent publication of the English translation of the third and final volume of his *Systematic Theology*,[1] his full magnum opus is now available to a wider audience. This offers an opportunity for a fresh evaluation of his overall theological method, and raises anew the question of its significance and relevance for the ongoing constructive task of theology.

After the appearance of the first volume, Pannenberg was criticized for not taking seriously the postmodern challenge to traditional conceptions of rationality and truth. A common complaint was that his attempt to justify theological statements is tied to the epistemology of Enlightenment "foundationalism," which searches for immediately self-justifying beliefs to ground the knowledge of the autonomous rational individual. Even where the term "foundationalist" was not used, many scholars saw Pannenberg's approach as unacceptably mired in modernist assumptions, as a rationalistic theology searching

---

1. W. Pannenberg, *Systematic Theology*, vols. 1-3, trans. G. Bromiley (Grand Rapids: Eerdmans, 1991-98). Hereafter noted as ST, with volume number. Originally published as *Systematische Theologie* (Göttingen: Vandenhoeck & Ruprecht, 1988-93).

1

for neutral and universally valid foundations. In this book, I will attempt to show that this popular reading of Pannenberg is a misinterpretation of his methodology; further, I will suggest that the structural dynamics of his approach offer significant resources for the *post*foundationalist task of theology in our postmodern culture. But first let us understand the charges against him.

Responding to Pannenberg's Systematic Theology

In a detailed review of the first volume of Pannenberg's ST, Francis Schüssler Fiorenza wonders why he failed to enter into dialogue with significant North American theologians and philosophers who have dealt with similar methodological and epistemological issues. Fiorenza suggests that dialogue with French deconstructionists, neopragmatists, and Reformed epistemologists might have strengthened Pannenberg's influence on those who are steeped in these discussions on this continent, and (at least the latter two) might have provided resources for "understanding the truth of religious affirmations without necessarily falling into the fideism, subjectivism, and flight to commitment that Pannenberg fears."[2] Fiorenza points out that the discussion on foundationalism and nonfoundationalism (or antifoundationalism) is central to the North American debate, noting the attempt to "go beyond relativism and objectivism in its understanding of the relation among truth claims and communities of discourse, the human self, and reality." Yet, Fiorenza concludes that finally "Pannenberg takes the approach of a more *foundationalist* scientific model of rationality."[3]

William Placher also illustrates this common response. He notes the vast difference between the academic situations of theology in Germany and North America. For the latter, the focus is on "rationality and relativism, oppression and particularity. Debates about gender, race, sexual preference and class form part of the academy's

2. Francis Schüssler Fiorenza, "Review Essay: Wolfhart Pannenberg's *Systematic Theology,* Volume One," *Pro Ecclesia* 2 (1993): 239, at 237.

3. Schüssler Fiorenza, "Review Essay," p. 239. Emphasis added.

agenda."[4] Placher admires Pannenberg's contribution, noting that he "may well be the most erudite living Christian theologian," yet he seems

> to live in a world where some significant paradigms can be assumed: a world where Western tradition as a whole remains essentially unproblematic, where people generally seem to know what counts as a reasoned argument, and where theologians know what counts as "the theological tradition." One may envy that world or hate it, feel nostalgia for it, dream of restoring it or dismiss it as good riddance. But many of us trying to write theology in this country find it to be a world in which we do not live.[5]

In 1992, The Canadian Theological Society sponsored a special panel discussion on ST, I, the results of which were published in *Calvin Theological Journal*. Brian Walsh complained of a disappointment with what he sees as Pannenberg's attempt to write a "contextless theology." Noting Pannenberg's claim to present "simply the truth" of Christian doctrine, rather than merely a "European" theology, Walsh suggests that "too many of us have come to believe that the truth must be contextual in order to be known and lived, for us to feel very comfortable with this proclamation."[6] In his contribution to the symposium, Rory A. A. Hinton suggests the need to correct the "overtly rational character" of Pannenberg's view of truth, and argues that for Pannenberg, the "unrevisable *starting-point* is human rationality."[7] James Olthuis is sur-

---

4. William Placher, "Revealed to Reason: Theology as 'Normal Science,'" *The Christian Century* 109 (1992): 194.

5. Placher, "Revealed to Reason," p. 195.

6. Brian Walsh, "Introduction" to "Pannenberg's 'Systematic Theology, Vol. I': A Symposium," *Calvin Theological Journal* 27 (1992): 306. When Walsh states that "truth must be contextual to be known and lived," does this assertion apply only to Walsh's own context, or is it true of all contexts? If the former, on what basis is he criticizing Pannenberg, for whose context the assertion may not apply? If the latter, he is making the same kind of universal claim for which he chides Pannenberg. We will often have the opportunity to note this self-exempting fallacy in many of Pannenberg's critics.

7. Rory A. A. Hinton, "Pannenberg on the Truth of Christian Discourse: A Logical Response," *Calvin Theological Journal* 27 (1992): 317. Emphasis added.

prised that "Pannenberg seems to know nothing in this volume of post-modern despair, the plight of the hopeless and homeless, the disenfranchised."[8] Stanley Grenz, also a participant in the symposium, was much more supportive of Pannenberg's general goal of the pursuit of truth, recognizing Pannenberg's qualification of all human knowledge as provisional due to the unfinished nature of creation. Yet he, too, voices concern over the lack of sensitivity to the "situation" of the theologian, and worries about Pannenberg's "thoroughgoing rationalism."[9]

Reinhold Hütter sees Pannenberg's project in ST as thoroughly modern, based on a particular reading of modernity that ignores difference and the other, and attempts to defend the truth of Christian faith by simply presenting it before the "tribunal" of modern rationality. He suggests that "Pannenberg's life-project seems to come to a conclusion at the very moment when the plaintiff, modernity, has become the defendant."[10] Paul Stroble interprets Pannenberg as affirming the possibility of a "context-neutral" standpoint in theological work.[11] Gabriel Fackre notes that Pannenberg's dialogue partners are mostly Western European males, suggesting that his affirmation of a "universal rationality" is weakened by his lack of interaction with liberation theology and feminist critique.[12] Faye Schott makes a similar complaint when she notes that Pannenberg's conception of the "debatability of claims" itself presupposes a view that was developed by dominant males, and so does not describe all

8. James H. Olthuis, "God as True Infinite: Concerns about Wolfhart Pannenberg's *Systematic Theology*, Vol. 1," *Calvin Theological Journal* 27 (1992): 319.

9. Stanley J. Grenz, "The Irrelevancy of Theology: Pannenberg and the Quest for Truth," *Calvin Theological Journal* 27 (1992): 310. Grenz offers more expansive reasons for both his concerns about and his appreciation of Pannenberg in "Wolfhart Pannenberg: Reason, Hope and Transcendence," *The Asbury Theological Journal* 46, no. 2 (Fall 1991): 73-90, and "Pannenberg and Evangelical Theology: Sympathy and Caution," *Christian Scholar's Review* 20, no. 3 (1991): 272-85.

10. Reinhold Hütter, review of *Systematic Theology, I*, by W. Pannenberg, in *Modern Theology* 9 (January, 1993): 93.

11. Paul Stroble, review of *ST, I*, by W. Pannenberg, in *Journal of the American Academy of Religion* 61 (Summer 1993): 375-77.

12. Gabriel Fackre, review of *ST, I*, by W. Pannenberg, in *Interpretation* 47 (July, 1993): 304-6.

human history.[13] Although Don Schweitzer sees Pannenberg's ST as a resource for those working from the "underside of history," he decries the fact that "the scandal of the situation of the socially oppressed and marginalized" finds no expression in his theology, which is written in relation "to the worldview of the relatively affluent modern subject, for whom the natural sciences tend to be highly authoritative."[14]

Concern about Pannenberg's model of theological rationality certainly predated the publication of ST. We will have opportunity to review the literature on Pannenberg in the following chapters, so a few representative comments should suffice. In a 1977 dissertation, David McKenzie said that Pannenberg's "primary purpose is to realize [the] Hegelian ideal of a rational religion."[15] Among the so-called "Reformed" epistemologists we find a critique of Pannenberg's method by David Holwerda, who finds him overly optimistic about the autonomous reason of the modern individual. He suggests that Pannenberg's "central thesis is that reason precedes faith and provides the *foundation* on which faith rests."[16] In the American *Festschrift* for Pannenberg, John Cobb recognizes that Pannenberg affirms the historical and culturally conditioned nature of anthropological investigation, but wonders whether he sees that theology, too, is thus conditioned, or "whether the goal of pure neutrality and

---

13. Faye Schott, "Comparing Eberhard Jüngel and Wolfhart Pannenberg on Theological Method and Religious Pluralism," *Dialog* 31 (1992): 132. In her 1990 dissertation "God Is Love: The Contemporary Theological Movement of Interpreting the Trinity as God's Relational Being" (Lutheran School of Theology at Chicago), Schott compares Jüngel, Jenson, and Moltmann to Pannenberg and finds the latter's "historical" approach generally helpful.

14. Don Schweitzer, review of *ST, II,* by W. Pannenberg, in *Journal of the American Academy of Religion* 64, no. 3 (Fall 1996): 687-88.

15. David McKenzie, *The Rational Theology of Wolfhart Pannenberg: A Philosophic Critique* (Ph.D. diss., University of Texas at Austin), p. 122. McKenzie expanded his critique in *Wolfhart Pannenberg and Religious Philosophy* (Lanham, Md.: University Press of America, 1980).

16. David Holwerda, "Faith, Reason and the Resurrection in the Theology of Wolfhart Pannenberg," in *Faith and Rationality,* ed. Alvin Plantinga and Nicholas Wolterstorff (Notre Dame: University of Notre Dame Press, 1983), p. 304. Emphasis added.

objectivity remains intact." Because Pannenberg does not dialogue with the voices of the third world and feminist thought, Cobb implies that his anthropology is merely an analysis of North Atlantic males and their experience.[17]

The concerns in English-speaking circles about Pannenberg's model of theological rationality continued as the other volumes of ST were published. Paul Molnar argues that Pannenberg "*grounds* the truth of theology as well as interpretation of individual and social history in experience rather than in God" and that such grounding "embodies the very subjectivism which Pannenberg criticizes in Barth."[18] Henry Jansen critiques Pannenberg for apparently "appealing to a neutral viewpoint,"[19] a move that he notes is clearly in contradiction to Pannenberg's explicit methodological statements elsewhere. George Sumner argues that Pannenberg's "aim of giving talk about the divine a 'secure place in the reality of human self-experience' fails in its *foundationalist* hope."[20] In a summary of his contributions to contemporary theology, Christoph Schwöbel interprets Pannenberg as finding it "essential that the theologian can establish certain *foundational* principles outside the perspective of faith that would support the claims to universality made within that framework."[21] Others have complained of the "rationalizing thrust" in his theology,[22] and of his embrace "the putatively autonomous exercise of reason."[23]

---

17. John Cobb, Jr., "Pannenberg and Process Theology," in *The Theology of Wolfhart Pannenberg: Twelve American Critiques with an Autobiographical Essay and Response*, ed. C. E. Braaten and P. Clayton (Minneapolis: Augsburg, 1988), pp. 66, 70.

18. Paul Molnar, "Some Problems with Pannenberg's Solution to Barth's 'Faith Subjectivism'," *Scottish Journal of Theology* 48, no. 3 (1995): 330. Emphasis added.

19. Henry Jansen, *Relationality and the Concept of God* (Amsterdam: Rodopi, 1995), p. 185.

20. George Sumner, "Pannenberg and the Religions: Conflictuality and the Demonstration of Power in a Christian Theology of the Religions" (Ph.D. diss., Yale, 1994), p. 305. Emphasis added.

21. Christoph Schwöbel, "Wolfhart Pannenberg," in *The Modern Theologians*, 2nd edition, ed. David F. Ford (Oxford: Blackwell, 1997), p. 204. Emphasis added.

22. Donald G. Bloesch, review of *Systematic Theology, III*, by W. Pannenberg, in *Christianity Today* (August 10, 1998): 70.

23. Kevin Corcoran, review of *Systematic Theology, II*, by W. Pannenberg, in *Perspectives* 11 (May 1996): 22.

What do his critics mean when they posit "foundationalism" as grounds for dismissing Pannenberg's method? What do they mean by complaining he is too "rational"? They cannot mean simply that he utilizes an inferential structure in argumentation, that one assertion supports another. In this weak form such a criticism is uninteresting, for inferential reasoning is evident (or at least attempted) in the arguments of even the most relativist of postmodern nonfoundationalists. For the "foundationalist" charge to work, it must either make the (strong) claim that Pannenberg's method is laden with the pernicious baggage of classical modernist epistemology, with its search for neutral, necessary, self-justifying beliefs that ground all knowledge, or at least make the (moderate) claim that Pannenberg is a "weak" foundationalist, accepting some set of beliefs as properly basic (defeasible, but not requiring justification). I will argue that neither of these claims is tenable.

It is interesting to note that in the German reception of Pannenberg's work we do not find the "anti-Cartesian" anxiety that is so pervasive among Anglo-Americans. As we examine Pannenberg's putative "foundationalism" in the following chapters, it will be helpful to recognize that the term "foundation" for German thinkers may not always carry the weight that it does for others in the western academy. We can see this in the following German responses to Pannenberg's ST. Greiner argues that the foundational or basic principle (Grundprinzip) in Pannenberg's theology is authentically Jesus-centered; i.e., the pivotal point of his whole theology is Jesus' eschatological revelation of the future.[24] For K. Gózdz, Pannenberg's foundational theological and philosophical assumption, his basic starting point, is Jesus Christ as the meaning of all history.[25] According to R. Nnamdi, Pannenberg sees the task of theology as reflecting on human existence in the light of revelation, informed by the trinitarian mystery disclosed to the church. This is the starting point of true knowledge, though it is mediated through

---

24. Sebastian Greiner, *Die Theologie Wolfhart Pannenbergs* (Würzburg: Echter, 1988), p. 320.

25. Krzysztof Gózdz, *Jesus Christus als Sinn der Geschichte bei Wolfhart Pannenberg* (Regensburg: Pustet, 1988), pp. 15, 241.

philosophical-anthropological concepts.[26] George Augustin interprets Pannenberg's foundation *(Begründung)* as christological; his
starting point *(Grundansatz)* is the totality of the meaning of all reality and the revelation of the end of history in the individuality and
universality of Jesus Christ.[27]

These statements will make the philosophical hair of most
postmodern Anglo-Americans crawl. For these continental scholars,
however, the term "foundational" has no denigrating connotation.
This suggests, as we will argue in more detail in the following chapters, that the use of the term "foundation" (especially by a German)
does not necessarily make a scholar "foundation*ist.*" English-
speaking respondents, too, have identified foundations in Pannenberg without accusing him of foundation*ism,* in the epistemically
deleterious sense. James Bridges, e.g., in comparing Pannenberg to
Rahner, argues that for both of these theologians, anthropology is a
foundation and critical principle for their methods; however, he
notes that this does not mean that their anthropological perspectives are "external" to theology.[28] Similarly, R. Pasqauriello identifies Pannenberg's philosophical "foundations" in his ontological
concepts of prolepsis, retroactivity, and negative mediation, without
thereby accusing him of collapsing into "foundationalist" epistemology.[29]

The form and style of Pannenberg's volume III follows that of
the first two volumes; the language of postmodern contextuality is
still not in the spotlight. Actually, it is not even on the stage. This
leaves us with a critical question, which Robert Jenson formulates
particularly well in his review of volume II:

26. Reginald Nnamdi, *Offenbarung und Geschichte: Zur hermeneutischen Bestimmung der Theologie Wolfhart Pannenbergs* (Frankfurt am Main: Peter Lang, 1993), pp.
15-19, 446.

27. George Augustin, *Gott eint-trennt Christus? Die Einmaligkeit und Universalität
Jesu Christi als Grundlage einer christlichen Theologie der Religionen: ausgehend von Ansatz
Wolfhart Pannenbergs* (Paderborn: Bonifatius, 1993), pp. 69-71.

28. James T. Bridges, *Human Destiny and Resurrection in Pannenberg and Rahner*
(New York: Peter Lang, 1987), pp. 4, 13ff.

29. Ronald D. Pasquariello, "Pannenberg's Philosophical Foundations," *Journal
of Religion* 56 (1976): 338-47.

If postmodernity is or is going to be something really and materially new, then [Pannenberg's] *Systematic Theology,* in its preoccupation with the great problems of modernity and its paradigmatic exemplification of one sort of modernist thinking, will probably be an historical artifact from the day of its publication. If, as I myself suspect, postmodernity is a purely negative phenomenon, so that such substance as our world may now have will continue to be that of the Enlightenment and later modernity's effort to "overcome" the Enlightenment, it may happen that Pannenberg's work is disregarded only long enough to be rediscovered.[30]

Jenson has correctly identified the problem. How one understands "postmodernity" will shape one's response to Pannenberg's method. With such a great cloud of scholarly witnesses against Pannenberg, it may seem hopeless to come to his defense. At the very least, however, we ought to attempt to bring his ST into dialogue with the discussions of rationality in our context to determine whether they might even today, as Jenson suggests, contain material ready to be "rediscovered." Is Pannenberg's theological method only fit to be swept into a North American dustbin by postmodern critique? Is he the last of the "foundationalists," a dying breed who would simply wither away if brought into the critical gaze of nonfoundationalist philosophers? Does he actually think his theological use of reason is completely immune from the influence of his European context?

This study will answer no on all counts. But this negative answer will require a critique of the assumptions behind the questions. Here we will be aided by bringing Pannenberg into dialogue with the emerging "postfoundationalist" view of rationality, a dialogue that will be at once critical and mutually enhancing. Clearly, it is admitted that Pannenberg has not constructively interacted with postmodern critiques of rationality, nor does he use the language of contextuality so prominent in the American academy. Might it be

---

30. Robert Jenson, review of *ST, II,* by W. Pannenberg, in *First Things* 53 (May 1995): 61.

possible, however, that Pannenberg's actual theological performance is consonant (at least partially) with postfoundationalism, which is all about affirming the contextuality of traditions and interpreted experience, without giving up the drive for intersubjective and transcommunal conversation? At the very least, we need to account for the fact that he appears to recognize many of the insights of postmodernity. Even before the publication of ST Pannenberg makes clear, in a response to John Cobb, Jr., that he is aware of the issues.

> Everybody, of course, works and speaks out of his or her own context. As I cannot escape my identity as a German Lutheran, so John Cobb will always sound like a North American Methodist. Regarding the third world, it would amount to intellectual imperialism if any one of us would claim to do what only theologians from those regions can do for themselves in order to appropriate the gospel and the heritage of other cultures to their own context. Nevertheless, one can expect of everyone who writes on anthropology (or on any other issue) that, whatever the personal point of view might be, he or she write on the general subject rather than simply voicing a partisan view. I tried to do that as well as I was able to, and if John Cobb or others think that my approach is too limited, let us discuss the matter in terms of the issues rather than assailing each other's contextual roots. This is the difference which I always had in mind when I advocated objective rather than confessional argument. Everybody's thought is historically and culturally conditioned, but it is something else to argue explicitly on the basis of partisan commitments. If that happens, the appropriate reaction might be that one partiality is as good as another, and then there can be neither genuine dialogue nor agreement anymore.[31]

---

31. W. Pannenberg, "A Response to My American Friends," in *The Theology of Wolfhart Pannenberg*, ed. Carl E. Braaten and Philip Clayton (Minneapolis: Augsburg, 1988), p. 330.

In spite of all the charges of modernist "foundationalism" and the claims that Pannenberg is hopelessly anchored in the Enlightenment view of reason, we find a strange ambivalence in the responses to his theology. Several thinkers have seen that Pannenberg does not easily fit into a taxonomy of rationality theories that dichotomizes modernist foundationalism and postmodernist nonfoundationalism. I will argue that many of Pannenberg's critics have misunderstood him precisely because they hold to this false dichotomy. Further, I will suggest that the emerging postfoundationalist model of theological rationality (outlined in Chapter Two) offers a viable "middle way" that both helps us critique Pannenberg for his failure to engage postmodernity, and provides us with a way to respond to Pannenberg that captures all the nuances of his complex method. The problem with previous interpretations of Pannenberg can be seen especially in the fact that it is difficult for scholars to decide whether his alleged foundationalism starts with anthropological assumptions or with theological assertions.

Anthropological or Theological Foundations?

The complaint that Pannenberg is a "foundationalist" goes in one of two ways. *Either* he is accepting the autonomy of reason and then basing Christian doctrine on the rational analysis of anthropological or philosophical concepts, *or* he is starting with a theological belief, such as Jesus' resurrection or the trinitarian idea of God, and then basing his philosophical and anthropological analysis on this foundation. Proponents of these mutually exclusive interpretations find some textual warrant in Pannenberg's writings, but attentive interpreters note the existence of opposing tendencies. As early as 1962, Pannenberg made clear his belief that systematic theology

> . . . takes place within the tension *between two tendencies*. On the one hand, it is concerned about the faithfulness of theology itself (and, beyond this, of the Christian church) to its origin, the revelation of God in Jesus Christ as this is attested in Scripture.

11

On the other hand, however, the task of theology goes beyond its special theme and includes all truth whatever.[32]

Rarely have scholars attempted to explain the relational unity that holds the two tendencies together.[33] This book aims to explain the relationality that constitutes the unity of these two tendencies, offering a new way of understanding Pannenberg and thus of responding to his ST. We will argue that Pannenberg can succeed in holding together the two tendencies, that he can help us find a "middle way," if we bring him into dialogue with the emerging postfoundationalist model of rationality.

Those who label him either as an "anthropological" or a "theological" foundationalist are faced with the task of accounting for statements and arguments in Pannenberg's writings that appear to contradict these readings. Let us examine the ambiguity in some of these previous interpretations, which assume that Pannenberg really has only one tendency, either starting with revelation or starting with reason, and that the opposing tendency leads him into confusion. Given the rigorous logic in Pannenberg's work over the last forty years, few critics have explicitly charged him with inconsistency.

Paul Molnar illustrates the "anthropological" foundationalist reading, as well as the inability to account for clear statements in

---

32. W. Pannenberg, "The Crisis of the Scripture Principle," in *Basic Questions in Theology,* vol. 1, trans. George Kehm (Philadelphia: Fortress Press, 1970), p. 1. Emphasis added. Hereafter noted as BQT, with volume number. BQT, I, represents pp. 3-201 of *Grundfragen systematischer Theologie: Gesammelte Aufsätze* (Göttingen: Vandenhoeck & Ruprecht, 1967). BQT, II, also translated by George Kehm (1971), represents pp. 202-398. The two volumes in English are the translation of the single volume in German. This sometimes leads to confusion, because Pannenberg published a second volume in German under the same name that was never translated fully into English: *Grundfragen systematischer Theologie: Gesammelte Aufsätze, Band II* (Göttingen: Vandenhoeck & Ruprecht, 1980). This latter text will be referred to in the footnotes as *Grundfragen, II.*

33. The few who have seen the importance of the relational unity of these two moves in Pannenberg's thought have not conceptualized and described his method in a way that captures all of its features. Three attempted descriptions will be examined and critiqued in the first part of Chapter Four below.

Pannenberg that contradict it. Molnar asserts that Pannenberg "grounds the truth of theology as well as interpretations of individual and social history in experience rather than in God."[34] He recognizes that Pannenberg, like Barth, asserts that only God can reveal God, but argues that this tendency is compromised because Pannenberg really "grounds our knowledge of God, Christ and revelation in our human experiences of anticipation."[35]

Schwöbel, too, sees Pannenberg as a foundationalist, suggesting that he employs "his conception of the non-thematic awareness of the Infinite that is given in the factual constitution of humanity" as a "foundational principle for securing the understanding of Christian truth-claims."[36] Yet in some paragraphs added to the 1997 edition (1st edition, 1989), Schwöbel recognizes that Pannenberg sees theology as "based on the revelation of God" and notes assertions that "counterbalance" Pannenberg's earlier work.[37] Schwöbel does not attempt to resolve this tension at a higher level of unity.

Holwerda, whose foundationalist (rationalist) charge against Pannenberg we noted earlier, also sees the tendency in his writing that opposes this interpretation. Quoting Pannenberg's comment that "the movement of faith is already operative in the very percep-

34. Molnar, "Some Problems," p. 325.

35. Molnar, "Some Problems," p. 338. Molnar's constant use of the term "grounds" shows that he has confused the *ordo cognoscendi* and the *ordo essendi*. As we will see, for Pannenberg it is the reality of God (order of being) that makes human knowledge possible. In the order of knowing, however, there is no "knowing" of God that bypasses human experience. Yet, this does not mean that human knowledge "grounds" (either ontically or noetically) knowledge of God. Molnar seems to have missed the point of Pannenberg's critique of Barth in two ways. First, Barth fails to realize that the "acknowledging" of God cannot bypass experience, because *all* knowing involves conceptual experience, and the concomitant physical neuronal firing of human consciousness. Second, the charge of subjectivism against Barth is aimed at his inability to argue intersubjectively with a proponent of some other religious claim. Molnar does not define "subjectivism," but by it he seems to mean "any attempt to claim universality for one's own subjective beliefs except such attempts of the Karl Barth type."

36. Schwöbel, "Pannenberg," pp. 204-5.

37. Schwöbel, "Pannenberg," pp. 188, 205.

tion of historical fact," Holwerda sees that this is "perilously close" to his own position, viz., that Christian belief in God is properly basic and leads to "the true understanding of reason."[38] In spite of Pannenberg's clear statements otherwise, Holwerda insists that his real goal is a verification of the Christian idea of God that "is established by reason *apart from faith.*"[39]

Pannenberg does indeed claim that anthropology is the "basis" of theology. The question is what he means by such a claim. When Pannenberg's critics attack his view of rationality, they are concerned with the way in which he relates the whole of anthropology[40] to the theological enterprise. For Pannenberg, anthropology is precisely the arena for epistemological and hermeneutical debate, and as such cannot be ignored by theology. These sciences have been for-

38. Holwerda, "Faith, Reason and Resurrection," pp. 307, 311.

39. Holwerda, "Faith, Reason and Resurrection," p. 278. Emphasis added. Here we find the somewhat unusual case of an American wishing that Pannenberg were *more* of a foundationalist, in this case a "modest" one. For a British example of this phenomenon, see Alister McGrath, "Christology and Soteriology: A Response to Wolfhart Pannenberg's Critique of the Soteriological Approach to Christology," *Theologische Zeitschrift* 42, no. 3 (May-June 1986): 222-36. McGrath argues against Pannenberg that "the most honest way of dealing with the problem is simply to assert that there is an *axiomatic correlation between the historical Jesus and the proclaimed Christ.* This does not solve the problem — but neither does it pretend to. . . . [All theology] ultimately begins from the Christian kerygma, and Pannenberg's, as we have shown, is no exception" (234). Holwerda and McGrath want Pannenberg to admit that all theological method is foundationalist (or fideist), including his own, and to accept this as appropriate.

40. Throughout this work, we will use the term "anthropology" broadly defined as the set of disciplines that aim to understand and explain the nature and behavior of human beings (including human biology, psychology, sociology, cultural anthropology, and history). These sciences are of course themselves human endeavors, which means we are dealing here with the task of human self-understanding. Because anthropology involves human reasoning about humans, the question of the nature and function of rationality pervades the self-reflective methodological discussions in and between these disciplines. This seems to be how Pannenberg generally uses the term anthropology, and so it will be followed here, unless specifically noted otherwise. Pannenberg typically uses the adjective "anthropologische" or "menschlich Wissenschaft." He uses but does not like the common term "Geisteswissenschaft," because he sees it as overly indebted to Hegel.

14

mative for the contemporary frame of mind,[41] which makes them important dialogue partners in the quest for understanding and theologically interpreting culture. As we hope to show, however, Pannenberg does not claim "neutrality" for the anthropological sciences, nor does he view their findings as the certain (or even defeasible) "foundation" upon which theology is built.

Although the most common form of the charge of foundationalism against Pannenberg is that he sees anthropology (human rational self-understanding) as the basis of theology, Pannenberg also at times appears to be basing anthropology (and human understanding of all things) on *theological* foundations, particularly on christology or the doctrine of God. Especially informative is a 1973 article in which Pannenberg discusses "The Christological Foundation of Christian Anthropology." In this exposition, he makes the astounding claim that "christology itself ought to have a constitutive value for general anthropology."[42] He is referring here not to "neutral" anthropology but to fundamental-theological anthropology, as we will see in our exposition of his 1983 *Anthropology in Theological Perspective* (ATP).[43] Even in his earlier anthropological work, we see statements pointing in this direction.[44] In addition, Pannenberg's well-known arguments for the resurrection of Jesus might also be considered a foundationalist move. In "Appearance as the Arrival of the Future" Pannenberg argues that the futurity of the reign of God in the ministry of Jesus Christ sheds light on the otherwise murky philo-

---

41. David Pailin follows Pannenberg on this point and offers a historical survey of the issue in *The Anthropological Character of Theology: Conditioning Theological Understanding* (New York: Cambridge University Press, 1990).

42. W. Pannenberg, "The Christological Foundation of Christian Anthropology" in *Humanism and Christianity* (Concilium, vol. 86), ed. Claude Geffré (New York: Herder and Herder, 1973), p. 87.

43. W. Pannenberg, *Anthropology in Theological Perspective*, trans. Matthew J. O'Connell (Philadelphia: Westminster, 1985). Hereafter noted as ATP. German: *Anthropologie in theologischer Perspektive* (Göttingen: Vandenhoeck & Ruprecht, 1983).

44. W. Pannenberg, *What Is Man?* trans. Duane Priebe (Philadelphia: Fortress, 1970), pp. 40, 146-49. Hereafter noted as WIM. German: *Was ist der Mensch? Die Anthropologie der Gegenwart in Lichte der Theologie* (Göttingen: Vandenhoeck & Ruprecht, 1962).

sophical problem of the simultaneous identity and difference of appearance and that which appears.[45]

Christology is not the only theological locus nominated as the basis of Pannenberg's system. M. W. Worthing is among those who point to the importance of the doctrine of God as the "foundation" of Pannenberg's approach.[46] In this case, Worthing is simply being descriptive, not making judgments about epistemic or hermeneutic propriety. Cornelius Buller views the "Divine love" interpreted in a trinitarian way as the "foundation" of Pannenberg's whole theological enterprise.[47] McKenzie is clearly aware of two "apparently conflicting motifs," viz., Pannenberg's attempt to hold together both the rational autonomy of the individual and the biblical view of an omnipotent deity. However, he finally concludes that Pannenberg is forced to be inconsistent with his method because he "begins and ends with God."[48] McKenzie elsewhere notes that Pannenberg "almost succeeds . . . [but] the synthesis cannot bear the tension of such radically-opposing forces."[49]

Does anthropology ground theology, or does theology ground anthropology? Our task will be to show that the solution to the problem of Pannenberg's alleged foundationalism is obscured by this way of asking the question. A similar situation underlies the reaction to Pannenberg's thematization of truth in systematic theology; some theologians are offended that he does not assume the truth of Christian doctrine, while others find it problematic that he assumes it is even possible or appropriate to argue for its objective truth. As we trace a path through the horns of the foundationalism *versus* nonfoundationalism dilemma, we will see that it is precisely at

45. W. Pannenberg, *Theology and the Kingdom of God* (Philadelphia: Westminster, 1969), p. 133. Hereafter noted as TKG.

46. M. W. Worthing, *Foundations and Functions of Theology as Universal Science: Theological Method and Apologetic Praxis in Wolfhart Pannenberg and Karl Rahner* (Frankfurt am Main: Peter Lang, 1996), p. 215. For Worthing's analysis of Pannenberg's view of the universality of truth claims, see pp. 193-95.

47. Cornelius Buller, *The Unity of Nature and History in Pannenberg's Theology* (Lanham, Md.: Littlefield Adams, 1996), p 21.

48. McKenzie, *Rational Theology*, p. 274.

49. McKenzie, *Religious Philosophy*, p. 145.

this point that we find what could become Pannenberg's unique contribution to the emerging postfoundationalist model of theological rationality.

Several scholars have seen Pannenberg's desire for a *via media* in the rationality debate. Although Schwöbel sees him as a foundationalist, he does recognize that Pannenberg is attempting "to find a *middle way* between the Scylla of a 'dogmatic' exposition of Christian doctrine based on revelation which fails to offer sufficient reasons for its assertions and the Charybdis of a 'rationalist' treatment of theology which only allows such statements as can be justified by means of reason alone."[50] In a 1993 dissertation, Gregory Jackson concludes, "I do not believe Pannenberg's work legitimately can be classified as either foundationalist or postmodernist, but that should not make his ideas passé in the eyes of postmodernism. Rather his approach to truth and rationality stands as a challenge to be considered both by foundationalists and postmodernists."[51]

An appropriate response to Pannenberg's theology must first move beyond the common misunderstanding of his view of the role of anthropology and human rationality in theology. For Pannenberg, theology is not undertaken *remoto deo*,[52] nor should it attempt an analysis of God *remoto homo* as in some forms of revelational positivism. Rather, for Pannenberg theology involves a reciprocal relational unity between a "fundamental" theological moment and a "systematic" theological moment, both played out on the terrain of a tensional field of existence, a field examined *sub ratione Dei*, in light of the relation of all things to God. That is, he does not base either theology or anthropology on the other in a foundationalist sense, but recognizes a real mutual conditioning between the two.

---

50. Schwöbel, "Pannenberg," p. 204. Emphasis added.

51. Gregory D. Jackson, "Creation and Reconciliation in the Theology of Wolfhart Pannenberg" (Ph.D. diss., Southern Baptist Theological Seminary, 1993), p. 301.

52. Eberhard Jüngel uses this phrase to criticize Pannenberg in *God as the Mystery of the World*, trans. Darrell L. Guder (Grand Rapids: Eerdmans, 1983), p. viii.

Preview

The ambiguities noted above suggest the need to question the adequacy and accuracy of the foundationalist *versus* nonfoundationalist way of framing the rationality debate. Neither of these options is able to capture Pannenberg's methodology. I will describe the contours of a new framework that holds promise for overcoming this dichotomy in Chapter Two, and the remainder of the book will aim to interpret Pannenberg in its light. The **central thesis** of the current project is that the methodological reciprocity operative in Wolfhart Pannenberg's theological anthropology (which will be exposited in Chapter Four) may be critically appropriated for the postfoundationalist task of theology, which is:

> to engage in interdisciplinary dialogue within our postmodern culture while *both* maintaining a commitment to intersubjective, transcommunal theological argumentation for the truth of Christian faith, *and* recognizing the provisionality of our historically embedded understandings and culturally conditioned explanations of the Christian tradition and religious experience.

The *post*foundationalist goal is to find a "middle way" between the dogmatism of foundationalism and the relativism of many forms of nonfoundationalism. Some theological representatives of each of these latter extremes will reject the possibility or desirability of *any* interdisciplinary dialogue. Among those representatives that *do* accept the need for theology to enter into conversation with other disciplines, the foundationalists will tend to deny the latter part of the postfoundationalist task (above), while the nonfoundationalists will reject the first part.

Three main objections might arise against my central thesis:

- *Objection 1:* the postfoundationalist model of theological rationality is implausible and the only options are foundationalism or nonfoundationalism,
- *Objection 2:* even if postfoundationalism is a viable option, the ba-

sic principle of Pannenberg's methodology makes him a foundationalist, and

- *Objection 3:* even if Pannenberg's theological method is theoretically consonant with the postfoundationalist task, in actual practice he operates as a foundationalist, basing his theological assertions on the findings of anthropology as he interprets them (or vice versa, basing his philosophical anthropological interpretations on privileged theological beliefs).

The middle three chapters of this book are aimed at rebutting these objections and demonstrating the fecundity of bringing Pannenberg's method into dialogue with the emerging postfoundationalist approach to theological rationality.

Chapter Two charts the territory of the philosophical discussions about rationality by introducing the "foundational" problem of theology. Attending to philosophical antecedents and some theological proponents, both foundationalism and nonfoundationalism are assessed for their strengths and weaknesses. The focus, however, is on the way in which these two views, which allegedly exhaust the options, are polemically defined in an exclusive disjunction. Many scholars have rejected this either/or mentality and are searching for a "middle way." The main task of Chapter Two is to outline the emergence of this *post*foundationalist option, explicating it and reconstructing it in the form of four relational "couplets," which aim to hold together belief and experience, truth and knowledge, individual and community, and explanation and understanding. This helps to differentiate it from foundationalism and nonfoundationalism, each of these tending to overemphasize one side or the other. A further distinctive move is found in postfoundationalism's attempt to link (without conflating) epistemology and hermeneutics. I will argue that this model is a plausible alternative that avoids the extremes that characterize the current debate. Further, this new approach to rationality promises to help us interpret Pannenberg in a way that captures the tension-filled relational unity of his "two tendencies."

Chapter Three buttresses the main thesis by bringing Pannenberg explicitly into dialogue with each of the four postfoundationalist couplets. First, in order to counter the claim that Pannenberg is inherently a foundationalist because of the key concept of his thought (variously rendered as reason, history, or prolepsis), I propose a new interpretation of his Grundprinzip (basic principle). For Pannenberg, theology is about understanding and explaining all things under the aspect of their relation to God *(sub ratione Dei)*. The quality of this relationality is itself the key, as I hope to show. For Pannenberg, the relation of all things to God is materially filled out by the concept of "true infinite" and its fulfillment in the trinitarian view of God. This Grundprinzip is traced through Pannenberg's thought to show the way in which it permeates his approach to epistemology and hermeneutics, and shapes material theological issues.

This interpretation is further confirmed by bringing Pannenberg into explicit dialogue with the four postfoundationalist couplets, showing the extent to which his methodology is consonant with this search for a middle way. The final section of Chapter Three illustrates the similarity between the distinctive postfoundationalist desire to link epistemology and hermeneutics and Pannenberg's attempt to use anthropology (as the "basis" for a theology of religions) as a link between the philosophy of religion and the history of religion. This comparison and analysis will help demonstrate that Pannenberg does not fit into either side of the foundationalist/nonfoundationalist dichotomy,[53] and has more in common with the *post*foundationalist move than might appear on the surface.

In spite of such *prima facie* similarities, it might be argued that in practice Pannenberg *founds* theology on anthropology (or vice versa). To disarm this objection, Chapter Four exposits the "reciprocity" of the "fundamental"[54] and "systematic" movements in Pannenberg's work generally, and critiques several proposed models that attempt to

53. Here we find another instance of a characteristic of his thought that was noted very early by Carl Braaten: "Pannenberg's theology obviously escapes ready-made labels." See Braaten, "The Current Controversy in Revelation: Pannenberg and His Critics," *Journal of Religion* 45 (1965): 234.

54. Perhaps Pannenberg's use of this adjective to describe one aspect of his approach has led many to leap to the conclusion that he is a fundamentalist or a "foundationalist." This facile judgment lacks warrant, as will be demonstrated in the following chapters.

conceptualize the relationality. To provide contextual background for understanding this reciprocal relation, I first offer a diachronic survey of his treatments of major anthropological themes over the last forty years. The general task of Chapter Four requires a thematization of "relationality" per se. Much of philosophical thought in the last two centuries has been aimed at critiquing "substance" metaphysics, and disclosing the inherently relational nature of being, knowing, and doing. Examples of differentiated relational unity include the undulatory and corpuscular characteristics of light, Michael Polanyi's descriptions of tacit and focal awareness in the single act of knowing, and Jean Piaget's interactionist model of assimilation and accommodation in the holistic adaptation of the developing person. Such models can help us to overcome the assumption that a conceptual relation requires one thing to be "based" on another in a linear foundationalist sense. Pannenberg himself points to the importance of the priority of the concept of "relation" as potentially helping to solve theological problems (ST, I, 367).

The extent to which Pannenberg's focus on relationality may be appropriated in a postfoundationalist way is the general concern of this book. In the final major section of Chapter Four, a new model of thinking about relationality is applied to Pannenberg's work; this model is borrowed from James E. Loder and W. Jim Neidhardt, who have adopted the Möbius band as a heuristic picture that graphically illustrates a special kind of differentiated relational unity. The final subsections of this chapter test this model by providing a detailed synchronic exposition of Pannenberg's treatment of the material themes of the traditional loci of theological anthropology (human nature, *imago Dei,* and sin) in both ATP and ST. By setting his "fundamental" theological anthropology and his "systematic" theological anthropology side by side, the goal is to demonstrate that Pannenberg does not start in a "foundational" sense either solely "from below" or "from above," but aims to hold the two together in a mutually conditioning relationship. These texts are where Pannenberg sets out self-consciously the two steps of his overall theological treatment of anthropology. Instead of "steps," it would be better to think of them as interlocking movements, twin moments, mutually shaping and supporting one another. It is this structural dynamic that is seen as the most valuable resource for the post-foundationalist discussion.

In the first volume of ST, he refers back to his *Theology and the Philosophy of Science* (TPS),[55] where he had "accorded fundamental theological rank to anthropology as the basis of a theology of religion." He immediately continues, however, by insisting, "I naturally have in view only a methodological priority and am not treating anthropology as materially the basis of theology."[56] Grasping this distinction between methodological and material priority is crucial for understanding Pannenberg. In TPS, Pannenberg set out his plan to hold together two distinct moves; one would take shape in ATP, while the other would find its culmination in ST. In *Sind wir von Natur aus religiös?*, in which Pannenberg responds to criticisms of ATP, he notes that there is an ironic moment[57] in the statement that anthropology is the basis of theology; because anthropology is abstract it must be brought into dialogue with concrete history (of religion). The latter occurs in systematic theology, where God's revelation has material primacy.

This complementary relation also holds for his use of the approaches "from above" and "from below." Pannenberg sees anthropology, or "from below" generally, as playing a crucial role in the Systematics. The general concepts of God, revelation, and religion (which all interface with anthropology) have a "transitional function" (ST, I, 198). In chapter 3 of ST, Pannenberg makes explicit a critical methodological turn.

> In the next sections we shall try to identify the anthropological elements of truth in the new theological approach in terms of the concept of religion. We shall do so in the interest of taking

55. W. Pannenberg, *Theology and the Philosophy of Science*, trans. F. McDonagh (Philadelphia: Westminster Press, 1976). Hereafter noted as TPS. Originally published as *Wissenschaftstheorie und Theologie* (Frankfurt am Main: Suhrkamp, 1973).

56. ST, I, 157-58 (translation emended). See also ST, I, 56-57, 417. We will see in the following chapters that a misunderstanding of the use of the term "basis" has led many scholars to misinterpret Pannenberg's methodology.

57. W. Pannenberg, ed., *Sind wir von Natur aus religiös?* (Düsseldorf: Patmos, 1986), pp. 165-66.

them up into ["Aufhebung"] the perspective of a theology that is oriented to the primacy of God and his revelation.[58]

So here the argument in ST turns around and becomes an exposition of revelation, exploring how it illuminates the phenomena of religion and human experience generally. Pannenberg unequivocally wants to see the *material* "basis" of theology as God. We will see that he holds the "fundamental" and "systematic" theological movements together, conceptualizing them as coinherent. This will clarify his intentions in ATP; although he was starting there with anthropology, he was not starting with it *in abstracto* or from a neutral perspective, but in light of its relation to theological themes, and especially the claims about the revelation of the one true God in Jesus Christ. We will see that the relation between ATP and ST was set out in TPS and that he has consistently followed it.

My final chapter will summarize the result of juxtaposing Pannenberg and postfoundationalism. His main contributions are recapitulated in light of the four couplets, with special attention to his efforts to disclose the mutual conditioning of anthropology and theology.[59] Throughout this book several critiques of Pannenberg

---

58. ST, I, 128. In the original German, Pannenberg puts "Aufhebung" in quotation marks for emphasis (*Systematische Theologie, I,* 143). The significance of this is missed in the English translation. Precisely how Pannenberg uses this term will be examined in Chapter Four.

59. Elsewhere I have attempted to clarify this reciprocity between anthropology and theology in Pannenberg by contrasting his approach to that of Karl Barth. See my "Constitutive Relationality in Anthropology and Trinity: The Shaping of the *Imago Dei* Doctrine in Barth and Pannenberg," *Neue Zeitschrift für systematischer Theologie und Religionsphilosophie* 39 (1997): 304-22. This analysis will be expanded in Chapter Four below. The mutual influence of anthropology and theology is not unique to Barth or Pannenberg; this reciprocal shaping may be traced, I believe, in all theological thought. For an example of this reciprocity in a doctrinal conception that crosses over both the patristic era and Protestant Scholasticism, see my "A Dubious Christological Formula: From Leontius of Byzantium to Karl Barth," *Theological Studies* 57 (1996): 431-46. For a nineteenth-century example, see my "Schleiermacher's 'Reciprocal Relationality': The Underlying Regulative Principle of His Theological Method," in *Schleiermacher on Workings of the Knowing Mind,* ed. Ruth Drucilla Richardson, 177-95 (Lampeter, Wales: Edwin Mellen, 1998).

will emerge, and these will be summarized and expanded in the second section of Chapter Five. A primary concern is his dismissal of postmodern hermeneutics; the nuanced analysis of the *post*foundationalist interpretation of this cultural and intellectual phenomenon may reveal a more adequate way to respond theologically. Clearly, we must go beyond Pannenberg at this juncture. Finally, we will identify some of the implications of this analysis for the constructive task of theology. How can we break down not only the *inter*disciplinary walls between theology and other disciplines, but also the *intra*disciplinary walls between philosophical, systematic, biblical, historical, and practical theology? Can we escape the seemingly perennial need to assess theological method, whether under the heading "theological foundations," or some other nomenclature? How can we stand critically and with integrity within the Christian tradition and "do theology" in the twenty-first century? These questions point us toward the central concerns of "postfoundationalism," to which we now turn.

CHAPTER TWO

The Emerging Postfoundationalist Model of Theological Rationality

The anxious reactions to Pannenberg's alleged "foundationalism" reviewed in Chapter One are shaped by the broader dialogue in the academy about the implications of the postmodern challenge for our understanding of epistemology, hermeneutics, and theological rationality. Much of the discussion presupposes that foundationalism and nonfoundationalism (negatively defined by each other) exhaust the available options. Both sides of this polemic share many of the same assumptions about the possibilities available to us in a description of human knowledge. Either we have absolute foundations for knowledge or truth is relative. Either the individual is endowed with universal reason or each community has its own form of rationality. Either our explanations are capable of achieving universality or we are only able to understand within the particularity of our own local context.

This antipodal structuring of the debate posits a dilemma, and the philosophical theologian is pressured to choose one of the horns. In recent years, however, a growing number of scholars have begun to explore the possibility of a "middle way" that transcends these options; they aim to go between the horns of this dilemma. Following J. Wentzel van Huyssteen, I will refer to this emerging view as the **postfoundationalist** model of theological rationality.

25

Over against the alleged objectivism of foundationalism and the extreme relativism of most forms of nonfoundationalism, a *postfoundationalist theology* wants to make two moves. First, it fully acknowledges contextuality, the epistemically crucial role of interpreted experience, and the way that tradition shapes the epistemic and nonepistemic values that inform our reflection about God and what some of us believe to be God's presence in this world. At the same time, however, a postfoundationalist notion of rationality in theological reflection claims to point creatively beyond the confines of the local community, group, or culture towards a plausible form of interdisciplinary conversation.[1]

Postfoundationalism aims to develop a plausible model of theological rationality that charts a course (to switch metaphors) between the Scylla of foundationalist dogmatism and the Charybdis of nonfoundationalist relativism. This approach argues for a more subtle set of distinctions for responding to the postmodern challenge.

*Post*foundationalist thinkers (as we will show below) recognize that postmodernism comes in both skeptical and affirmative forms. After "modernity," some postmodernists take a negative stance toward the very idea of epistemology, arguing that all we have left is a hermeneutics whose task is deconstruction. Others see in the collapse of modernist notions of knowledge a call to the reconstruction of epistemology. Postfoundationalists want to accept the challenge of postmodernity, but they do this in order to take up the task of refiguring the ideals of truth, progress, and reason, rather than expunging them from the philosophical vocabulary. Robert Kegan expresses this well in his distinction between deconstructive and reconstructive approaches to postmodernity. Both see the need to identify unacknowledged ideological partiality in the disciplines. The deconstructivist concludes all claims to truth are unacceptable. "In contrast, the reconstructive approach would have an equal interest in bringing the limits of the disciplines and its theories to center stage in our learning, but for the purpose of nourishing the very

---

1. J. Wentzel van Huyssteen, *Essays in Postfoundationalist Theology* (Grand Rapids: Eerdmans, 1997), p. 4.

process of reconstructing the disciplines and their theories . . . as long as life goes on, the process will need to go on."[2]

Supporting the postfoundationalist move is a particular vision of the relation between modernity and postmodernity. Rather than asserting that the latter means the end or annihilation of the former, postfoundationalist thinkers affirm a more dialectical or dynamic relation between the two. Postmodernism is defined as a to-and-fro movement, constantly challenging the foundationalist assumptions of modernity.[3] They are not defined as poles on the opposite sides of a continuum, nor as two horns of a dilemma. Instead of settling for this bogus dichotomy, postfoundationalism sees the primary value of postmodernism in its relentless interrogation of the remnants of the facile foundationalisms of the Enlightenment. It is precisely the failure to see this dialectic that leads many nonfoundationalists to stop the interrogation, inadvertently allowing new (unchallenged) foundations to shape their models of rationality.

At this stage, there is no "school" of postfoundationalism.[4] However, several contemporary thinkers in the debate display obvious

2. Robert Kegan, *In over Our Heads: The Mental Demands of Modern Life* (Cambridge, Mass.: Harvard University Press, 1994), p. 330.

3. E.g., van Huyssteen, *Essays,* p. 278.

4. "Post" in postfoundationalism, as I am using the term, does not mean "against" or "completely apart from" or even simply "after." It includes the idea of being "after," but intentionally aims to accommodate the aspects of the foundationalist approach that made it seem so intuitively correct, allowing it to dominate the epistemological landscape for so long. "Post" is not simply "anti" or "non," because the model we see emerging does not reject the idea that we do have traditions and foundations (metaphorically speaking) from which we enter conversation. Postfoundationalism also aims to accommodate the helpful intuitions of the *non*foundationalist critique without embracing its extreme relativist forms and their concomitant self-referential incoherence. One can think, then, of "post"-foundationalism as trying to identify the operation of rationality between these two extremes. The prefix "epi-" might be suggestive here. "Epifoundationalism" would indicate the existence of "foundations," but recognize the need for human thought to move constantly around, under, beside, within, and upon these foundations in an ongoing reconstructive process. This might capture the value of the nonfoundationalist "web" metaphor, and avoid the "edifice" imagery of foundationalism. For the sake of following scholarly parlance, we will embrace the term "postfoundationalist" as defined above.

family resemblances (to borrow Wittgenstein's phrase). In order to draw these similarities into sharper relief, my strategy is to define a "postfoundationalist" as one who would assert a particular kind of relationality as obtaining between four conceptual pairs:

- experience and belief
- truth and knowledge
- individual and community
- explanation and understanding

These four dyads offer a helpful apparatus for understanding the new postfoundationalist move because they illuminate the dichotomous framing of the debate between foundationalism and nonfoundationalism. Each of these latter models privileges one side of each dyad over the other, and tends to miss their dynamic relational unity. The postfoundationalist model of rationality will be presented in terms of four relational "couplets," which are designed to accommodate the intuitions and concerns of both the foundationalists and the nonfoundationalists, but in a way that transcends the various polemical definitions assumed by both sides.

It is important here at the beginning to differentiate between two dimensions of the debate. Both foundationalists and nonfoundationalists make assertions about *epistemology* and about *hermeneutics*. The epistemic aspect of the problem is the focus of the foundationalists, who fear that the very concept of knowledge itself is at risk in the discussion. In conceptualizing the relation between epistemology and hermeneutics, the foundationalist will tend to privilege the former and ignore or downplay some of the recent developments in the latter. Conversely, nonfoundationalists tend to focus on the hermeneutic side of the issue, and emphasize the untenability of the modernist approach to theory justification. The hermeneutic dimension of the debate is about how one *justifies* one's interpretations (or beliefs) as reasonable. For the nonfoundationalist, we cannot get "behind" or "under" our beliefs to justify them; all we have is the criterion of coherence with other beliefs within our culturally conditioned web.

As we will see in the last section of this chapter, the attempt to link epistemology and hermeneutics in a particular kind of relational unity is one of the distinctive characteristics of the emerging postfoundationalist model. This move, which subtends the four relational couplets outlined below, is designed to overcome the fallacy of nonfoundationalism without falling back into foundationalism. We will then be in a position to bring Pannenberg into dialogue with this new theory of rationality in Chapter Three.

The "Foundational" Problem in Theology

The issue of "foundationalism" has clearly become a *foundational* problem in theology. This can be seen in the promulgation of titles like *Faith after Foundationalism*[5] and *Theology without Foundations*.[6] These texts are about theological method and rationality. How do we justify theological claims to knowledge and theological interpretations of experience? Such methodological discussions used to be found under the heading of "theological foundations," which typically came at the beginning of theological systems. Philosophical justification of a methodology was provided as a secure foundation upon which the system was then constructed. After the collapse of foundationalism, many see this *praeambula fidei* approach as no longer plausible.

However, the very existence of nonfoundationalist justifications of (nonfoundationalist) theological method demonstrates that the *task* itself cannot be abandoned. It is precisely here that the "postfoundationalist task of theology" emerges most clearly. The adjective "foundational" as used in the title of this section is palpably amphibolous. On the one hand, it points to the seriousness of the problem, but on the other hand it serves to illustrate that there is something pre-analytically intuitive about the metaphor of "foundations" when describing the structure of knowledge and argumentation.

5. D. Z. Phillips, *Faith after Foundationalism* (San Francisco: Westview, 1995).

6. S. Hauerwas, N. Murphy, and M. Nation, eds., *Theology without Foundations* (Nashville: Abingdon, 1994).

We should avoid assuming, on the one hand, that the use of the word "foundation" automatically entails that an argument or an author is foundational*ist* or, on the other hand, that the absence of the term in the presentation of an epistemic or hermeneutic theory is assurance that the author has successfully evaded the quagmire of foundational*ism*. In the following sections, we will see counter-examples of both assumptions. This should help us overcome the allergic reaction to the term "foundation," while still avoiding "foundational*ist*" epistemology and hermeneutics.

If we recognize the metaphorical nature of the term "foundation," we might agree that we all have noetic and hermeneutic foundations in a general innocuous sense, upon which we "base" our beliefs. This may refer simply to the dynamics of inferential patterns in thinking. The negativity of the label "foundationalist" derives from the specific question of *how we relate* to our beliefs. Even the nonfoundationalist has a "basis" for theological beliefs. She may accept a Lakatosian model of science because she thinks there are good reasons to accept it, or he may leap into Rortyan relativism because he has reasons for thinking this is the best or only philosophical option. The belief (for example) that "narrative shapes our experience" inferentially supports (and so in a metaphorical sense functions as a "foundation" for) the methodological decisions of some nonfoundationalist theologians.

To be distinctive, postfoundationalism must be about more than just criticizing our assumptions; it must be about criticizing the *way* we criticize our assumptions. Critical reflection on theological method involves constantly revisiting and reconstructing our beliefs and theories to account for our experience and the necessary conditions that must be posited to explain that experience. Even if this is not admitted in the case of some nonfoundationalists, it is evident in their argumentative performance. We do not have to abandon the metaphor of foundations, so long as we recognize it is a metaphor, and spell out the disanalogies (just as we should with the nonfoundationalist metaphor of a "web" of beliefs). It is important to capture our pre-analytic intuition that being rational includes having good reasons as a basis for our beliefs. This means that we can and should still speak of the postfoundationalist task as a response to a "foundational" problem in theology; namely, the problem of articulating how theological claims may be rationally justified after the *fall* of foundationalism without the *fallacy* of nonfoundationalism.

Foundationalism versus Nonfoundationalism

The postfoundationalist argues that the underlying problem is the way in which these two philosophical options have been cast as opposites. It aims to join nonfoundationalism in moving beyond foundationalism, but wants first to challenge more deeply the dichotomous assumptions that have been uncritically accepted by both sides. The dangers in each view are in the extremity of their claims, when they move beyond initially helpful intuitions to more exclusive and radical statements. As we will see below, *foundationalism,* in the "classical" sense, was a part of the Enlightenment project: human reason could attain absolute and certain knowledge based on self-evident foundational experiences or *a priori* propositions, from which necessary and universal conclusions could be reached. So reason is seen as *absolute.* The positive intuition here is that some beliefs seem to be based on other beliefs, about which we feel more sure than other beliefs. The problem that led to the fall of foundationalism per se is the insistence on apodicticity, and the belief that the constant critique of assumptions could be halted.

Nonfoundationalism (or antifoundationalism) is diametrically opposed to this approach. It asserts that we have no foundational beliefs that are independent of the support of other beliefs; rather, we subsist in a groundless web, attempting merely to maintain coherence in our local praxis. Justifying beliefs is only a matter of determining whether they cohere with all the other beliefs in our own particular web or context. So reason in this view is often seen as *relative.* The positive intuition here is that certainty is not a feasible goal in the search for knowledge, but the fallacy lies in the inherent danger of collapsing into self-referentially incoherent relativism.[7]

7. The concept of a "context" is parasitic on intercontextuality. How can I know

This "foundational" problem in theology is not new, nor is it a problem only for theologians. Although one commonly hears of "Cartesian anxiety," the fear of noetic vertigo goes back at least as far as Plato and his search for *episteme* (knowledge) in contrast to *doxa* (opinion). The goal for both ancient and modern (Enlightenment) thinkers was to find absolutely secure foundations for knowledge that would guarantee certainty. In the literature on epistemology and rationality, this approach is called "classical" foundationalism.[8] It is this model of human knowledge, and usually its modern manifestations in Cartesian rationalism, Lockean empiricism, or German idealism, that has come under such fierce attack by nonfoundationalists in the second half of the twentieth century.

In its "classical" form, this aspect of foundationalism can be seen from Plato to the Logical Positivists. Plato's goal was knowledge of eternal forms; but how does one know when an adequate grasp of a "form" has been achieved? Here Plato appeals to intuition where the mind is flooded with light. This illuminationist imagery deeply influenced Augustine and many other early theologians. Similarly, in the *Posterior Analytics,* Aristotle asserts that first principles must simply be intuitively grasped by the mind. But here we have a dilemma. If we stop with intuition (whether Platonic or Aristotelian), and refuse to give reasons for why this is the correct intuition, we have no basis for judging between alternative visions. If we do offer reasons for the intuition of choice, we are now relying on these reasons and no longer on the intuition. But how do we justify *these* reasons? Precisely at this point it becomes clear that classical foundationalism cannot accomplish its goal of halting the infinite regress in the

---

that I am "in" a context, unless that context can be differentiated from an "other" context, which of course implies a higher awareness of a relation between the contexts? Relativism asserts that "all assertions are only true (or false) within their own context." However, that assertion itself, which is intended to apply to all contexts, is strangely exempted. If it is false, it is false. If it is true, it is false. We have here the well-known self-refuting nature of relativism.

8. As we will see below, the definition of the term "foundationalism" is the subject of much debate, and scholars differentiate between types of foundationalism, such as "classical" and "modest."

search for foundations of knowledge; thought can always return to challenge the basis of thought.

Harold Brown offers a good summary of this classical model and shows its failure. In spite of many obvious differences, all versions of the "classical" model insist that for a belief to be rationally justified, it must be *universally* valid, there must be *necessary* relations between it and the other components of the argument, and it must be the result of following precise *rules*. The rationalists, empiricists, and idealists all accepted these criteria but argued over what the rules were and how to determine universal validity. They argued about how to defend the foundations, and which rules to follow, and how we get the self-evident foundations in the first place. Brown points out the problem:

> . . . rational beliefs must be based on reasons. On the classical model of rationality, reasons are provided by the information we begin with, along with the rules that establish the connection between this information and the proposition believed. But as soon as the model is put this starkly, two questions arise . . . on what basis do we select the information from which to begin, and on what basis do we select our rules?[9]

We then ask how to justify beginning with *those rules* that helped select the first rules, or the information that led us to the selection of the original information, and we are threatened again by an infinite regress. The classical foundationalist tries to solve this problem by positing self-justifying or self-evident rules or beliefs. But how do we know we are following the right rules? We need rules to help us get to the right rules. And then we need rules to get at those rules, *ad infinitum*.

A similar regress results when we try to discover how we know something is self-evident, or when we inquire about the foundation for the proposed foundation. Simply put, the problem is identifying criteria for determining which rules or beliefs are self-justifying. The classical model of rationality has also been criticized as self-

---

9. Harold Brown, *Rationality* (London: Routledge, 1990), p. 38.

referentially incoherent. Its own assertion about the criteria for rationality does not meet the criteria; the assertion of the classical definition of foundationalism is not universal, self-evident, or the result of rule-following.

The problem is perhaps most clearly evinced in the Cartesian incarnation of classical foundationalism. In his *Meditations* (1641), Descartes posited as a foundation for knowledge his famous "clear and distinct ideas," which one can identify by their clarity and distinctness. This circle is so vicious, it is surprising it exerted such a powerful influence. Descartes's goal was *certainty* (following the ideal of mathematics), to know that something "is so and can't be otherwise." In order to accomplish this, he suggested his well-known phrase *cogito ergo sum;* I cannot doubt that I (as doubting thinker) exist. So the foundation of all knowledge is the certainty of the existence of the self, which is bound up with the certainty of the existence of God (the infinite) as the condition for the finite existence of the thinker. His famous dualism between mind and matter, thinking thing *(res cogitans)* and extended thing *(res extensa),* was designed to buttress an epistemological foundationalism that did not rely on empirical evidence, but was based on innate ideas in the mind.

Although John Locke, the father of modern empiricism, differs from Descartes in significant ways, they share the same conception of the goal of reason. Locke, too, aimed for certainty, but he thought it could be had only by sense experience. In his famous refutation of the concept of innate ideas in *An Essay concerning Human Understanding* (1689), Locke argued that faith ends when we have knowledge. He speaks of faith making the determination for assent, when reason comes short (IV.18). That is, reason provides a certain amount of evidence, and the role of faith is to make the leap the rest of the way so that we can assent to revelation. However, Locke reserves for reason the right to decide which propositions are in fact revelation. These can only be on the level of probability, not certainty. The latter is reserved for beliefs that are self-evident to the senses, and these form the foundation for all true knowledge. Here the circle returns: What reasons do we have for asserting that a belief is self-evident to the senses?

In the preface to the second edition of *Critique of Pure Reason* (1787), Immanuel Kant said that his goal was to limit knowledge to make room for faith. The purpose of his distinction between phenomena and noumena was to set the boundary of *knowing*. Although we cannot *know* an object as a thing in itself, we may *think* an object as a thing in itself. "Knowing," in Kant's view, means that one has proved the possibility of an object, either because it has actually been experienced sensibly, or because one has shown (through the transcendental method of pure theoretical reason) that it is *a priori* necessary. But Kant insists that we can "think" whatever we please, as long as it is not contradictory. Of course merely thinking a thing is insufficient to show its real possibility; to tackle this latter task, Kant proposes that we identify sources in the use of *practical* reason. Pure practical reason provides us with the "practical postulates" of freedom, God, and immortality. The main point for our current analysis is to note that for Kant all knowledge had to be founded either on the *a priori* forms of perception and understanding, or on the postulates of practical reason. In either case, the possibility of rational knowing rested on the firmness of the foundations provided. So Kant's idealism also falls under the rubric of foundationalist attempts to achieve certainty, although his attempt was aimed at an integration (which was also a transcendence) of rationalism and empiricism.

We might trace other foundationalist thinkers, but let us conclude this brief survey with the "verification principle" of the Logical Positivists: only sentences that express statements which either are analytic or are empirically verifiable may be considered cognitively meaningful. This might be seen as the last popular attempt to salvage the modernist model of rationality. The well-known Vienna Circle in the 1920s to 1930s (Schlick, Carnap, Neurath, Reichenbach) argued that only scientific statements were meaningful; a synthetic assertion is meaningful only if it can be verified empirically. However, this foundationalist model failed, too, because, among other reasons, it was unable to account for the success and progress of science. Further, it was ultimately seen as self-defeating; the verification principle itself could not be verified empirically.

Postmodernism was born, then, out of the death throes of

foundationalism. However, this does not force a conclusion that the only option is a relativist nonfoundationalism. Nonfoundationalism, for its part, is not a "school," although it has been described as a "research program." However, one of the defining characteristics of nonfoundationalism is a view of postmodernity as primarily a negative (or negating) phenomenon; it exists primarily as a criticism, a negating, of foundationalism. For D. Z. Phillips, for example, nonfoundationalism means giving up on the need for justifying the grammars of our respective discourses.[10] This move not only gives up the search for certain foundations, but also throws out the task for which foundationalism was developed: intersubjectively justifying our beliefs as reasonable. The *post*foundationalist wants to throw out the bath water (modernist certitude), but not the baby (the search for transcommunal criteria of rationality).

Nonfoundationalist John Thiel illustrates the common polarization; for him, foundationalism and nonfoundationalism are "mutually constituted positions."[11] Thiel traces the development of the twentieth-century philosophers from whom nonfoundationalist theologians take their cue, which include W. Sellars, W. V. O. Quine, Richard Rorty, and Donald Davidson. He notes that the main ancestors of nonfoundationalism (through these other philosophers) are pragmatism (especially Peirce and James) and the linguistic turn (Wittgenstein). In their discussions of rationality and hermeneutics, these thinkers and their epigoni emphasize the role of the community with its web of belief and localized praxis, as well as the importance of a consensus that allows for the playing of "language games."

Thiel's version of nonfoundationalism is one of the best examples of the "either/or" mentality that has structured the current debate. After stating that Christian practices draw their meaning from particular religious frameworks, he insists that *there is no alternative* to these practices except the foundationalist illusion of a universal reasoning to justify belief."[12] For Thiel, foundationalism and

---

10. Phillips, *Faith after Foundationalism,* p. 227.
11. John Thiel, *Nonfoundationalism* (Minneapolis: Fortress, 1994), p. 2.
12. Thiel, *Nonfoundationalism,* p. 102. Emphasis added.

nonfoundationalism exhaust the options. It is precisely this assumption that is challenged by a *post*foundationalist model. The problem with versions of nonfoundationalism like this is their apparent lack of awareness that philosophy is conditioning their own theological method. Some quotes from Thiel show this clearly:

> Modern apologetics sometimes indulges its secular audience by accommodating Christian explanation to non-Christian expectations. The correlational method is easily employed in ways that accord *priority to philosophical construction* rather than to the normative canons of Christian interpretation.[13]

This is ironic, for Thiel's entire book is an argument that we should accord priority to the philosophical construction of Wittgenstein and company. Are Rorty and Quine part of the "normative canon" of Christian interpretation? Thiel insists that foundationalists are trying to do something that the best philosophers tell us is impossible, without argument for why these are the "best" philosophers. How can this be anything other than giving priority to nonfoundationalist philosophical construction?[14]

Thiel notes that nonfoundationalist theologians like Lindbeck, Thiemann, and Hauerwas "use the metaphor of foundations to name an extrabiblical theory or a supposedly universal human experience such a theory purports to represent."[15] This odd definition of foundationalism is clearly suspect. It assumes that nonfoundationalism itself as a theory is not extrabiblical. In fact, this is what Thiel claims: "*Foundationlessness* . . . refers to Christian faith as it has been normatively expressed, practiced, and experienced through the

---

13. Thiel, *Nonfoundationalism*, p. 99. Emphasis added.

14. The nonfoundationalist narrative theologian who wants to avoid the word "foundation" has trouble with the fact that the narrative of the Bible itself posits Jesus Christ as the "foundation" of Christian faith. E.g., 1 Corinthians 3:11, "For no one can lay any foundation other than the one that has been laid; that foundation is Jesus Christ." The term "narrativity," on the other hand, is not in the Bible, and so (on the narrativist's own terms) requires philosophical justification for its inclusion in a depth description of Christian religious practice.

15. Thiel, *Nonfoundationalism*, p. 86.

ages."[16] Of course, the question that immediately arises is how Thiel knows that nonfoundationalism is the true interpretation of Christian faith. On what basis does he make this claim; it seems we are right back to the dilemma of an infinite regress, which Thiel has tried to halt by an appeal to the *practice* of foundationlessness.

We have here a case of the self-exempting fallacy, a characteristic of many nonfoundationalist theological discussions. I am not suggesting here that theology can or ought to avoid making critical use of philosophy; I agree with Augustine that theology can be in a sense "true philosophy." But the problem with many nonfoundationalists is that they think they are being *neutral,* and so the assumptions of radically relativist philosophies wander around naked and unnoticed in their writings. In fact, many self-described nonfoundationalists have explicitly tried to respond to the charge of relativism. To the extent they succeed, these thinkers move toward, and contribute to the articulation of, the postfoundationalist model.

The Search for a "Middle Way"

My goal thus far has simply been to offer a broad outline of the two most common approaches to explaining knowledge and rationality, showing how they are conceived as polar opposites. The possibility of finding a "middle way" that overcomes and transcends this dichotomy is what postfoundationalism is all about. The purpose of this section is to introduce the thinkers that are the main contributors to the emerging postfoundationalist model of theological rationality.

The contours of this model have been most clearly outlined by J. Wentzel van Huyssteen. In his *Essays in Postfoundationalist Theology,* he summarizes the move in the following way.

> To reject foundationalism in theology, however, is not to embrace nonfoundationalism or antifoundationalism per se — in any case not a type of antifoundationalism that claims that one

16. Thiel, *Nonfoundationalism,* p. 87.

can engage in theological reflection without attention to the explanatory nature and epistemic status of theological truth-claims. . . . Moreover, a postfoundationalist shift to a fallibilist epistemology, which honestly embraces the role of traditioned experience, personal commitment, interpretation, and the provisional nature of all of our knowledge-claims, avoids the alleged necessity of opting for either foundationalism or antifoundationalism.[17]

Here van Huyssteen points to a middle way, a third epistemological and hermeneutic option that avoids the extremes of both dogmatic foundationalism and relativist nonfoundationalism. My development of the four postfoundationalist couplets below will draw heavily on van Huyssteen's writings. While he serves as the leading proponent for the model, several other thinkers will be examined to buttress and explicate the four couplets. The core value they all hold in common is the commitment to finding a middle way.

Philip Clayton proposes a synthesis of formal factors (Popper) and contextual factors (Kuhn) in a new model that he calls a "formal-semantic" theory.[18] This is his attempt to overcome the stalemate between the two competing models of rationality in philosophy of science. Clayton has written extensively on Pannenberg and, as we will see below, he spells out and expands on the implications of his former teacher's work in a way that is more up to date with contemporary philosophy of science. Further, Clayton has explicitly affirmed the value of the term "postfoundationalism" over against "postmodernism," which is so multivalent.[19]

Another example is Andy F. Sanders, a Dutch theologian who proposes the phrase "traditionalist fallibilism" as a middle way between relativism and foundationalism.[20] Sanders is especially inter-

17. van Huyssteen, *Essays,* p. 228.

18. P. Clayton, *Explanation from Physics to Theology* (New Haven: Yale University Press, 1989), p. 66.

19. P. Clayton, *God and Contemporary Science* (Grand Rapids: Eerdmans, 1997), p. 4.

20. A. Sanders, "Traditionalism, Fallibilism and Theological Relativism," *Nederlands Theologisch Tijdschrift* 49 (1995): 195. Much of the philosophical back-

ested in religious epistemology and theories of justification in the rationality debate; his goal is to develop a model of human knowledge in which "truth is still in." His work is particularly helpful in clarifying the epistemological implications of interdisciplinary dialogue for religious belief, as we will see in our discussion below of the relation of truth and knowledge.

Also consonant with the postfoundationalist model is Mikael Stenmark, who suggests the model of "presumptionism" as a *via media* between "formalism" and "contextualism." The core of his proposal is the principle of presumption: "It is rational to accept a belief unless there are good reasons to cease from thinking that it is true."[21] He distinguishes this from the two extremes of formalism and contextualism. Formalists accept (among other things) the *evidentialist* principle ("it is rational to accept a proposition or belief only if there are good reasons to believe it is true") and the *rule* principle ("a belief, action or evaluation is rational only if it is obtained by following the appropriate rules"). The other extreme is defined in the *contextual* principle: "what is rational or irrational can be determined only internally, from within a context (practice); there exist no context-independent standards of rationality."[22] Stenmark refers to the actual way rational agents reason as their "practice," and notes that contextualism implies a view of rationality that is practice-*determined*, while formalism attempts to define rationality in a way that is practice-*independent*. Because his "presumptionism" is intended to be practice-*oriented*, accepting the shaping influence of the rational practices within which we are socially embedded, but also maintaining that the *nature* of rationality is universal (although its standards are person-relative), Stenmark appears to be in the stream of the emerging postfoundationalist movement.

Although they do not address *theological* methodology in any de-

---

ground for Sanders's approach is developed in his book *Michael Polanyi's Post-Critical Epistemology* (Amsterdam: Rodopi, 1988). Sanders also treats these issues in "Criticism, Contact with Reality and Truth," *Tradition and Discovery* 23, no. 3 (1996-97): 24-37.

21. M. Stenmark, *Rationality in Science, Religion, and Everyday Life* (Notre Dame: University of Notre Dame Press, 1995), p. 212.

22. Stenmark, *Rationality*, pp. 42, 56, 303.

tail, the works of philosophers Nicholas Rescher, Susan Haack, and Calvin Schrag appear to belong in the postfoundationalist group. Nicholas Rescher proposes "contextualistic rationalism" as a middle way between rationalism and relativism.

> Against dogmatic uniformitarianism, it seeks to defend a doctrine of pluralism in cognitive and social theory. But against the widespread current of relativistic indifferentism it seeks to defend the appropriateness of taking a committed and definite position, even in the face of views that differ from one's own . . . such a view seeks to occupy a *middle ground* [emphasis added] between a traditionalistic rationalism that sees our cognitive and practical problems as admitting of only one possible solution dictated by reason alone, and a postmodern relativism that dissolves every sort of position into the indifferentism of personal interests. . . .[23]

Rescher affirms a type of coherentism, but his model is consciously developed to avoid relativism. In several works, he attempts to clarify the value of our realist intuitions and affirms truth as an ideal.

Calvin Schrag also points to the fall of foundationalism, which he shows has been rightly challenged by postmodern critique. The mistake of modern epistemology was assuming that *episteme* must be conceptualized as a universal, vertical, ahistorical logos "designed to provide a foundational support for every instance of knowledge."[24] This assumption is the linchpin of the debate. The foundationalist affirms the universal logos (so conceived), and the nonfoundationalist vigorously denies it. The former puts all the epistemic eggs in this basket, while the latter eschews the use of baskets completely and aims to explain rationality without the help of any "logos." But as Schrag urges, "So long as one stays within [this] framework of inquiry . . . the battle lines will continue to be drawn

23. N. Rescher, *Pluralism: Against the Demand for Consensus* (Oxford: Clarendon, 1993), p. 2.

24. C. Schrag, *The Resources of Rationality: A Response to the Postmodern Challenge* (Bloomington: Indiana University Press, 1992), p. 168.

between a logocentric epistemology and a doxastic flux of historical becoming, congealing into a differend that neither party can surmount."[25] We will see below that Schrag contributes to a middle way with his concept of "transversal" rationality.

Susan Haack has explicitly proposed a middle way between foundationalism and coherentism, which she argues "do not exhaust the options."[26] She calls her approach "foundherentism," a neologism designed to emphasize the need for a *via media* that overcomes the antipodal structuring of the debate. Her model will be particularly helpful in the discussion of the relation of belief to experience.

In this brief survey, it has become clear that we are not simply dealing with a single "middle way." Rather, there are several dichotomies that must be overcome. However, the various emphases are mutually supporting and cannot be wholly understood in abstraction from the others. To clarify the distinctions between foundationalism and nonfoundationalism, we can ask of each model how it views the relation between the four pairs: experience and belief, truth and knowledge, individual and community, explanation and understanding. We will see the following emphases in *foundationalism:* experience as the basis of belief, the unity of truth, reason in the individual, and the universality of explanation. *Nonfoundationalism* will be characterized by the following emphases: the web of belief as conditioning experience, the plurality of knowledge, the rationality of the community, and the particularity of understanding. *Postfoundationalism* attempts to accommodate the legitimate intuitions of these emphases without collapsing into either extreme. I will explicate this emerging model in terms of four relational couplets, each aiming to overcome the polarizing tendencies of foundationalism and nonfoundationalism.

---

25. Schrag, *The Resources of Rationality,* p. 168.

26. Susan Haack, *Evidence and Inquiry: Towards Reconstruction in Epistemology* (Oxford: Basil Blackwell, 1993), p. 19.

The Four Couplets of Postfoundationalism

The following couplets are my own reconstruction of an emerging model of theological rationality; no single thinker has articulated them precisely in this way. Therefore, the four couplets are proposed as representing the assertions of an "ideal type" postfoundationalist.

(PF1): interpreted experience engenders and nourishes all beliefs, and a network of beliefs informs the interpretation of experience.

(PF2): the objective unity of truth is a necessary condition for the intelligible search for knowledge, and the subjective multiplicity of knowledge indicates the fallibility of truth claims.

(PF3): rational judgment is an activity of socially situated individuals, and the cultural community indeterminately mediates the criteria of rationality.

(PF4): explanation aims for universal, transcontextual understanding, and understanding derives from particular contextualized explanations.

In what follows, we will examine each of these couplets, referring to the writings of the authors mentioned above, to determine the extent to which they navigate between the extremes of emphasis in foundationalism and nonfoundationalism. Notice that the first part of each couplet aims to capture the positive intuitions of the former, while the second part articulates the concern of the latter. This analysis is not intended to be exhaustive, but merely to serve as background for bringing Pannenberg into dialogue with the postfoundationalist model in Chapter Three.

1. Experience and Belief

How are we to understand the relation between our beliefs and our experience? Is there a balance between the foundationalist stress on the "basis of experience" and the nonfoundationalist emphasis on the "web of belief"? To what extent do our experiences justify our beliefs, and how do our beliefs determine what we experience? When the issue is the justification of beliefs, foundationalism is best contrasted with "coherentism,"[27] a nonfoundationalist construal of rationality which argues that experiences are embedded in networks of belief, and that this linguistically shaped "web" limits and mediates all experience. Foundationalists, on the other hand, justify beliefs by appealing to their groundedness in experience (whether conceptual or sensual); the direction of rational support flows only from experience to belief.

These are often seen as the only options. Ernest Sosa claims we must decide between metaphors: "Contemporary epistemology must choose between the solid security of the ancient foundationalist pyramid and the risky adventure of the new coherentist raft."[28] The raft metaphor suggests that we are at sea and must reconstruct our knowledge one plank at a time without the ease and safety of a firm foundation. The postfoundationalist approach aims for a middle way, challenging both metaphors:

(PF1): interpreted experience engenders and nourishes all beliefs, and a network of beliefs informs the interpretation of experience.

The key concept in the first part of the couplet is the phrase "interpreted experience," and it is specifically aimed against foundationalist conceptions that would allow some beliefs to bypass experience or to enter the web "neutrally," without being interpreted. This is a central concept in the writings of van Huyssteen.

> Because we relate to our world epistemically only through the mediation of interpreted experience, the observer or the knower

27. This term will be defined more carefully below, borrowing from the analysis of Haack and Stenmark.

28. Ernest Sosa, "The Raft and the Pyramid: Coherence versus Foundations in the Theory of Knowledge," *Midwest Studies in Philosophy,* vol. 5: *Studies in Epistemology* (Minneapolis: University of Minnesota Press, 1980), p. 3. Notice that the "raft" metaphor also suggests that we are supported by *something* (water), even if it is not as solid as we might like. Similarly, "webs" have to be supported somehow, or the metaphor falls down completely.

is always in a relationship to what is known, and thus always limited in perspective, in focus, and in experiential scope. In this sense beliefs are both brought to experience and derived from it, and our interpreted experience thus becomes the matrix within which meaning and knowledge arise.[29]

For van Huyssteen, this is true not only for theology, but also for natural science and all other types of human inquiry. Once we recognize that all beliefs emerge out of (and are nourished by) already interpreted experience, this frees us to explore critically the experiential roots of our beliefs without feeling compelled to throw out our commitment to the explanatory power of those beliefs.

This opens up space for overcoming the dilemma. Van Huyssteen suggests a *balance* that affirms both "the way our beliefs are anchored in interpreted experience" and "the broader networks of belief in which our rationally compelling experiences are already embedded."[30] This overcomes the nonfoundationalist worry about a linear justification of rationality that moves only from experience to beliefs. It also responds to the foundationalist anxiety about attempts to divorce our reasons for believing something from our experience of the world.

The metaphors of "engendering" and "nourishing" in the first part of (PF1) capture the idea that experience gives rise to beliefs, but avoid the idea of a unilateral determinism. Van Huyssteen argues that we need two complementary criteria for justifying beliefs: *experiential* adequacy and *epistemological* adequacy.[31] These refer to the twin demands that, on the one hand, our beliefs adequately account for our experience, which will always be compelling to us, and that, on the other hand, our beliefs be justified by their explanatory power relative to criteria external to the system. To accomplish this, the postfoundationalist model calls for a broader theory of experience than either the traditional empiricist or rationalist views, or

29. van Huyssteen, *Essays,* p. 20.

30. J. W. van Huyssteen, *The Shaping of Rationality* (Grand Rapids: Eerdmans, 1999), p. 37.

31. van Huyssteen, *Essays,* p. 71.

the isolated, incommensurable linguistic webs of nonfoundationalism. Here van Huyssteen finds a resource in thinkers like Jerome Stone, with his "transactional realism."[32] Such a move avoids the naïve realism often found in early foundationalist epistemology as well as the skepticism of nihilist anti-realism, arguing instead for "the fiduciary rootedness of all rationality"[33] but in a way that acknowledges the fallibility and provisionality of our beliefs.

The second clause in (PF1) is oriented toward challenging the nonfoundationalist assumption that webs of belief limit and *determine* what is experienced. However, the postfoundationalist does acknowledge that the network of belief *informs* the interpretation of experience. It is precisely the reciprocal relation between belief and experience that sets the postfoundationalist model apart from its rivals. To bolster this aspect of the model, van Huyssteen has argued for a "critical realism" that affirms the embedded nature of human knowledge and existence.[34] He holds onto the goal of developing criteria for judging between webs of belief, and continues to insist that experience shapes our ongoing interpretations and contributes to the justification of our beliefs.

As a resource for the postfoundationalist treatment of the relation of belief to experience, the "foundherentist" model developed by Susan Haack is particularly helpful. In her *Evidence and Inquiry*, she defines foundationalism (as a theory of justification) as involving two theses:

(FD1) Some justified beliefs are basic; a basic belief is justified independently of the support of any other belief; and

(FD2) All other justified beliefs are derived; a derived belief is justified via the support, direct or indirect, of a basic belief or beliefs.[35]

---

32. Jerome Stone, *The Minimalist Vision of Transcendence* (Albany: State University of New York Press, 1992).

33. van Huyssteen, *Essays*, p. 44.

34. J. Wentzel van Huyssteen, "Postfoundationalism in Theology and Science: Beyond Conflict and Consonance," in *Rethinking Theology and Science: Six Models for the Current Dialogue*, ed. Niels Henrik Gregersen and J. W. van Huyssteen (Grand Rapids: Eerdmans, 1998), p. 37.

35. Haack, *Evidence and Inquiry*, p. 14.

Haack explicitly includes "weak" foundationalist approaches (like Reformed epistemology) in this category. Indeed, "classical" is only one type of foundationalism, as philosophers like Nicholas Wolterstorff have urged.[36] Even after the demise of Logical Positivism, Alvin Plantinga and others describe themselves as foundationalists (of a "modest" or "weak" sort). They insist that some beliefs are "properly basic," but argue about what kinds of belief qualify for this status. The classical foundationalists of the Enlightenment tended to suggest beliefs that are self-evident, incorrigible, and/or "evident to the senses." Plantinga, on the other hand, suggests that experiences that meet specific conditions, whether perceptual experiences ("being appeared to") or memory experiences ("being appeared to pastly"), are what justify the holding of beliefs; such experiences are "the *ground* of my justification, and, by extension, the ground of the belief itself."[37]

Because of this ambiguity in the use of the term, I think it is wise to follow Mikael Stenmark in defining a "foundationalist" (of any type) as one who asserts that the relation between human beliefs is asymmetrical,[38] i.e., that there are two types of belief: basic and nonbasic. The former are justified non-inferentially or immediately, while the latter are justified by inferential appeal to basic beliefs. This allows us to include the "Reformed" epistemologists under the heading of "foundationalist" even if they do not accept the "classical" criteria for the basicality of beliefs. D. Z. Phillips[39] follows a similar categorization.

Haack addresses several of the problems with the foundationalist theory. She notes that foundations (once identified) are either rich *or* secure, never both. That is, when a foundation is extremely secure, it is not very helpful. The *a priori* analytic assertion, "bachelors are unmarried males," does not support very many other

36. N. Wolterstorff, "Introduction," in *Faith and Rationality*, ed. A. Plantinga and N. Wolterstorff (Notre Dame: University of Notre Dame Press, 1983), p. 3.

37. A. Plantinga, "Reason and Belief in God," in *Faith and Rationality*, ed. A. Plantinga and N. Wolterstorff (Notre Dame: University of Notre Dame Press, 1983), p. 79.

38. Stenmark, *Rationality*, p. 44.

39. Phillips, *Faith after Foundationalism*, pp. 24ff.

beliefs. On the other hand, rich concepts or robust beliefs do not make very stable foundations because they are always open to challenge. She also criticizes the idea that any belief can be immune from support from some other belief. She offers the illustration of a person who believes she perceives a dog. It seems that such a person would be more justified in the belief that she sees a dog if she also has other beliefs that support it, such as that she is not under hypnosis, that there are no large lifelike toy dogs around, etc. In other words, the belief that she perceives a dog is not basic in the sense that it is not supported at all by other beliefs.

Haack is no more hopeful about the coherentist model for justifying beliefs. She defines coherentism as asserting:

(CH)   A belief is justified if and only if it belongs to a coherent set of beliefs.

Here Haack has three major complaints. First, coherentism seems "too much to ask." Is it possible for a person to think through all of his or her beliefs to ascertain whether all of them are interdependent and coherent? Surely, this may be an ideal but it hardly seems possible. If it is actually impossible, then no one could ever be justified in holding *any* belief. Second, Haack discusses what she calls the "drunken sailors" argument. If beliefs are holding each other up, what is holding the beliefs up? Of course, we are dealing with metaphors here, but some questions for the strict coherentist are: where did we get these beliefs, why do we choose these beliefs, and how are they holding each other up? This is closely related to a third concern, Haack's "consistent fairy story" objection. Quite simply, the coherentist vision has no way of indicating the truth of its beliefs, so long as it maintains strict adherence to its strong assertions about the criteria of justification as involving *only* coherence.

As a middle position between foundationalism and coherentism, Haack proposes *foundherentism*, which asserts two theses:

(FH1)   A subject's experience is relevant to the justification of his or her empirical beliefs, but there need be no privileged class of empirical beliefs justified exclusively by the support of experience, independently of the support of other beliefs, and

(FH2) Justification is not exclusively one-directional, but involves pervasive relations of mutual support.[40]

Haack sees her proposal for foundherentism as overcoming several dichotomies that have shaped the philosophical discussion, dichotomies such as foundationalism vs. coherentism, externalism vs. internalism, causal vs. logical, and inductivist vs. deductivist.[41] The ambition of breaking false dichotomies makes her a valuable resource for theologians struggling to develop a postfoundationalist model of rationality.

> Considered as theories of empirical justification, the point is, foundationalism and coherentism *do not exhaust the options;* there is logical space in between. At its simplest, the argument is this: foundationalism requires one-directionality, coherentism does not; coherentism requires justification to be exclusively a matter of relations among beliefs, foundationalism does not. . . . A theory such as the one I favour, which allows the relevance of experience to justification, but requires no class of privileged beliefs justified exclusively by experience with no support from other beliefs, is neither foundationalist nor coherentist, but is *intermediate between the traditional rivals.*[42]

Against the foundationalist, she insists that justification of beliefs is not one-directional, but against the nonfoundationalist she wants experience (not merely other beliefs) to play a crucial role in justifying the rationality of a belief. The debate about experience and belief, however, is only one of the battlegrounds on which the battle over the definition of rationality is waged. Inherently connected are the other conceptual pairs we have outlined, and demonstrating the way in which the postfoundationalist model attempts

40. Haack, *Evidence and Inquiry,* p. 19.
41. Haack, *Evidence and Inquiry,* pp. 2, 4.
42. Haack, *Evidence and Inquiry,* p. 19. Emphases added.

to find a middle way between these other sets of horns will contribute to a more complete understanding of the impact of this emerging view of rationality and its impact on the task of theology.

2. Truth and Knowledge

What is truth? How can we *know* that we know anything? These are the kinds of epistemological questions that fuel the debates between philosophers. The classical foundationalist emphasized the drive for certain and objective knowledge of the truth. In this view, the multiplicity of truth claims is due only to unclear thinking (opinion, *doxa*). The nonfoundationalist, on the other hand, points to the obvious plurality of knowledge claims, and argues that all knowing is subjectively bound to the knower; in its deconstructivist and relativist forms, this leads to a denial of the existence of "truth" independent of the subject. The postfoundationalist couplet that aims to transcend this dichotomy is:

(PF2):   the objective unity of truth is a necessary condition for the intelligible search for knowledge, and the subjective multiplicity of knowledge indicates the fallibility of truth claims.

Several important concepts cohabit this assertion. We see a distinction (but not a strong bifurcation) between objectivity and subjectivity, between unity and multiplicity, between truth and knowledge. The key conceptual tools used by the postfoundationalist in linking these pairs are the terms "intelligibility" and "fallibility." The goal is to maintain the foundationalist vision of truth as an ideal that drives our inquiry, but to avoid arrogating one's current knowledge as the total and final metanarrative, a danger against which the nonfoundationalist rightly warns.

To understand the role of intelligibility and fallibility in the postfoundationalist model, it is necessary to touch again upon van Huyssteen's version of "critical realism." The connection is made explicitly: "As a broader, holist approach a *fallibilist*, experiential program of postfoundationalist critical realism can . . . link theology, philosophy of religion, and the sciences in their common search for *intelligibility*."[43] The call for a weak form of critical realism already played a significant role in van Huyssteen's earlier work:

> A critical-realist stand is realistic because in the process of theological theorizing this concept enables us to recognize the cognitive and referential nature of analogical language as a form of indirect speech. It is also critical, however, because the role of metaphoric language in theology would teach us that models should never be absolutized or ideologized, but should retain their openness and provisionality throughout the process of theorizing.[44]

In his more recent work, van Huyssteen clearly recognizes that such a move is necessary for finding a "safe epistemological space" for the task of theology, space that avoids both the absolutism of foundationalism and the relativism of nonfoundationalism. The emphasis on "intelligibility" aims to accommodate the foundationalist intuitions about truth as an ideal, and the insistence on "fallibility" accommodates the nonfoundationalist worry about absolutism and hegemonic totalization.

The nonfoundationalist is right in noting that much of theology in the past has been based on an epistemic foundationalism that is no longer tenable. We can see it operative in Thomas Aquinas, for example, who was so influential in Christian theology's claim to be a "science" after the rise of the first universities in Europe in the thirteenth century. Of course, *scientia* was understood in Aristotelian terms as being based on first principles, derived from axioms, etc. Up until the eleventh century, the term *theologia* referred to only one aspect of Christian teaching, namely, the doctrine of God (which included God's existence, attributes, and triunity), while the salvific acts of God in history witnessed to in Scripture were dis-

---

43. van Huyssteen, *Essays*, p. 52. Emphases added.

44. J. W. van Huyssteen, *Theology and the Justification of Faith: Constructing Theories in Systematic Theology*, trans. H. F. Snijders (Grand Rapids: Eerdmans, 1989), p. 142.

cussed under the rubric *oikonomia* (economy). But with the emergence of universities, all Christian doctrine came to be studied as *facultas theologica,* with the other "sciences." To make theology a science in the Aristotelian sense, Thomas posited the articles of faith (sacredly revealed) as the first principles; the *Summa Theologiae* derives its propositions from these principles in Scripture as well as from "the Philosopher." Thomas could pull this off (even in the University) because everyone accepted them by authority. Today, since the Enlightenment attack on appeals to authority, this route appears blocked.

Two more recent examples of foundationalism in theology are Friedrich Schleiermacher and Karl Barth. Schleiermacher appealed to "Feeling," which is presupposed in the self-consciousness of every human being. From this, he deduced the "feeling of absolute dependence" as the foundation for his *Glaubenslehre.*[45] For Karl Barth the "act of faith," the risk one takes in affirming the self-authenticating Word of God, leads to a positing of this Word as an epistemic foundation. The truth of this Word is self-evident for those who receive it in faith; on this incorrigible foundation, Barth builds his *Church Dogmatics.*[46] The obvious problem here is that proponents of other religions (or other Christian denominations) can assert the same self-evidence for *their* faith; how are we to judge between them?

Ironically, Barth has also been deeply influential on *non*foundationalist theologians, particularly the "Yale school" through the work of George Lindbeck. This historical fact suggests the possibility that this latter approach may in fact be crypto-foundationalist, a model that has fallen back into fideism without noticing it, as van

---

45. Elsewhere I have demonstrated how the relationality that constitutes human self-consciousness functions regulatively in Schleiermacher's dogmatics. See my "Schleiermacher's 'Reciprocal Relationality': The Underlying Regulative Principle of His Theological Method," in *Schleiermacher on Workings of the Knowing Mind,* ed. Ruth Drucilla Richardson, 177-95 (Lampeter, Wales: Edwin Mellen, 1998).

46. For the way in which anthropology (surreptitiously) shapes Barth's methodology, see my "Constitutive Relationality in Anthropology and Trinity: The Shaping of the *Imago Dei* Doctrine in Barth and Pannenberg," *Neue Zeitschrift für systematische Theologie und Religionsphilosophie* 39 (1997): 304-22.

Huyssteen and others have charged.[47] It is important to understand this complaint against nonfoundationalist theology in order to grasp the distinctiveness of the *post*foundationalist model.

Lindbeck's proposal is for a nonfoundationalist "cultural-linguistic" model of theology. He argues that the "most fruitful" philosophy of our day has shown that religions resemble languages and cultures and that this is the best way to study religion. In this model, doctrines function as rules that guide speech and behavior in the linguistic community (church). Lindbeck distinguishes between three kinds of truth: propositional truth, symbolic truth (efficacy), and categorial truth (adequacy). Doctrines function at the latter level. They are true insofar as they are adequate for socializing new members into the Christian community and its ongoing narrative. He admits it sounds odd to claim the Niceanum is not making first-order truth claims, but this is what he argues. In fact, he argues even more strongly that the *innovative* aspect of his proposal is the argument that the regulative function is "the *only job* that doctrines do in their role as church teachings."[48] His rule theory insists that doctrines attain propositional or ontological reference *only insofar* as in "performing" these utterances they are *made* true. A religious utterance "acquires the propositional truth of ontological correspondence only insofar as it is a performance, an act or deed, which helps create that correspondence."[49]

This proposal has several problems, but let us limit our focus to the issue of foundationalism.[50] Lindbeck makes a claim in the preface for the "neutrality" of his proposal. This is hardly tenable in light of postmodern epistemological criticism, and is clearly inconsistent with his claim later in the book to be an antifoundationalist. He com-

47. van Huyssteen, *Essays,* p. 24.

48. George Lindbeck, *The Nature of Doctrine* (Philadelphia: Westminster, 1984), p. 19. Emphasis added.

49. George Lindbeck, *The Nature of Doctrine,* p. 65.

50. For a more detailed critical analysis of Lindbeck's proposal, see my "Truth Happens? The Pragmatic Conception of Truth and the Postliberal Research Program," *The Princeton Theological Review* 4, no. 1 (February (1997): 26-36. Lindbeck's view is a post–linguistic-turn version of William James's conception of truth, and it fails for the same reasons (among others).

plains that the propositionalist and experiential-expressivist views of doctrine try to offer a "common framework" by which to compare religions, and suggests that his cultural-linguistic approach avoids this.[51] But on what grounds does he argue this? From what "neutral" territory does he support his contention that religions are primarily languages and doctrines are grammatical rules? Clearly (his relativistic reading of) Wittgenstein is a "common framework" from which he hopes to judge the pragmatic "adequacy" of all doctrines.

In Lindbeck's actual argumentation, his definition of the *nature* of doctrine is the one *proposition* that is not susceptible to communal relativization; it is a foundation that is immediately justified and basic for his model. It is assumed to be *true* for experiential-expressivists (for example) as well as for postliberals. Lindbeck asserts that the text absorbs the world. But there is one thing that is immune from this absorption: Wittgensteinian rule theory. The very condition for stating the text's ability to absorb is not absorbed by the text. In fact, Wittgenstein absorbs both the text and Lindbeck's reading of it. This suggests that Lindbeck has privileged a philosophical theory over the nature of doctrine. He wants to describe the "nature" of doctrine, but he claims to have done so by describing its (only) "function." But what does he claim for *his own theory:* Is it "categorially" true or "propositionally" true? That is to say, if his theory is just adequate for socializing members into the postliberal research community, then it is limited to his particular language game, and does not describe the "nature" of doctrine. But surely he seems to think he is actually describing a state of affairs: he believes it is the case that this is what doctrine actually *is.* Lindbeck claims that the innovative aspect of his proposal is that the regulative function is the *"only job"* of doctrine. But his cultural-linguistic theory (borrowed from Wittgenstein) is doing some other job, and has more referential power than the doctrines he is describing.

Ironically, in spite of his antifoundationalist claims, Lindbeck exemplifies one of the most obvious *foundationalist* pitfalls.[52] He says

---

51. F. LeRon Shults, "Truth Happens?" p. 49.

52. In "Lindbeck's New Program," *The Thomist* 49 (1985): 468, David Tracy argues that Lindbeck fails to save himself from the charges of relativism and fideism.

doctrines are "rules" and that the ones from Nicea are authoritative. But how do we know these are the right rules? By what rules did he arrive at the decision to pick Nicea instead of some others? Cult leaders around the world would list different rules and they would claim, as he does, that their rules are adequate for socializing their new converts into their community. If Lindbeck did provide the rules for that decision (choosing Nicea), then we would ask where he got *those* rules, *ad infinitum*. So it falls into an infinite regress, which Lindbeck seems to try to halt by appealing to *his* community: ecumenical scholars and church leaders who want to maintain "difference without disunity." But this has nothing to do with what we *mean* by truth; we can be united without agreeing, just as we can agree without being united.

The goal of the *post*foundationalist model is to move beyond the hidden fideism of nonfoundationalist thought, which ironically emerges out of its relativism. As Roger Trigg has pointed out, if all reasoning is trapped in and reducible to particular social practices, then we can never reason about social practices. But then the statement that all reason is a social practice is reducible to a social practice and should not be granted any more credibility than the statement that it is not reducible to a social practice. If the fragmentation of reason is complete, then we cannot make any claims about reason at all, including the claim that the fragmentation of reason is complete. The making of the claim presupposes the reasonableness of the judgment, which disproves the claim. Trigg further notes that "it is hard to think that religious practices can long endure after people have given up any idea of the objective reality of God."[53]

Similarly, van Huyssteen notes that if this kind of nonfoundationalism were true, "then any social or human activity could in principle function as a test case for rationality."[54] This would leave us with no way to judge between the many rationalities of the postmodern world. While postfoundationalists acknowledge the ideal of objectivity, this does not entail *objectivism:* "Over against the

---

53. Roger Trigg, *Rationality and Science: Can Science Explain Everything?* (Oxford: Blackwell, 1993), p. 163.

54. van Huyssteen, *Essays,* p. 245.

objectivism of foundationalism and the extreme relativism of most forms of nonfoundationalism, some of us want to develop a postfoundationalist model of rationality that is thoroughly contextual, but that at the same time will attempt to reach beyond the limits of its own group or culture in interdisciplinary discussion."[55]

As mentioned above, the key conceptual tools for finding the middle way in this case are the notions of intelligibility and fallibility. Here van Huyssteen finds resources in the work of Nicholas Rescher and Andy Sanders. The postfoundationalist does not claim to "have" the truth, but argues that the truth as an ideal is what "pulls" our search for optimal intelligibility.[56] Rescher refers to this ideal as a *focus imaginarius* that canalizes and structures human inquiry.[57] In a more recent work, Rescher explicitly deals with the concept of "objectivity," which he believes cannot simply be discarded. He aims to rehabilitate the commitment to objectivity.

> For what a relativistic indifferentism to truth and rightness in effect achieves is to destroy the very conception it presumably elucidates. Where a factual question is at issue ("Was there indeed a Nazi holocaust that killed more than six million people in execution camps?") an answer that is supposed to hold true for X but not for Y is not an answer at all. And the same situation obtains where a moral question is concerned ("Is it morally acceptable to foster an ideological program by killing people?"). A physics, a history, a morality that abandons its claims to impersonal cogency is simply no physics, no history, no morality at all.[58]

---

55. van Huyssteen, *Essays,* p. 245.

56. For van Huyssteen, intelligibility is "the supreme value that determines rationality" (*Essays,* p. 163).

57. N. Rescher, *A System of Pragmatic Idealism,* vol. 1 (Princeton: Princeton University Press, 1992), p. 94.

58. N. Rescher, *Objectivity: The Obligations of Impersonal Reason* (Notre Dame: University of Notre Dame Press, 1997), p. 2. Rescher notes that much of feminist thought has dismissed the concept of truth, even as an ideal. It is important to balance Rescher's complaint with a recognition that many streams of feminist philosophy have indeed affirmed the necessity of the concept of truth. E.g., in *Eros for the*

To that list, the postfoundationalist wants to add theology. As van Huyssteen urges, "there is more to our religious and theological language than just what happens to be useful to us."[59] Theology must aim to accommodate the realist intuitions of Christian faith.

In articulating her "foundherentism," Susan Haack addresses the issue of truth, suggesting that we should accept the pre-analytic intuition that for the criteria of justification of beliefs to be good, they should be "truth-indicative." In order to highlight the fact that it is individual persons who are justified in their beliefs (avoiding an epistemology without knowers), and to emphasize that the justification of beliefs is gradational, she proposes the following *explicandum*: "A is more/less justified, at time t, in believing that p, depending on. . . ." The *explanans* is a matter of the "experiential anchoring and explanatory integration of the subject's evidence with respect to a belief."[60]

For Haack, such "evidence" may be either empirical in the broadest sense, or introspective, or both. She concludes that "if any truth indication is available to us, satisfaction of the foundherentist criteria of justification is as good an indication of truth as we could have."[61] She explicitly excludes "religious" experience. It is precisely here that the postfoundationalist theologian will want to part company, and argue that in fact part of our interpreted experience is the experience of that which is ultimate, of a source of the intelligibility of the cosmos. Excluding such experience can only be based on *a priori* naturalistic assumptions. Van Huyssteen wants to hold on to the possibility that the search for intelligibility may lead us to

---

Other: Retaining Truth in a Pluralistic World (University Park: The University of Pennsylvania Press, 1996), p. 12, Wendy Farley argues that "the reality of other beings is the touchstone of my attempt to retrieve an idea of truth that is not destroyed by the false alternatives between relativism and absolutism, and that does not depend upon inhabiting a 'view from nowhere' in order to discern this reality." This drive for a middle way shows affinities with the postfoundationalist model.

59. van Huyssteen, "Critical Realism and God: Can There Be Faith after Foundationalism?" in *Essays*, p. 42.

60. Haack, *Evidence and Inquiry*, p. 139.

61. Haack, *Evidence and Inquiry*, p. 220.

point to some form of ontological unity, and maybe even to a personal God[.] This notion of a personal God may serve to make sense of (and thus may be experientially more adequate to) great swathes of experience that without this notion would simply baffle us. . . . Our commitment to a mind-independent reality called God thus would not only arise *from experience,* but in a very specific sense also *for experience.* . . .[62]

However, this does not inevitably lead to the bugaboo of a totalizing metanarrative; it is precisely the function of "fallibilism" in postfoundationalist thought that serves to protect against it. If we want to avoid fideism, we must hold onto the ideals of truth, objectivity, and rationality, while at the same time acknowledging the provisional, contextual, and fallible nature of human reason.[63]

Andy F. Sanders proposes the phrase "traditionalist fallibilism" as a middle way between relativism and foundationalism.[64] He traces briefly the failure of foundationalism and the well-known self-defeating nature of relativism, illustrating the latter in theologian Sally McFague. Sanders then emphasizes that "fallibilism" avoids self-defeat, because it is aware that even the belief in fallibilism may be mistaken, but since it does not deny we can have true beliefs, it may consistently offer reasons for accepting fallibilism. Sanders's conception of "traditionalism" is another attempt at a middle way; in this case between the blind acceptance of tradition and the acceptance (or critique) of tradition based on evidence. He offers an alternative that aims to "comply with the intellectual virtue of participating in the quest for truth"[65] without accepting the foundationalist thesis that this requires a detached and impartial viewpoint. Here we can see a drive to account for the commitment of the theologian herself within the theory of religious knowledge and justification of beliefs, without thereby giving up on

62. van Huyssteen, *Essays,* p. 102.
63. van Huyssteen, *Essays,* p. 259. The concept of "fallibility" is an essential aspect of the postfoundationalist model; see also van Huyssteen's *The Shaping of Rationality,* chapters 3 and 4.
64. Sanders, "Traditionalism," p. 195.
65. Sanders, "Traditionalism," p. 207.

intersubjective criteria. This connection between the individual and his or her tradition provides a nice segue to our next conceptual pair.

3. *Individual and Community*

The first two couplets are more oriented toward epistemological questions, i.e., the nature of and conditions for our knowing, although they inevitably ramify into hermeneutic issues as well. For the latter two dyads, the focus is more on hermeneutic questions, although they are derived from and have implications for epistemological issues. As we will see in the final section of this chapter, it is the attempt to link epistemology and hermeneutics in a particular way that characterizes postfoundationalist thinking.

Foundationalism tends to privilege the individual in discussions of reason. The Platonists believed that the individual human *nous* participates in the divine logos. Enlightenment thinkers assumed that individuals had access to "Reason" as a kind of neutral tribunal that would guide them to the truth if the proper rules were followed and the conclusions were necessarily derived from the right foundations. This meant all individuals can and ought to come to the same conclusion, irrespective of context, tradition, or language. The individual standing in a neutral Archimedean point, wholly independent of tradition, became the ideal. Some scholars have also critiqued the "weak" foundationalism of "Reformed" epistemology as focusing too heavily on the individual, ignoring the communal factors that shape rational judgment.[66]

Nonfoundationalism, on the other hand, has affirmed the postmodern critique of individualism. Historicist hermeneutics has illustrated the dependence of rationality on the historical context out of which it operates. After Wittgenstein effected the "linguistic

---

66. E.g., James Beilby, "Proper Basicality, Warrant and Religious Diversity: An Appraisal of Plantinga's *Warranted Christian Belief*" (unpublished paper presented at the Midwest Meeting of the American Academy of Religion, April 17, 1998, St. Paul, Minn.).

turn," it is difficult to deny that the language games in which we live do indeed have a profound effect on our interpretations. We are shaped by the cultural systems and traditions into which we are born. In its relativist forms, nonfoundationalism takes this to the extreme and argues that language games are incommensurable, and that each community determines its own rationality. Finding transcommunal criteria for justifying rationality is impossible.

As with the other polarities, *post*foundationalism aims to accommodate the intuitions of both sides without collapsing into absolutism or relativism.

(PF3): rational judgment is an activity of socially situated individuals, and the cultural community indeterminately mediates the criteria of rationality.

The postfoundationalist insists that the locus of rational choice is the individual agent, yet also affirms that what a person judges to be rational is affected by the cultural-historical group of which he or she is a part. For van Huyssteen, "rationality not only involves evaluation against the standards of a community of inquiry, but also assures that the personal voice of the individual rational agent is not silenced in this ongoing process of collective assessment."[67] In this way he acknowledges the nonfoundationalist sensitivity to the hermeneutical conditioning effected by being situated in a community of inquirers, but refuses to give up the intuition of the foundationalist that it is the individual who actually *makes* a rational judgment.

We may find resources for the postfoundationalist model in several authors. In an important essay, Clayton and Knapp argue that the standards of the community shape the evaluative decisions of the personal rational agent.[68] This does not mean that only consensual agreement is rational, for this would block the voice of the prophet, visionary, or genius. They emphasize that the rational

67. van Huyssteen, "Postfoundationalism in Theology and Science," p. 30.
68. P. Clayton and S. Knapp, "Rationality and Ethics," *American Philosophical Quarterly* 30, no. 2 (April 1993): 151-61.

agent's *self-conception* plays an implicit and central role in each judgment over against the epistemic community's general standards.[69] This is a move away from modernist notions of universal, acontextual standards, yet it provides an indispensable role for the individual precisely in the relation of the self to the community.[70] Individuals are shaped by their communal situation, but most individuals do not believe that *any* presently existing community fully represents their sense of what a community should be, i.e., a place where they may achieve "ideal" selfhood.

Individuals make decisions for reasons that appear good to them, reasons that are shaped by cognitive, pragmatic, and evaluative factors. These dimensions of rationality are mediated (but not determined) by the community. This allows the postfoundationalist to make a critical distinction. In the words of Nicholas Rescher,

> . . . rationality as such is self-identically uniform. *What rationality is* is something that is fixedly defined by the conception itself — by the item that constitutes the topic of discussion. However, variation enters in with consideration regarding *what is rational*, seeing that different people operate in different circumstances.[71]

But what are the dynamics by which rationality operates "between" the individual and the community? How does the postfoundationalist avoid the pitfalls of individualistic dogmatism and communitarian relativism? For van Huyssteen, the move is "from individual judgment to communal evaluation to intersubjective conversation."[72] However, the original judgment is in turn shaped by the tradition of the community. While we can and do trust in and

69. Clayton and Knapp, "Rationality and Ethics," p. 152.

70. The use of "community" in the singular here is not meant to imply a clearly delineated or static set; rather, the "community" to which the self relates is a complex, intermingled, and overlapping matrix of communities.

71. Rescher, *Pluralism*, p. 12.

72. J. W. van Huyssteen, "Tradition and the Task of Theology," *Theology Today* 55, no. 2 (July 1998): 224.

rely on these traditions as they guide our lives, this does not mean that we accept them uncritically or that we set out each piece of the tradition for radical criticism. Following Sanders, we can conceive of tradition in a way "which allows its adherents to be both fully committed and yet open to suggestions and criticisms from all quarters."[73]

Delwin Brown has contributed greatly to a more nuanced conception of tradition and its role in theological construction. He is especially critical of the nonfoundationalist move that attempts to define the rationality of Christian faith with criteria wholly internal to the tradition (e.g., Lindbeck). Brown insists that theology "must be answerable to canons of critical inquiry defensible within the various arenas of our common discourse and not merely within those that are Christian."[74] Postfoundationalism aims to overcome this ghettoization of Christian theology. Yet, it overcomes it not by reverting to acontextual universal norms, but by engaging in interdisciplinary dialogue across contexts in search of more adequate explanations.

For van Huyssteen, tradition clearly conditions the present, but this does not mean that we are prisoners of our traditions. He focuses on the crucial question whether it is possible to choose between traditions, which he answers affirmatively:

> . . . first, we should be able to enter the pluralist, interdisciplinary conversation between research traditions with our full personal convictions, while at the same time reaching beyond the strict boundaries of our own intellectual contexts; second, we should indeed be able to justify our choices for or against a specific research tradition in interdisciplinary conversation.[75]

Such justification of a tradition is not through direct testing or neutral analysis, but through bringing one's own commitment into an

---

73. Sanders, "Traditionalism," p. 214.

74. Delwin Brown, *Boundaries of Our Habitations* (Albany: State University of New York Press, 1994), p. 4.

75. van Huyssteen, "Tradition and the Task of Theology," pp. 221-22.

ongoing and open dialogue with other traditions. For van Huyssteen, nonfoundationalist theologians who appeal to their own communities, and rely only on intrasystemic criteria for judgment, have really fallen into what he calls *crypto-foundationalism*. That is, they are simply positing their own tradition as the foundation for knowledge.

A brief analysis of the work of Nancey Murphy may serve as a case study to illustrate this problem. In her *Theology in the Age of Scientific Reasoning,*[76] she concedes that since the time of Hume theology has been increasingly unable to ground its statements in authority. Murphy then tries to adopt a nonfoundationalist rationality which she thinks gets around Hume *via* philosophy of science, specifically through the work of Imre Lakatos. Instead of Kuhnian "paradigms" that replace each other through revolutions, Lakatos spoke of "research programs" in science that work alongside each other. We can judge between these programs by assessing whether they are progressive or degenerative. A program is progressive if *inter alia* it continues to predict novel facts. Each program has a "hard core" of beliefs that are surrounded, so to speak, by a set of auxiliary hypotheses that form a protective belt. The "negative heuristic" of each program is an attempt to avoid falsification of the hard core by constantly adjusting the auxiliary hypotheses. A "positive heuristic," which is a long-term policy for research, is typically found only in mature research programs.

Murphy argues that theology can be construed to meet all these criteria, including the criteria that it has data and that it can predict novel facts. She views theological "data" as the results of Christian communal discernment; these experiments are *repeatable* as in science. In fact, in her conclusion she claims that methodologically theology ought to be *indistinguishable* from science.[77] We can get together as Christians and discern a consensus on our tradition, and then repeat this process like an experiment to support the "progressive" nature of our theological research program. In her new

76. Nancey Murphy, *Theology in the Age of Scientific Reasoning* (Ithaca: Cornell University Press, 1990).

77. Murphy, *Theology in the Age of Scientific Reasoning,* p. 198.

Lakatosian theology, Murphy places the existence of God in the hard core of her program. In a move analogous to that of Lindbeck, she is willing to accept that the criteria for what goes in this core is determined by the context of what she calls Christian epistemic practice. This is where van Huyssteen charges Murphy with closet foundationalism.

How does one justify the placing of Christian beliefs in a "hard core"? This seems to be what I would call a "centripetal" foundationalism; placing the foundations in the "center" instead of at the "base." As van Huyssteen puts it,

> Lakatos's criterion of relative empirical progress could hardly be used to adjudicate between competing theological theories or schools. In the end, we are left with no idea how one of Murphy's most startling claims could ever be justified: that the more acceptable — and progressive — theological program(s) may claim to provide (superior?) knowledge of God and of God's relation to the world.[78]

He concludes that her appeal to her (anabaptist) community seems to be simply a covert form of foundationalism. Postfoundationalism, on the other hand, insists on developing transcommunal and intersubjective explanations; it is committed to engaging the broader interdisciplinary dialogue without first immunizing a "hard core" of beliefs.

The question to theological nonfoundationalists is whether their models are adequately protected against the self-defeating relativism and radical contextualism that come with many deconstructivist forms of postmodern philosophy. In the case of Lindbeck's postliberalism and Murphy's Lakatosian model,[79] their

78. van Huyssteen, "Is the Postmodernist Always a Postfoundationalist?" in *Essays*, p. 86.

79. It is important to note that Murphy has shown a greater sensitivity to the charge of relativism in her more recent works, although it is debatable whether she has provided an adequate response. See, e.g., her "Textual Relativism, Philosophy of Language and the Baptist Vision," in *Theology without Foundations*; see also *Reasoning and Rhetoric in Religion* (Valley Forge, Penn.: Trinity Press International, 1994), pp.

attempts to halt the fall into relativism by starting with the particularity of the Christian form of life or the hard core of Christian belief seem to be *foundationalist* moves. Ironically, both foundationalism and nonfoundationalism end up as (or are at "bottom"?) strategies for immunizing our most basic epistemic and hermeneutic assumptions. Postfoundationalism tries to break out of this dichotomy with a to-and-fro move that continually interrogates precisely these assumptions.

The works of philosopher Calvin Schrag are particularly helpful to the postfoundationalist model in overcoming this dichotomy between individual and community. He rejects the relativizing tendency of postmodern deconstructivists who want to throw out the whole idea of "rationality" as having any commonality across disciplines or traditions.

> Whereas the vertical grounding of metaphysically and epistemologically oriented modes of thought sought a view from the other side of history, the horizontal multiplicity celebrated in postmodernity offers only a fragmented vision from this side of history. This privileging of horizontality in postmodernism has its own disturbing consequences. It leaves us with a heterogeneity of socio-historical assemblages of discourse and action in which paralogy and incommensurability, rupture and overturn, have the final word. In such a scheme of things the relativization of all forms of thought and all contents

236f. In her *Anglo-American Postmodernity* (Boulder, Colo.: Westview, 1997), she explicitly acknowledges we must attempt to make rational assessments of large-scale traditions, even though this is quite difficult (p. 192). In this context and others, she moves in this direction by building on the work of Alasdair MacIntyre, a thinker who has been influential on her thought at least since 1989; see her article, with James McClendon, Jr., "Distinguishing Modern and Postmodern Theologies," *Modern Theology* 5, no. 3 (April 1989): 203f. In *The Shaping of Rationality,* van Huyssteen acknowledges this move in Murphy's thought, but suggests that she has not yet fully accounted for the epistemic role of religious commitment in her theory, nor developed a sufficiently broad theory of experience to protect her from the charge of crypto-fideism (ch. 2). To the extent that Murphy's work is moving in this direction, she might be a resource and contributor to the emerging postfoundationalist model.

of culture is difficult to avoid . . . [W]e cannot think and act except through an engagement with the tradition. The task is to stand in a *critical* relation to the tradition. It is thus that our project, simplified possibly to the extreme, comprises an effort to split the difference between the vertically grounded conceptions of reason and the horizontality of the postmodern anti-logos of becoming. . . . The logos is reconstituted but it is not left behind. It continues to register its effects (and it is discernible only through its effects) in a transversal binding or gathering of the multiplicity and flux of our socio-historical practices.[80]

Schrag accepts the contextuality and fallibility of our knowledge, but does not assume that this automatically entails relativism; rather he sees reason as having a binding effect across contexts.

Perhaps the most important contribution to the specific issue of the relation of individual and communal factors in rational judgment is Schrag's refiguring of the dialectics of participation (*in* the community/tradition) and distanciation (*from* the community/tradition). He tries to show how these terms, common in hermeneutical discussions, might be seen not as simply juxtaposed in a linear way, nor as one determining the other in a hierarchical way, but rather as in a relation of "transversal interplay" that connects "the performance of reason with our communal discourse and our communal action."[81] Critically appropriating the work of Jürgen Habermas, Schrag proposes that we speak of participation and distanciation as the "twin moments" of praxial critique. The dialectic between them is "socio-pragmatic," jettisoning neither the rational subject, nor the communal concerns and practices out of which the identity of that subject emerges.

Participation without distanciation congeals into traditionalism and conservatism, paving the way to a tyranny of custom. It is thus that the "critical" moment of praxial critique, which carves out a space for disagreement and dissent, needs to be se-

80. Schrag, *Resources of Rationality*, p. 166.
81. Schrag, *Resources of Rationality*, p. 63.

cured. Although distanciation without participation remains bereft of its background conditions, participation without distanciation remains blind to resources for critical assessment and evaluation.[82]

Unlike the foundationalist, who privileges the subject over against the tradition and community, and unlike the nonfoundationalist, who subordinates the individual to the group or narrative, Schrag illustrates the postfoundationalist attempt to hold them together in a dialectical fashion.

In a more recent work, *The Self after Postmodernity*, Schrag argues that even if we accept the postmodernist deconstructive jettisoning of the old modernist notion of "self," construed either as a substance or a transparent mind, this does not mean that all other construals of the self are outlawed. He opts for a praxis-oriented self, "defined by its communicative practices, oriented toward an understanding of itself in its discourse, its action, its being with others, and its experience of transcendence."[83] Most important for our current purpose is his third chapter, "The Self in Community," which offers a profile of the self after postmodernity as discovering and constituting itself in relation to other selves. The self is conditioned, but not determined, by a particular tradition. It is precisely the existential experience of becoming a self (over against but still a part of the community) that discloses the nature of the communalized self. Once again, Schrag calls for overcoming the bogus dichotomies that are merely conceptual constructs of theoretical positions: universal versus particular, ahistorical versus historical, etc. Instead, he calls for a praxial critique that emerges out of the space of our communal relations. The self in community, then, is

. . . historically embedded, existing with others, inclusive of predecessors, contemporaries, and successors. Never an island entire of itself, the self remains rooted in history but is not suffo-

---

82. Schrag, *Resources of Rationality*, pp. 64-65.

83. Schrag, *The Self after Postmodernity* (New Haven: Yale University Press, 1997), p. 9.

cated by the influx of historical forms and forces. The communalized self is *in* history, but not *of* history. It has the resources for transcending the historically specific without arrogating to itself an unconditioned and decontextualized vision of the world.[84]

The postfoundationalist model, therefore, sees individual and communal factors as mutually conditioning elements in the shaping of rationality. The community with its particular tradition mediates criteria for what is considered reasonable to the individual as he or she participates in the life-world of the group. The individual agent, however, is the locus of the act of rational judgment, and is only able to make judgments because of the distanciation involved in his or her self-differentiation from the community.[85] This means the individual may bring his or her commitments into the dialogue with other traditions or disciplines, but without immunizing them against the critique that inevitably comes in transcommunal and intersubjective conversation.

4. Explanation and Understanding

The final postfoundationalist couplet focuses specifically on the interdisciplinary location of theology by responding to a dichotomy that has shaped the strong separation in western culture between the natural sciences, which aim to explain things according to universal laws, and the human sciences, which aim to understand things in their particularity. Of great importance in the emergence of this bifurcation was the distinction made by Wilhelm Dilthey[86]

84. Schrag, *The Self after Postmodernity*, p. 109.

85. Elsewhere I have emphasized the importance of understanding and including the development of the *individual* in discussions of rationality. See my "Structures of Rationality in Science and Theology: Overcoming the Postmodern Dilemma," *Perspectives on Science and Christian Faith* 49, no. 4 (December 1997): 228-36.

86. Dilthey (1833-1911) was a German philosopher who was deeply influential in the critique of positivism and the rise of historicism. As we will see below, his writings continue to play a role in the debate about rationality and methodology in

between *Erklärung* (explanation) and *Verstehen* (understanding). The former has to do with including a particular phenomenon under a general rule, the latter with considering a particular in light of the whole of its context. This separation was also shaped by the philosophical roots of modern science, epitomized in "mechanistic" natural science which eventually dispensed with the need for hypotheses like "God" (Laplace) or "mind" (Behaviorism). Here we see the results of a bifurcation of value and fact, of the exclusion of concerns about *res cogitans* from descriptions of *res extensa*. In large part, Hegel's emphasis on *Geist* can be seen as a reaction to a situation in which humans felt like insignificant aliens in a huge (non-spiritual) world-machine.

This background is important for seeing how the distinction between "explanation" and "understanding" played a role in the separation of the sciences and humanities.[87] The basis of Dilthey's divorce of the human sciences from the natural sciences was the view that while the latter "explained" things, it offered no resources for "understanding," which is a unique function of the human mind. Dilthey utilized this distinction in affirming the uniqueness of the human sciences, or *Geisteswissenschaften* (the term illustrates the influence of German idealism *via* Hegel), as opposed to the *Naturwissenschaften*.

How does this influence the debate between foundationalists and nonfoundationalists about theological method? The foundationalist will tend to model theology as much as possible after the natural sciences, aiming to offer absolute "explanations," necessarily derived by following specific rules, which are or aim to be clearly true regardless of tradition or context. This is evident, for example, in Charles Hodge's famous comment that "the Bible is to the theologian what nature is to the man of science,"[88] which assumed a

---

the "human sciences." In Chapter Three, we will see that Pannenberg has critically appropriated much of Dilthey's thought.

87. Elsewhere I have traced the deleterious effects of this bifurcation, and argued for the importance of the link between intelligence and intelligibility in the human search for meaning. See my "Integrative Epistemology and the Search for Meaning," *Journal of Interdisciplinary Studies* 5, no. 1 (1993): 125-40.

88. Charles Hodge, *Systematic Theology*, vol. 1 (Grand Rapids: Eerdmans, 1981), p. 10.

nineteenth-century positivist view of scientific method. The foundationalist will aim to rise above (operate rationally beyond) the pre-understanding which the individual brings to the interpretation of an event or text, and "explain" the text objectively from a neutral position.

The nonfoundationalist, on the other hand, embraces the turn to "understanding" and lists theology as one of the disciplines whose aim is "Verstehen" (defined as empathic understanding). This approach concedes that all understanding is conditioned (some would say determined) by the historical context within which the understanding occurs. Interpretation and language go all the way down and all the way back up. The nonfoundationalist sees understanding as rooted in particular traditions (contexts) which have their own coherence, and eschews the chimerical goal of an explanation that could escape its context and make contact with other incommensurable traditions. The nonfoundationalist will be content with securing for theology a place among the human sciences, and limiting its role to the analysis of language games, or to a depth description of the forms of life of particular faith communities.[89]

The *post*foundationalist rejects the strict methodological opposition between "human" and "natural" science, seeing this dichotomous division of labor as an expression of the outdated distinctions between thought and matter in Descartes, or between mind and nature in German idealism. Instead, the postfoundationalist model stresses the mutual conditioning of two movements in human rationality.

(PF4): explanation aims for universal, transcontextual understanding, and understanding derives from particular contextualized explanations.

---

89. Here nonfoundationalists assume that secular scholars of religion have given up on "explanation" and that theology must conform if it wants to be academically respectable. In fact this is not at all the consensus in religious studies. See, e.g., Catherine Bell's review of several books in "Modernism and Postmodernism in the Study of Religion," *Religious Studies Review* 22, no. 3 (July 1996): 179-90.

For van Huyssteen, theology is inherently interdisciplinary, and must not give up its call to "reach beyond the walls of our own epistemic communities in cross-contextual, cross-cultural, and cross-disciplinary conversation."[90] This attack on the nonfoundationalist strategy of hiding in the safe haven of Verstehen models of inquiry does not mean a decision for the opposite approach; i.e., a foundationalist insistence on acontextual, atraditional, certain and absolute explanations. The postfoundationalist critiques both as rooted in a false dichotomy, and argues for a middle way that offers a more compelling vision of theology's interdisciplinary task.

The dialogue between theology and (natural) science is the matrix out of which the postfoundationalist model has emerged. Without conflating these modes of inquiry, the postfoundationalist sees real similarities between them. Although different in scope, focus, and content, they share common resources of rationality, including the quest for intelligibility. Since the contextualist shift in philosophy of science (Kuhn), it is clear that even the explanations of "hard" science are shaped by the interpretive traditions (the "understandings") of the historical contexts in which they are embedded. In trying to overcome the opposition between explanation and understanding, van Huyssteen argues that in all sciences, "the subjectivity of interpreting belongs right in the heart of the explanatory task."[91] However, this does not lead to relativism but to an ongoing rational reconstruction of our understanding. In this view, "theological explanations attempt to establish a link between the inherited beliefs and practices of a specific religious tradition and the contemporary experience of its adherents."[92]

For van Huyssteen, then, the task of theology is *both* to understand and to explain. He criticizes the rejection of the latter part of that task in some forms of narrative theology. He is critical especially of the approach of Ronald Thiemann, who contrasts "descriptive" theology with all forms of "explanation." Thiemann seems to

---

90. van Huyssteen, *Essays,* p. 4.

91. van Huyssteen, "Theology and Science: The Quest for a New Apologetics," in *Essays,* p. 232.

92. van Huyssteen, "Theology and Science," *Essays,* p. 234.

think the latter always implies a foundationalist epistemology. This nonfoundationalist mode is, according to van Huyssteen,

> . . . a peculiar brand of neo-Wittgensteinian fideism. On this view religious beliefs have no need for explanatory support and in the end can hardly be seen as more than a groundless language game . . . pure narrative theology leads not only to a relativistic understanding of justification, truth, and knowledge, but also to an epistemological relativism that would be fatal for the cognitive claims of theological statements.[93]

The nonfoundationalist ignores the first part of (PF4), the recognition that explanations are universal *in intent*.[94] Explanation *aims* for the crossing of ever-widening boundaries and contexts, even if these "crossings" are never final. By giving up on explanation, the nonfoundationalist move (at least in some of its narrative modes) "is a retreat into the ghetto of a world created by rather than illuminated by the scriptural text."[95] The foundationalist, on the other hand, misses the second part of (PF4), or denies it for fear that conceding the situatedness of all "understandings" will inevitably lead to relativism.

By emphasizing the back-and-forth movement between traditioned understanding and universally intended explanations, the postfoundationalist escapes relativism without retreating into absolutism. Theological rationality involves a fallible search for intelligibility, open to constant interdisciplinary dialogue. Attempts to understand involve seeking the best explanation, and explanations emerge out of and lead to new interpretive understandings. Rather than being mutually exclusive, both tasks are intrinsic to the search for maximal intelligibility.

In the postfoundationalist response to the separation of expla-

93. van Huyssteen, "Narrative Theology: An Adequate Paradigm for Theological Reflection?" in *Essays*, p. 186. Cf. Ronald F. Thiemann, *Revelation and Theology: The Gospel as Narrated Promise* (Notre Dame: University of Notre Dame Press, 1987).

94. Cf. van Huyssteen, "Experience and Explanation: The Justification of Cognitive Claims in Theology," in *Essays*, p. 162.

95. van Huyssteen, "Narrative Theology," *Essays*, p. 189.

nation and understanding, once again Calvin Schrag is extremely helpful. Borrowing the concept of "chronotope" from literary theorist Mikhail Bakhtin, Schrag emphasizes the spatio-temporal background of the interplay between whole and part.[96] In this interplay, he wants to refigure "understanding" and "explanation" as twin tasks in a discursive event, understanding as we explain and explaining as we understand. In *understanding* a part of a discourse, we identify it as an instance of a certain genus, the whole. *Explanation* focuses on the parts of the discourse and distinguishes them. He calls for holding these two tasks together in discursive practice. This view of "transversal" (instead of "universal") rationality is particularly illuminating for interdisciplinary dialogue, because it points to the operation of rationality between forms of knowing; it "lies across" disciplinary activities.

The term chronotope intends to convey a view of space and time not as abstract frames of reference, but as vibrant and vitalized "existential dwellings." For Bakhtin, discourse involves "dialogic imagination," which includes what he calls centripetal and centrifugal forces. Schrag explains: "The centripetal indicates the centralizing, homogenizing, and hierarchical forces of language and culture. The centrifugal marks the decentralizing, dispersing, and dismantling functions and forces."[97] Schrag sees the spatio-temporal dimensions of rationality, which shape the configuration of discourse and action, and the event of interpretation as mutually constitutive. This brings him to a discussion of the interplay of whole and part, the central issues in the distinction between understanding and explanation. Here he attempts to refigure these moments, from the perspective of chronotopal interpretation,

> as integral moments within a whole/part interplay. We understand a portion of discourse by taking it as an exemplification of a genre or type. . . . But such understanding is never complete, always subject to further revision, threatened by ambiguity, and susceptible to breakdown. . . . It is the task of explanation to fo-

96. Schrag, *Resources of Rationality*, p. 86.
97. Schrag, *Resources of Rationality*, p. 84.

cus on the distinguishable "parts" of discourse (phonemic and lexical units, grammatical structures, semantical elements) and provide an analytical explication of their functions, always cognizant of the role of these specific functions within the gestalt of discourse as an emergent whole. It is thus that understanding and explanation move to and fro between whole and part, enabling understanding and explanation to work side by side as twin halves of an august discursive event, allowing us to understand as we explain and explain as we understand.[98]

Schrag notes that deconstructivist postmodernists make the same move the Sophists did in ancient Greek culture, viz., despising the logos. So this twentieth-century move is not entirely new, but it has taken relativism to a new radical extreme. For Nietzsche, knowledge is nothing but desire; for Foucault, knowledge is nothing but power. Schrag wants to accommodate the postmodern intuition of the importance of contextuality, but without scuttling reason completely. "These moments of rationality, exhibiting a logos-effect of gathering, circumvent both the synchronic verticality of totalitarian hegemony and the diachronic horizontality of anarchic multiplicity. This enables us to speak of the transversal logos."[99] He argues that

> Reason remains transversal to the various forms of our personal and social forms of life. It lies across them diagonally; it is neither vertically transcendent to them nor horizontally immanent within them . . . the dynamics of transversal rationality falls out as a convergence without coincidence, an interplay without synthesis, an appropriation without totalization, and a unification that allows for difference.[100]

A transversal (rather than universal) conception of the logos allows for whole and part (one and many) to be dialectically related without subsumption. The relation of whole and part will play an im-

98. Schrag, *Resources of Rationality*, p. 86.
99. Schrag, *Resources of Rationality*, p. 163.
100. Schrag, *Resources of Rationality*, p. 158.

portant role in our analysis in the following chapter of Pannenberg's own treatment of understanding and explanation.[101]

Of all the authors I am calling postfoundationalist, Philip Clayton offers the most extensive treatment of the distinction and connection between understanding and explanation with reference to theological method. In his *Explanation from Physics to Theology*, Clayton's general theme is epistemology, but his specific concern is to show how the explanatory practices of science and religion may both be seen as "rational," which he specifies as "intersubjective criticizability."[102] He carefully traces the divorce of the natural from the human sciences, a divorce related to the distinction between nomothetic disciplines, which sought explanations of general laws, and ideographic disciplines, which are interested in understanding how a particular fits into a whole or pattern.

In an attempt to mediate these extremes, Clayton proposes "explanation *with* understanding" as a theory of social scientific explanation. Accepting aspects of the nonfoundationalist critique, he wants to see both natural and social science as hermeneutical, but at the same time insists that this does not throw out the possibility of judging a belief to be an experientially adequate and *intersubjective* explanation. So he recognizes "understanding as a necessary precondition for social scientific explanation."[103]

Clayton also traces the emergence of the *Verstehen* tradition (from Dilthey onward) that emphasized the distinctiveness of the human sciences. Against this tradition, Clayton wants to maintain that the social sciences are *primarily explanatory,* although they also involve and even require "empathic understanding." Clayton especially emphasizes the two "semantic levels" of rationality in the human sciences. In natural science, there is one framework of interpretation, viz., the scientist's. But in social science, there is not only the

---

101. Interestingly, Nancey Murphy's more recent work recognizes the importance of seeing the mutual conditioning of the concepts of whole and part. See *Anglo-American Postmodernity*, p. 34.

102. Clayton, *Explanation from Physics to Theology*, p. 9. Clayton alludes to Pannenberg at various places in this work, especially in the final chapter, where he concludes with a discussion of Pannenberg's method (166f.).

103. Clayton, *Explanation*, p. 100.

social scientist but also the social agent. In other words, the *objects* of the science are also agents who are operating out of semantic worlds.[104] This makes Popper's aim of finding a single type of explanation for all science very problematic. Equally problematic, on the other hand, are the Verstehen theorists and their extreme "antipositivist" successors, who try to make social science distinctive by attempting to avoid Erklärung.

Clayton's mediating position aims to recognize the shaping influence of contexts of meaning, but simultaneously allows for general standards or criteria for explanation in social science. So he calls his approach a "formal-semantic" theory.[105] He argues that both understanding and explanation are indispensable. Both natural and social science try to interpret a domain of phenomena to make it comprehensible — in this sense, both are hermeneutical. But we do not have to throw out explanation, or to use the term equivocally in the different disciplines. To this end, Clayton proposes that we define "understanding" broadly as an intuitive grasping of patterns of meaning, and "explanation" as a rational reconstruction of these interrelated structures in a primarily theoretical context. Explanation and understanding are interdependent. Explanations are attempted answers to why-questions. In the social sciences, empathic "understanding" is a necessary prerequisite to such explanation.

The latter part of Clayton's book argues that religious beliefs generally, and theology as a discipline specifically, involve "explanation." This is entailed by the fact that religious and theological claims are constative by their very structure; they intend to make assertions about something outside themselves. The fact that theology refers to a realm of "ineffability," however, should make us wary of facile comparisons between theology and other disciplines. In this context, Clayton summarizes a basic conviction of the position we are calling postfoundationalism:

> . . . to reject foundationalism is not to fall automatically into the
> waiting arms of the antifoundationalists, who claim that theol-

---

104. Clayton, *Explanation,* p. 61.
105. Clayton, *Explanation,* p. 66.

ogy can be pursued without attention to the nature and epistemic status of its truth claims. To the contrary, the whole debate between foundationalism and antifoundationalism is probably based on the *false dichotomy* of an *outdated epistemological dilemma*. The shift to a fallibilist epistemology avoids, I believe, the alleged necessity of being either a foundationalist or an antifoundationalist.[106]

The postfoundationalist model is precisely the attempt to find a middle way between the horns of this outdated epistemological dilemma. Supporting the move beyond the four forced dichotomies we have just reviewed is a more central conceptual move that attempts to understand and explain rationality through a linking of epistemic and hermeneutic concerns.

Rationality: Linking Epistemology and Hermeneutics

In addition to proposing the couplets as a resolution of the polarizations that have ossified the foundationalist-nonfoundationalist debate, the postfoundationalist model (as I am reconstructing it) also aims for an intercalation of the four couplets themselves. It does this by insisting on a constitutive reciprocal relation between epistemology and hermeneutics. Here we arrive at the central concern of the postfoundationalist model of rationality. Is it possible to accommodate the postmodern critique of *episteme* without collapsing into relativist hermeneutics? Conversely, is it possible to accommodate the modernist search for epistemological justification without returning to foundationalist absolutism? The postfoundationalist task of theology, as we defined it in Chapter One, is:

> to engage in interdisciplinary dialogue within our postmodern culture while *both* maintaining a commitment to intersubjective, transcommunal theological argumentation for the truth of Christian faith, *and* recognizing the provisionality of our histori-

106. Clayton, *Explanation*, p. 152. Emphasis added.

cally embedded understandings and culturally conditioned explanations of the Christian tradition and religious experience.

In order to accomplish this, postfoundationalism aims to show that epistemology and hermeneutics are inherently linked, mutually conditioning rather than mutually exclusive. In the search for apodictic knowledge of the truth, the foundationalists privileged epistemology as the primary enterprise of philosophy. Nonfoundationalists, on the other hand, tend to disparage epistemology and valorize instead the play of hermeneutics as philosophy's task.[107] As modernity shaped foundationalism, so (negative forms of) postmodernity informed the nonfoundationalist model of what constitutes rationality in human inquiry.

The postfoundationalist, however, does not view postmodernism as the "end" of modernism, nor merely as its negation. Rather, it calls for "splitting the difference" between them, to use Schrag's phrase. This means a shuttling back and forth between their concerns, a constant interrogation of modernist foundations from the point of view of historicist hermeneutics. Postfoundationalism refuses to replace the valid search for epistemologically adequate and intelligible explanations with mere hermeneutical understandings. At the same time, it demands a radical engagement with postmodern critique that incorporates the modern concern for justified true belief.

Van Huyssteen describes this central benefit of postfoundationalism as allowing "for the creative fusion of hermeneutics and epistemology."[108] He insists that "hermeneutics and epistemology will therefore always go together very closely"[109] in a postfoundationalist model of rationality. In his most recent book, *The Shaping of Rationality,* he again utilizes the metaphor of "fusion." In the postfoundationalist model, "a fusion of epistemological and hermeneutical concerns will enable a focused (though fallibilist) quest for

107. Richard Rorty, e.g., heralds the death of epistemology in *Philosophy and the Mirror of Nature* (Princeton: Princeton University Press, 1979). One might ask, of course, how he *knows* this.

108. van Huyssteen, *Essays,* p. 4.

109. van Huyssteen, *Essays,* p. 22.

intelligibility through the epistemic skills of responsible, critical judgment and discernment."[110]

Because the term "fusion" might imply a conflation or a melding of the two in a way that obscures the important differentiation between them, I prefer the term "link" for the relation of epistemology and hermeneutics, although this might be too weak. Here we find the need for a plethora of descriptors, including intercalation, inmixing, entwinement, etc. In Chapter Four, I will thematize this relational unity and attempt a more thorough presentation of this "linking." The key is to insist that this is not a static relation, but a dynamic one. It is important to realize that the postfoundationalist approach is not merely a middle way between two poles, but rather a dynamic integration, an intercalation of concerns, a movement back and forth without halting at or reifying either moment. In other words, its "middle way" involves challenging the assumptions that led to the formulation of the dilemma in the first place. Rather than a continuum or a simple bipolarity, the postfoundationalist wants to conceptualize modernism and postmodernism, with their respective emphases on epistemology and hermeneutics, as two differentiated yet mutually conditioning or reciprocally related movements:

Modernist   ⟶   Postmodernist
Epistemology   ⟵   Hermeneutics

Although this drive to link epistemology and hermeneutics is not always explicitly stated in the work of van Huyssteen, it is implicit in the way he works out the issues reflected in my four postfoundationalist couplets. To illustrate this, let us examine each one again briefly. In the relation between experience and belief, this drive is most clear in van Huyssteen's emphasis on the interpreted nature of all experience as part of his version of critical realism. The postfoundationalist "makes tentative claims through the epistemic

---

110. van Huyssteen, *The Shaping of Rationality*, p. 33. He uses the fusion metaphor in several other places, including "Tradition and the Task of Theology," p. 228.

access provided by interpreted religious experience."[111] Experiential epistemology and interpreted belief are unthinkable apart from each other. "All contextual, experiential, and hermeneutical issues in theological theorizing presuppose an epistemological model of rationality."[112]

Interpreted experience is also key to the relation between truth and knowledge. Emphasizing the relational character of our being in the world, van Huyssteen insists that our knowledge of reality is always mediated by our interpretation of experience. Nevertheless, we can maintain the ideals of truth and objectivity that are tied to the epistemological enterprise because, according to the post-foundationalist, any hermeneutical endeavor presupposes them. However, our claims to truth are not absolute because our interpretation of the reality we experience is fallible. This suggests the need for humility as well as courage in articulating our provisional argumentation for the truth of the Christian faith.

The implications of the linking of epistemology and hermeneutics for the relation of individual and communal factors in rational judgment are most vividly disclosed in the issue of biblical interpretation. Here van Huyssteen has criticized both naïve modernist methods of interpreting Scripture as well as nonfoundationalist attempts to read the text using wholly internal criteria. He notes the connection of the two central problems:

> the *epistemological* problem of determining criteria for assessing the truth-claims and cognitive status of theological statements [and] *hermeneutical* criteria for distinguishing between good or bad receptions of Christianity's classic text, and thus for assessing the validity of different interpretations of this text.[113]

The complaint against foundationalism is that it tends to miss the communal factors, the historical shaping of the traditional understandings out of which the individual operates. The complaint

111. van Huyssteen, *Essays*, p. 51.
112. van Huyssteen, *Essays*, p. 176.
113. van Huyssteen, *Essays*, p. 184. Emphasis in original.

against nonfoundationalism is that it attempts to immunize particular interpretations from critique by appealing only to these communal factors.

The couplet of explanation and understanding is the most relevant for the interdisciplinary location of theology. By illustrating that natural science, too (and indeed every mode of human inquiry), is already hermeneutically conditioned, the postmodern critique dispels the common myth that science is about reason and theology is about faith. All explanations emerge out of a fiduciary rootedness, but the quest for intelligibility also involves a drive to search beyond these roots for broader understandings through crosscontextual, cross-cultural, and cross-disciplinary dialogue. From out of our own traditions (whether theological or scientific) we must strive to account for our own faith commitments as they are humbly brought into dialogue with other traditions. This means that on the journey into interdisciplinary discussion, we do not have to *leave our commitments behind* (like the foundationalist), nor are we compelled to *stay behind with our commitments* (like the nonfoundationalist). The postfoundationalist wants to do theology on the move, "between" epistemology and hermeneutics.

This distinctive feature of the postfoundationalist model is only now beginning to emerge clearly, and will require significant clarification and articulation. Our purpose in the next chapter is to bring Pannenberg into dialogue with this model in order to explore the extent to which his methodology exhibits the "family resemblances" of postfoundationalism. Pannenberg himself has never been fond of postmodern hermeneutics, usually dismissing it as a fad. However, in the actual performance of his theological argumentation over the last four decades, specifically at the juncture where anthropology serves as a link between his fundamental and systematic theology, Pannenberg may offer us help in thinking through the structural dynamics of the postfoundationalist task of theology.

CHAPTER THREE

Pannenberg's Theological Method

My goal is to demonstrate that Wolfhart Pannenberg can no longer be facilely labeled a "foundationalist," or dismissed for his allegedly modernist view of reason, as so many Anglo-American theologians apparently believe. On the contrary, his approach holds much in common with the emerging postfoundationalist model outlined in Chapter Two. What follows is a new interpretation of Pannenberg's methodology that not only sheds light on why he has been seen as a foundationalist, but also illustrates his family resemblance to the postfoundationalists. In the first section I argue that the key concept of his theological method is not reason, history, or prolepsis (all of which easily lead to foundationalist readings); rather, it is the conceptualization of theology as understanding and explaining all things *sub ratione Dei* (under the aspect of the relation to God).

With this view of his basic principle, we can then more easily bring Pannenberg into explicit dialogue with the four postfoundationalist couplets. In each case, we will see that he resolves these epistemological and hermeneutical tensions on the soil of anthropology, but always in reference to the "relation to God." This analysis will help us examine (in the last section of this chapter) the way in which anthropology functions for Pannenberg as a link between philosophy of religion and history of religion in his overall call for a "theology of religion." The structural dynamics of this relational link may then be appropriated for the postfoundationalist attempt to link epistemology and hermeneutics in a new theory of rationality.

Because this is the distinctive characteristic of postfoundationalism (as we argued above), Chapter Four is devoted to expositing Pannenberg's anthropology, illustrating how its relation to theology helps in overcoming the dichotomy of "from below" and "from above." As we will try to show, his use of anthropology is not intended to provide a neutral or absolute foundation; rather, theological anthropology is for him a field of inquiry which is constituted by a back-and-forth movement, involving the two reciprocally related moments of "fundamental" and "systematic" theology. Although Pannenberg hinted at this in his earlier works, it has only become clearly manifested with the publication of his three-volume ST.

The Search for Pannenberg's "Grundprinzip"

In most of the comprehensive scholarly treatments of Pannenberg's thought, we find an attempt to identify a "key concept" or "basic principle" (*Grundprinzip*) in his theological method. It is important to come to terms briefly with these attempts before proposing a new way of understanding his method. My proposed reading of his Grundprinzip not only accommodates and incorporates all of the insights of these three common interpretations, but also provides the background for illustrating his confluence with the post-foundationalist couplets.

The Usual Suspects: Reason, History, Prolepsis

While most Pannenberg scholars recognize the importance of several elements in his thought, the attempts at identifying a single basic principle in his theology have tended to fall into three general camps, privileging either "reason," "history," or "prolepsis" as the key concept. Those who believe his view of "**reason**" is central to his theological program emphasize his treatments of verification, validation, truth, or analogy (theological language and knowledge).

These authors tend to stress the centrality of TPS and other related works on methodology. Many others see the key concept as "**history**." This is the most popular reading of Pannenberg on the continent, although it has several English-speaking proponents as well. These authors tend to stress the programmatic role of the early *Revelation as History* and related articles. Such a concept is also evident, however, in ATP, which argues that the most concrete form of human existence is historical. On the other hand, some scholars argue that the key concept is anticipation or "**prolepsis**" of the future; this is intrinsically related to the revelation of the proleptic structure of all reality in the resurrection of Jesus, which discloses the ontological priority of the future. Such interpretations naturally emphasize, therefore, the early *Jesus — God and Man* (JGM)[1] and the various treatments of future ontology.

Our task in this subsection is to offer a brief historical review of some of the major treatments of Pannenberg's theology, noting along the way the waxing and waning of these three popular interpretations. This overview is not intended to be exhaustive, but merely to outline in broad strokes the general scholarly reception of Pannenberg's project. All three themes were already noted in the first doctoral dissertation produced on Pannenberg's theology, by J. Wentzel van Huyssteen in 1969 in The Netherlands.[2] While he focused on the element of the rational in Pannenberg's thought, he explicitly recognized that it might also be called a "theology of history." History and reason were seen as the key concepts by van Huyssteen, although he also noted the significant role of Pannenberg's use of proleptic categories and the ontology of the future.

In 1965, when Pannenberg was still a new "young voice" from Germany, American theologian Carl Braaten summed up his observations that theologians across the liberal-conservative spectrum were embracing aspects of his thought by noting that "Pannen-

---

1. W. Pannenberg, *Jesus — God and Man,* 2nd ed., trans. L. Wilkins and D. Priebe (Philadelphia: Westminster, 1977). Hereafter noted as JGM. German: *Gründzuge der Christologie* (Gütersloh: Gerd Mohn, 1964).

2. J. W. van Huyssteen, *Theologie van die Rede: Die funksie van die rasionele in die denke van Wolfhart Pannenberg* (Kampen: J. H. Kok,1970).

berg's theology obviously escapes ready-made labels."[3] Richard John Neuhaus introduced him to American theologians in 1969 with his more personal "Profile of a Theologian" in the English edition of Pannenberg's *Theology and the Kingdom of God*. Neuhaus made the judgment that "reason" was the central concept of Pannenberg's theology,[4] and this was a common theme in the early North American response.

In 1973, three separate comprehensive treatments of Pannenberg's theology appeared in English. These responded mainly to Pannenberg's view of history and his christology, represented in *Revelation as History* (1961)[5] and JGM (1964). In 1967, James Robinson declared that "a new school had been launched,"[6] and all three of the 1973 monographs on Pannenberg tended to agree that, if not a "school," at least a major new way of doing theology had been introduced. It is important to remember that all three of the major treatments appeared in 1973, so they did not treat the arguments of Pannenberg's TPS, which appeared in the same year.

For Allan Galloway, Pannenberg's novelty was his understanding of the relation of history to theology. For Barth, Bultmann, and Tillich, history caused problems for theology. For Pannenberg, on the other hand, it provides answers. Here we see a "new relationship between historical research and systematic theology, whereby history becomes a source of confidence rather than doubt and theology becomes the source of a credible philosophy of history."[7] Galloway complains that Pannenberg relies too heavily on history and fails to develop a sufficient systematic metaphysics.

---

3. Carl Braaten, "The Current Controversy in Revelation: Pannenberg and His Critics," *Journal of Religion* 45 (1965): 234.

4. Richard John Neuhaus, "Profile of a Theologian," in *Theology and the Kingdom of God*, p. 43.

5. W. Pannenberg, *Revelation as History*, with Rolf Rendtorff, Trutz Rendtorff, and Ulrich Wilkens, trans. David Granskou (New York: Macmillan, 1968). German: *Offenbarung als Geschichte* (Göttingen: Vandenhoeck & Ruprecht, 1961).

6. James M. Robinson, "Revelation as Word and as History," in *Theology as History*, ed. James M. Robinson and John B. Cobb, Jr. (New York: Harper and Row, 1967), p. 12.

7. Allan D. Galloway, *Wolfhart Pannenberg* (London: George Allen & Unwin, 1973), p. 11.

Twenty-six years later, after the publication of Pannenberg's ST, we will need to reevaluate the relation of history and philosophy in his method.[8]

D. H. Olive also emphasized the importance of history in Pannenberg's thought, but treated his attitude toward reason somewhat more thoroughly. Although he worries that it removes certainty from Christian faith, he sees the restoration of reason to a determinative place in theology as a strength of Pannenberg's approach.[9] In this relatively brief work, Olive points to Pannenberg's conception of theology as a "universal science" and applauds (even if quietly) the refusal to surrender claims to truth in theology.

Frank Tupper was the author of the third assessment during this same year; his treatment was much more exhaustive than the first two.[10] The central part of his book treated the familiar themes of revelation as history, christology "from below," and the futurity of God. However, the first and third major parts of his book offered a significant attempt to weigh the impact of Pannenberg's approach on the broader systematic task of contemporary theology. Although Tupper's overall assessment was extremely positive, he did point to two weaknesses in Pannenberg's work, viz., the failure to deal adequately with the action *of God* in the cross and the failure to thematize sin and the evil side of humanity. Both of these concerns reflect a call for a more systematic-theological treatment of these themes. As we will try to show below in Chapter Four, looking retrospectively at these early works, we can now see them as the first of two inherently related moments in the theological task.

After a fifteen-year hiatus (in the English-speaking world), a new

---

8. This is the task of the last section of Chapter Three below. Galloway's judgment of Pannenberg's influence was certainly premature: "Pannenberg's approach to theology signals the end of the age of the great 'prima donnas' in theology — the age of the multi-volume monograph in which a whole system of theology was elaborated as the achievement of an individual" (133).

9. Don H. Olive, *Wolfhart Pannenberg* in Makers of the Modern Theological Mind, ed. Bob E. Patterson (Waco: Word Books, 1973), p. 98.

10. E. Frank Tupper, *The Theology of Wolfhart Pannenberg* (Philadelphia: Westminster, 1973).

crop of comprehensive treatments of Pannenberg's theology appeared during 1988-1990. To honor his sixtieth birthday, Carl Braaten and Philip Clayton edited an American festschrift, *The Theology of Wolfhart Pannenberg.*[11] Taken together, the essays in this book offer a comprehensive response to the major themes of Pannenberg's theology up to that point. The ST had not yet been published.

The author in this collection who came closest to trying to identify Pannenberg's basic principle was Philip Clayton, who suggested that "anticipation" is at the heart of his method. He calls the concept of anticipation "the central systematic principle of his theology."[12] This insight emerged as Pannenberg thought through the logic of Jesus' resurrection, and his eschatological message about the coming kingdom of God. In this chapter, as well as in other articles, Clayton criticizes Pannenberg for insisting that anticipation has *ontological* as well as epistemological import; he suggests that a "future epistemology" would be sufficient and avoid the problems philosophers have seen in Pannenberg's ontological priority of the future.[13] In another article, Clayton recognizes the key concept of history, for he identifies the following as the *Grundmotiv* of Pannenberg's entire corpus: "both history and God can be conceptualized only in a reciprocal relationship with each other."[14] Yet, the principles of history and future are not exclusive, for Clayton in the same article notes that "undeniably, some type of an 'eschatological ontology' is foundational to his entire theological project."[15]

---

11. Carl E. Braaten and Philip Clayton, eds., *The Theology of Wolfhart Pannenberg: Twelve American Critiques, with an Autobiographical Essay and Response* (Minneapolis: Augsburg, 1988).

12. Philip Clayton, "Anticipation and Theological Method," in *The Theology of Wolfhart Pannenberg,* p. 131. Clayton notes that "in his seminars Pannenberg often worked to get his students to grasp the systematic impulse or principle that underlies every systematic theology. Without a doubt, his is the insight into the structure of anticipation" (128).

13. Philip Clayton, "Being and One Theologian," *The Thomist* 50 (October 1988): 667.

14. Philip Clayton, "The God of History and the Presence of the Future," *The Journal of Religion* 65, no. 1 (June 1985): 103.

15. Clayton, "The God of History," p. 106.

David Polk, who contributed a chapter to the Braaten/Clayton volume, published a book devoted wholly to Pannenberg in 1989.[16] Polk is a process theologian, and the gist of his critique is that Pannenberg is not. The book is based on a dissertation done at Claremont under process theologian John Cobb, Jr. Of all of his concerns, the one most salient to our current question is Polk's emphasis on the futurity of God as the driving ontological concept of Pannenberg's theology. As a process theologian, this sounds to him like determinism, even if from the future.[17] As we will see below, Pannenberg aims to resolve this problem through a specific conception of the relation of God to the world, worked out in terms of the relation of the economic and immanent Trinity.

In 1990, Stanley Grenz published what was up to that point the most comprehensive English treatment of Pannenberg's systematic theological method.[18] This book is a concise summary of the contents of *Systematische Theologie,* which Grenz provided based on the already published volume I, and notes from Munich lectures that would become the other two volumes. Grenz's basic argument is that Pannenberg's theology is guided by a drive to provide a "reason for the hope" of the Christian faith. He notes that "generally the systematic presentation of the Christian faith offered by a theologian centers on one or more specific motifs that form a core illuminating the whole."[19] Grenz argues that the two themes of reason (necessitated by the public nature of theology) and hope (the material theme of God's eschatological salvation) combine to form the basic principle of Pannenberg's theology.

In 1996 Cornelius Buller offered an analysis of Pannenberg's theology focusing on the way in which he argues for "the unity of nature and history." As might be guessed from the title, Buller argues that universal history is the key category by which Pannenberg pro-

---

16. David P. Polk, *On the Way to God: An Exploration into the Theology of Wolfhart Pannenberg* (Lanham, Md.: University Press of America, 1989).

17. David P. Polk, "The All-Determining God and the Peril of Determinism," in *The Theology of Wolfhart Pannenberg,* ed. Braaten and Clayton, pp. 167f.

18. Stanley J. Grenz, *Reason for Hope: The Systematic Theology of Wolfhart Pannenberg* (Oxford: Oxford University Press, 1990).

19. Grenz, *Reason for Hope,* p. 9.

poses to understand all of reality.[20] Buller's general concern is to show that Pannenberg can help overcome the dichotomy between spirit and nature that caused much of the ecological crisis in contemporary culture, and aid in the development of an ethical response. For the purposes of our brief review, the main point is to show that the concept of history continues to play a role in the search for Pannenberg's basic principle.

The continental reception of Pannenberg's thought has tended to focus primarily on the new ideas about revelation and history in his theology, and secondarily on his view of theological rationality. Although his new christological approach evoked substantial discussion, the early comprehensive book-length treatments of his work tended to emphasize his "theology of history."[21] The basic conclusion of most of the major German and French interpreters of Pannenberg seems to be that the core of his theology is the view of *history* and that this is the key to understanding him. While I agree that an emphasis on history must be incorporated in any valid interpretation of Pannenberg, I believe that there is something going on in his theology even deeper than his commitment to revelation as history.

In his 1988 *Die Theologie Wolfhart Pannenbergs*,[22] S. Greiner pro-

---

20. Cornelius Buller, *The Unity of Nature and History in Pannenberg's Theology* (Lanham, Md.: Littlefield Adams Books, 1996), p. 21.

21. Just a glance at some of the titles illustrates the focus on this theme. Krzysztof Gózdz, *Jesus Christus als Sinn der Geschichte bei Wolfhart Pannenberg* (Regensburg: Pustet, 1988); Kurt Koch, *Der Gott der Geschichte: Theologie der Geschichte bei Wolfhart Pannenberg als Paradigma einer Philosophischen Theologie in ökumenischer Perspektive* (Mainz: Matthias-Grünewald Verlag, 1988); Günther Klein, *Theologie des Wortes Gottes und die Hypothese der Universalgeschichte. Zur Auseinandersetzung mit W. Pannenberg* (Munich: Chr. Kaiser, 1964); Pannenberg responded to Klein in *Theology as History* (see pp. 123, 258, 263); Reginald Nnamdi, *Offenbarung und Geschichte: Zur hermeneutischen Bestimmung der Theologie Wolfhart Pannenbergs* (Frankfurt am Main: Peter Lang, 1993); Ignace Berten, *Geschichte, Offenbarung, Glaube. Eine Einführung in die Theologie Wolfhart Pannenbergs,* trans. from the French *Histoire, Revelation et Foi* by Sigrid Martin (Munich: Claudius Verlag, 1970); Denis Müller, *Parole et Histoire: Dialogue avec W. Pannenberg* (Geneva: Labor et Fides, 1983).

22. Sebastian Greiner, *Die Theologie Wolfhart Pannenbergs* (Würzburg: Echter, 1988).

duced a comprehensive treatment of Pannenberg from an explicitly Catholic perspective. He noted that the last full assessment of Pannenberg in German had been by Berten in 1970, which was a German translation of the 1969 French text. This represents a gap in the literature similar to that in the English-speaking world. Elsewhere on the continent, the French theologian P. Warin had assessed the whole of Pannenberg's approach as a "théologie de la raison" in 1981.[23] In Holland, M. E. Brinkman had published a summary of Pannenberg's work to date (1979), focusing on the concepts of God and humanity in his theology.[24] Greiner's book was mostly an exposition of Pannenberg's thought to introduce him to those in the Catholic theological world who were not familiar with the themes of his theology.

Although Greiner's primary aim was not to explain the underlying structure that guides Pannenberg's theology, he did argue that "eschatology" was the key concept; specifically, the future is the "pivotal point" *(Angelpunkt)* of Pannenberg's whole system.[25] A similar interpretation was made by Eberhard Jüngel after the publication of volume I of Pannenberg's *Systematische Theologie.* Jüngel sees the concept of prolepsis (or anticipation) of the future as the key concept *(Schlüsselbegriff)* that guides all of Pannenberg's argumentation.[26] Elisabeth Dieckmann is primarily interested in his concept of "person," and its application to God and humans, but she, too, notes that Pannenberg's emphasis on the ontological priority of the future is the aspect of his work that will probably have the most impact on wider theological reflection.[27] Clearly, anticipation of the future is crucially important for Pannenberg, but here, too, I want

23. Pierre Warin, *Le Chemin de la Théologie chez Wolfhart Pannenberg* (Rome: Gregorian University, 1981).

24. M. E. Brinkman, *Het Gods- en Mensbegrip in de Theologie van Wolfhart Pannenberg* (Kampen: J. H. Kok, 1979).

25. Greiner, *Die Theologie,* p. 315.

26. E. Jüngel, "Nihil divinitatis, ubi non fides," *Zeitschrift für Theologie und Kirche* 86, no. 2 (1989): 207.

27. Elisabeth Dieckmann, *Personalität Gottes — Personalität des Menschen: Ihre Deutung im theologischen Denken Wolfhart Pannenbergs* (Altenberge: Oros Verlag, 1995), p. 363.

to argue that his commitment to the God of the future is supported by a deeper basic principle.[28]

All three of these common choices for Pannenberg's Grund-prinzip easily lend themselves to a foundationalist reading of his method. If reason is seen as dominant, his method can easily be read as simply another page in the history of the (moribund) Enlightenment modernist approach to epistemology. If "universal" history is the starting point, then it may appear that a foundationalist longing for an absolute metanarrative permeates Pannenberg's interpretation of the findings of historical research. If the anticipation of "totality," based on the priority of the future, is a metaphysical (or epistemic) self-justifying assumption that grounds his system, we would seem to have some form of foundationalism. My argument is that such readings of Pannenberg privilege one (or a set) of his works over others, and miss the structural dynamics that lie across the whole *corpus* of his authorship.

Sub ratione Dei: The "True Infinite" and the Trinity

In this subsection, I will take two major steps. First, I will try to show that the attempt to understand and explain all things *sub ratione Dei* (under the aspect of their "relation to God") is the basic principle in Pannenberg's approach, which he takes over with some important modifications from Thomas Aquinas. This interpretation will be buttressed by references in Pannenberg's work spanning almost forty years. Second, I will outline the precise nature of this "relation," which Pannenberg spells out through the reciprocally related concepts of the "true infinite" and the Trinity, which are correlated to his understanding of the "fundamental" and "systematic" movements in theology. I hope to show how this Grundprinzip subtends the other three "key concepts" commonly identified by

28. I am not denying that these are key concepts in Pannenberg's theology; rather, I am arguing that none of them captures *the* basic principle that drives his theological method. As we will see in our review of the literature in the next two chapters, reason, history, and prolepsis were and continue to be dominant and central themes in Pannenberg's theology.

Pannenberg scholars.[29] This interpretation suggests that Pannenberg is not a foundationalist in the pernicious sense; demonstrating this in more detail is the goal of bringing him into dialogue with the four postfoundationalist couplets in the next section.

Already in 1958 we see in embryonic form an emphasis on a dynamic relation to God as the *terminus a quo* of theology: "the single legitimate point of departure of theological cognition lies in the historical situation wherein man is met by the revelatory action of God."[30] This way of putting it is shaped by the early influence of Barth, but Pannenberg's willingness to engage philosophical metaphysics is more clear by 1962, when he indicated that the task of theology involves understanding "all being in relation to God [*auf Gott hin*]."[31] In the preface to BQT, I, he says:

> . . . the question of the theology of history, in the last analysis, has to do with the *one theme of all theology* which is, quite properly, built into its name. To say that the revelation of God is not a supernatural event which breaks into history perpendicularly from above but rather that it is the theme of history itself, the power that moves it in its deepest dimension, is to say something about *God and his relation to the world*. . . . The studies of truth, reason, and faith [in BQT, II] trace the roots of these themes to a relation to the eschatological future.[32]

29. In a June 4, 1997, private conversation in Munich, Pannenberg confirmed my interpretation of his basic principle as *sub ratione Dei*, acknowledging that it was more basic than the other key concepts of reason, history, and prolepsis. Of course, Pannenberg's agreement is neither a necessary nor a sufficient condition for accepting this interpretation, so what follows is an attempt to demonstrate the thesis through textual analysis and argument.

30. W. Pannenberg, "Christliche Glaube und menschliche Freiheit," *Kerygma und Dogma* 4 (1958): 274-75. Quoted and translated by Tupper, *The Theology of Wolfhart Pannenberg*, p. 70.

31. BQT, I, 1. See also the 1961 article "Kerygma and History" where Pannenberg asserts that "God can be spoken of only in relation to the whole of reality because, since the critical question of Greek philosophy about the true form of the divine, only one who was the author of all things and all events could seriously be called God," BQT, I, 94.

32. BQT, I, xv. Emphasis added. See also p. 14.

In *An Introduction to Systematic Theology* Pannenberg credits Thomas Aquinas as the first to "state clearly that everything in theology is concerned with God."[33] Albertus Magnus and Thomas argued that this is the case even though Christian doctrines treat many other things besides God, viz., aspects of created reality. However,

> Thomas stressed that these things enter into theological discussion only inasmuch as they are related to God (*sub ratione Dei;* see Summa Theologica 1.2 a 2; cf. 1.1 a 7 ad 1). To this extent God is the unifying point of reference for all the objects and themes of theology and in this sense he is its absolute subject. (ST, I, 5)

The importance of the "relation to God" can be traced at every point in his work, from the early articles to his magnum opus. In his 1967 response to the discussion in *Theology as History,* Pannenberg is already suggesting that the point of the emphasis on "history" is its relevance for the question of the reality of God. The task of theology is to speak about God in critical thought, but "the divinity of God can only be conceived in relation to the whole of reality."[34]

In his 1973 massive programmatic treatment of theology in the context of *Wissenschaftstheorie,* he utilizes the phrase *sub ratione Dei* and spells it out in more detail.

> That God is the true object of theology is sufficiently shown by the history of the concept of theology. We saw above that the term "theology" originally had the narrow sense of the doctrine of God, as distinct from "economy," the doctrine of God's plan of salvation and its accomplishment in salvation history, from the creation to the eschatological fulfillment. The later extension of the concept of theology to cover the area of the divine economy was justified by the argument that everything studied within this comprehensive theology was studied from the point of view of its relation to God (*sub ratione Dei*). If the *concepts* of the

33. Wolfhart Pannenberg, *An Introduction to Systematic Theology* (Edinburgh: T. & T. Clark, 1991), p. 13.

34. W. Pannenberg, "Response to the Discussion," *Theology as History,* p. 241.

objects with which theological investigation is concerned are not separated from the *relations* within which they stand, but the relations are seen as the expression of the reality of the objects, the examination of the various objects of theological study *sub ratione Dei* becomes not merely a subjective approach unrelated to their objectivity, but the approach which is appropriate to them and to the nature of theological objects as such. It is only this consideration *sub ratione Dei* which distinguishes the treatment of a wide range of topics in theology from their treatment in other disciplines which concern themselves with the same areas but from different points of view. (TPS, 298)

He emphasizes that the success of this *sub ratione Dei* approach depends on the possibility of showing that the reality of God as all-determining reality is implicit in all finite reality (TPS, 330). This is already an allusion to the importance of the concept of the infinite for Pannenberg, which we will see in more detail below. This relation of the infinite God to finite creation will have to be thought out in connection to the incarnation of Jesus Christ, and this is precisely how Pannenberg sees the task of christology:

This poses the task of thinking about Christology in connection with God's relation to the world in general and especially in connection with his relationship to humanity in the course of its history. But this would have to be done in such a way that Jesus' history would be shown as providing the key to understanding human history and to God's relation to the world in general. (JGM, 406, "Afterword")

Pannenberg does not use the phrase *sub ratione Dei* in his treatments of anthropology or history, but he clearly sees his task there as understanding and explaining human experience under the aspect of its relation to God. For example, he argues that "because selfness is ultimately grounded in the relation to God, persons can be free in the face of their social situation" (ATP, 241). In response to misinterpretations of ATP Pannenberg did have occasion to use the phrase. He was criticized for not sufficiently addressing the Reformation doctrine of justification in that monograph; his response points to the fact that ATP was not intended as a systematic-theological presentation. For Pannenberg, the proper place for fully setting out such doctrines would be in the context of a "whole presentation of Dogmatics *sub ratione Dei*."[35]

In *Metaphysics and the Idea of God* (MIG), he reiterates that Christian theology "is essentially an inquiry [*Wissenschaft*] into God and his revelation. Everything else that occurs within theology can become a theme for the theologian only 'in relation to God,' as Thomas Aquinas put it: *sub ratione Dei*."[36] Only in light of these statements about the "relation to God" as the theme of theology are we able to understand Pannenberg's insistence that systematic theology is a "systematic doctrine of God and nothing else" (ST, I, 59). Theology is about God, but to speak of God one must also speak of "the world, humanity and history as they are grounded, reconciled and consummated in God" (ST, I, 60). These triads are an allusion to the overall structure of his *Systematic Theology*, but the salient point here is that every presentation of a systematic locus is for Pannenberg couched in and aimed at an attempt to understand and explain all things under the aspect of their relation to God.

Clearly, the theme of "relation to God" is central in Pannenberg's method. However, it might be argued that this is the case for *every* theological system. In a sense this is true; all theology deals with the relation of God to the world. Because the concept of "relation" is notoriously ambiguous, it is necessary to show the material uniqueness of Pannenberg's view. More than simply emphasizing the importance of the content of this relation, however, I am suggesting

35. W. Pannenberg, "Schlußdiskussion," in *Sind wir von Natur aus religiös?* (Düsseldorf: Patmos, 1986), p. 135. My translation. "Ich glaube gar nicht, daß das zwischen uns strittig sein kann, aber dieses Recht der Priorität Gottes vor dem Menschen, das ja für die Rechtfertigungslehre im reformatorischen Verständnis konstitutiv ist, kann in einer systematischen Darstellung eigentlich nur im Zusammenhang einer Gesamtdarstellung der Dogmatik *sub ratione Dei* ausgeführt werden."

36. W. Pannenberg, *Metaphysics and the Idea of God,* trans. P. Clayton (Edinburgh: T. & T. Clark, 1990), p. 73. Hereafter noted as MIG. German: *Metaphysik und Gottesgedanke* (Göttingen: Vandenhoeck & Ruprecht, 1988).

that Pannenberg has thematized this relationality in a more radical way than most theologians and embraced it as the basic principle of his method, so that it is folded into and illuminates all aspects of his theological presentation.

In the theological world, the last half-century has seen a kind of "relational turn," a rigorous thematization of relationality, with special attention on implications for the doctrine of the Trinity.[37] Also in the non-theological disciplines, we find a turn to relationality as a decisive concept. For example, one can think of "object relations" theory in psychology, systems theory in sociology, and field theories in physics. Pannenberg's corpus engages all of these relational thought-forms and many more.

Pannenberg is aware that what I am calling the "relational turn" should not be naïvely adopted by theology. He is careful throughout his writings to distinguish his views from relational conceptualizations that dissolve the idea of substance or essence completely, and from theological approaches (like some forms of process theology) that so emphasize the God-world connection that their distinction is blurred. I believe that Pannenberg has seen that the turn to relationality affects not only material doctrinal decisions (e.g., as in christology, wherein one finds the key to the relation of God to his creation), but also that this turn very radically affects formal methodological patterns. So he finds the thematization of relationality to be important in understanding the regulation of theological knowledge, as well as in explaining constitutive and transformative dynamics in anthropology, christology, and all other loci.

Pannenberg quotes Thomas Aquinas in his adoption of the phrase *sub ratione Dei*, but he clearly refigures the concept based on his understanding of the relational turn. Here are the words of Thomas:

37. This thematic has been identified by authors such as Colin Gunton, *The One, The Three and The Many* (Cambridge: Cambridge University Press, 1993); H. Jansen, *Relationality and the Concept of God* (Amsterdam: Rodopi, 1995); and Catherine M. LaCugna, *God for Us* (San Francisco: HarperCollins, 1991). This renewed interest in trinitarian doctrine is helpfully traced by Ted Peters, *God as Trinity* (Philadelphia: Westminster, 1993). Peters sees Pannenberg as going further than others in this direction.

Now all things are dealt with in holy teaching in terms of God [*sub ratione Dei*], either because they are God himself or because they are relative to him as their origin and end. . . . All these indeed are dwelt on by this science, yet as held in their relationship to God [*ordinem ad Deum*]. . . . All other things that are settled in Holy Scripture are embraced in God, not that they are parts of him — such as essential components or accidents — but because they are somehow related to him.[38]

In Pannenberg's view, Thomas did not affirm "a real relation which defines the essential distinctiveness of the one who relates himself. Similarly, although the creature is defined by dependence on the Creator, the relation to God is also not a real relation (Summa, 1.45.3 ad 1; cf. 13.7)."[39] For Thomas, relations to the world are not properly predicated of the divine essence because they are not real (definitive) but conceptual relations on God's part.

It is at this point that Pannenberg appeals to the philosophical roots of the relational turn. Influential on Thomas (especially at this point) was the approach of Aristotle, for whom the category of "relation" was an accident that did not describe an essential part of a "substance." Because there is no composition of substance and accidents in the divine essence, Thomas had to see the Trinity, which posited relations (and therefore accidents) in God, as a "supernatural truth of faith." On this hypothesis, only with a concept of causative substance could Thomas predicate of God's essence the attributes that are ascribed to him as the "first cause" of all creaturely things. In modern thought, however, Kant reversed the order so that substance was subordinate to the category of relation, and for Hegel the concept of essence itself is relationally structured. This philosophical turn set the concept of relation above that of substance.

For Pannenberg, this "introduction of relation into the concept of substance not only raises problems but also *offers opportunities to*

---

38. Thomas Aquinas, *Summa Theologiae*, Blackfriars edition, vol. 1 (New York: McGraw-Hill, 1964), p. 27 (I, Q. 1, Art. 7).

39. Pannenberg, ST, I, 362. See also p. 365.

solve others that have thus far seemed to be insoluble."[40] The most important problem for our purposes is the relation of God to the world. Pannenberg's appropriation of aspects of the relational turn makes his *sub ratione Dei* approach radically different from that of Thomas. Both the "relation" is different, and the concept of "God" is different. The first is explicated in terms of the **true infinite**, the latter in terms of his robust view of the **trinitarian God**. Let us look at each of these and their interconnection.

In 1972 Pannenberg was not using the term "true infinite," but the concept is there in less precise form: "if we conceive of God as finite, we have not conceived of God at all. . . . I try to overcome an idea of infinity which has become connected with an eternity that would mean timelessness."[41] Pannenberg wants to insist that finite and infinite, temporal and eternal, are not *merely* opposed to each other; this would mean the eternal God was defined by the distinction from the temporal, and God's infinity would be defined merely as that which is not finite. In a 1975 article, he speaks of the intercalation or entwining *(Vershränkung)* of time and eternity, without the dissolution of the distinction between them.[42] Later, he would express his view positively as a notion of eternity as constituting time; by speaking of God as the "power of the future," he means that "the future of finite entities is the point where time and eternity coincide."[43] This finds more careful articulation in ST:

> Strictly, the infinite is not that which is without end but that which stands opposed to the finite, to what is defined by some-

40. ST, I, 367. Emphasis added. Cf. MIG, 73. See also Carver T. Yu's analysis (and critique) of the leitmotif of being as "being-in-itself" from Greek philosophy to modern times, *Being and Relation* (Edinburgh: Scottish Academic Press, 1987). Although he does not refer to Pannenberg, Yu also finds the biblical ideas of history, reality, and human experience to be inherently relational.

41. "A Theological Conversation with Wolfhart Pannenberg," *Dialog* 11 (Autumn 1972): 294.

42. "Zeit und Ewigkeit in der religiösen Erfahrung Israels und des Christentums," in *Grundfragen, II,* 199-202. Cf. ST, I, 408.

43. W. Pannenberg, "Providence, God and Eschatology," in *The Whirlwind of Culture,* ed. D. Musser and J. Price (Bloomington, Ind.: Meyer-Stone, 1988), p. 178.

thing else. . . . To be finite is to be in distinction from something and to be defined by the distinction. The relation of something to something else is an immanent definition of the something itself. From this fact Hegel derives his famous thesis that the Infinite is truly infinite only when it is not thought of merely as the opposite of the finite, for otherwise it would be seen as something in relation to something else and therefore as itself finite. (ST, I, 397)

Pannenberg believes that the idea of the true infinite is best understood in terms of the biblical understanding of the holiness of God and of the essence of God as Spirit. The holiness of God "is truly infinite, for it is opposed to the profane, yet it also enters the profane world, penetrates it, and makes it holy." The biblical conception of God as Spirit includes the "thought that God gives existence to the finite as that which is different from himself, so that his holiness does not mean the abolition of the distinction between the finite and the infinite" (ST, I, 400).

Pannenberg traces the failure of various philosophical systems to solve the issue of the true infinite because of their inability to posit relationality in the unity of the essence of God. How can the one divine essence be truly infinite and yet also be really related to the world? Pannenberg argues that "the principle of the unity of the immanent and economic Trinity in the doctrine of God embraces these relations" (ST, I, 367). Although it pervades the entire ST (see summary below), this trinitarian answer is worked out in detail in chapters 5 and 6 of volume I.

Before examining his attempted trinitarian solution, it is important to stress the importance of the "true infinite" concept. Here we have a distinction that transcends yet embraces the distinction between God and the world. This special distinction has been emphasized by many theologians over the centuries, but recently it has been radically thematized. Robert Sokolowski describes it in this way: "(God plus the world) is not greater than God alone."[44] He dis-

---

44. Robert Sokolowski, *The God of Faith and Reason: Foundations of Christian Theology* (Washington, D.C.: The Catholic University of America Press, 1995), p. 8.

tinguishes this conception of God, which he finds in Anselm, from the "pagan" conception of divinity in which God is always a "part" of the world, even if the highest part. In his *Proslogion* Anselm seems to have assumed this special kind of distinction in his famous concept of "that than which nothing greater can be conceived." If the world and God together were "more" than God alone, then we have something "greater" than God; namely, God and the world. So Anselm's conception of God seems to presuppose a distinction that transcends the nature of normal finite distinctions. As Diogenes Allen puts it, "The relation between God and the world (the relation of Creator and creature) is less basic than one of the terms of the relation, namely God. In other words, God is more fundamental than the relation between God and the world."[45]

Many of the phrases and concepts that Pannenberg has used over the years, such as "all-determining Reality," are more clearly understood when we examine them in connection with the infinity of God, understood in terms of this special distinction. The key point for Pannenberg is that God is not exhaustively defined by his relation to the creation.[46] This means God does not "exist" as creaturely finite things exist. God is not one existent being among others. Only in this context can we understand his early suggestion that "in a restricted but important sense, God does not yet exist."[47] For Pannenberg, the problem of human freedom is also solved by the concept of true infinite, even when he does not use the term. Human freedom is constituted by our openness to the infinite power that gives us existence. God's power does not share in the genus "power" as finite things do. This is spelled out in several essays.[48]

---

45. Diogenes Allen, *Philosophy for Understanding Theology* (Atlanta: John Knox, 1985), p. 10. For helpful analysis of this unique distinction in Christian thought, see David Burrell, *Freedom and Creation in Three Traditions* (Notre Dame: University of Notre Dame Press, 1993), pp. 60ff., and Austin Farrer, *Finite and Infinite*, 2nd ed. (Westminster: Dacre Press, 1959), pp. 61ff.

46. This is already clear in early writings like *Theology as History*, pp. 253-55 and BQT, II, 138ff.

47. TKG, 56. In "A Theological Conversation," *Dialog* (1972): 294, Pannenberg qualified this claim by adding, "from a finite point of view."

48. E.g., *The Idea of God and Human Freedom*, trans. R. A. Wilson (Philadelphia:

Similarly, the problem of "analogy," which was the topic of Pannenberg's Habilitationschrift,[49] is resolved in light of this special distinction. In BQT, II (133-34), he noted that the "philosophical" concept of God was developed on the assumption that knowledge of God as origin could be inferred from "effects." This idea lived through the theological conceptions of scholasticism ("first cause") and modernity ("absolute subject"). Arguing against any form of *analogia entis* that would allow a movement from the finite to the infinite, Pannenberg rejected "analogy" as the basic form of theological speech, and opted instead for "doxology." We will have the opportunity to examine his concept "analogy" (along with many other issues) in light of the postfoundationalist couplets below.[50]

The crucial point for our interpretation of his Grundprinzip is that although God is not exhausted by the relation to the world, because he is truly infinite, at the same time God is really related to the world. "Of course God could have not created a world. But if He created a world, and since He did, the divine identity of God, the existence of God is inseparable from His Kingdom in His Creation."[51] Before the publication of ST (and afterwards as well), some interpreters saw a tension in Pannenberg at this point. In a review of *Grundfragen systematischer Theologie, Band II,* Philip Clayton notes Pannenberg's comment that "the reality of God is not simply set over against the finite, but at the same time contains it in itself," and his description of the kingdom of God as God's "presence in the creation and the creation's in him without dissolving their difference." But Clayton thinks simply making these assertions alone

---

Westminster, 1973), pp. 131ff. German: *Gottesgedanke und menschliche Freiheit* (Göttingen: Vandenhoeck & Ruprecht, 1971). See also ST, I, 388. The issue of omnipotence, too, is explained in terms of the true infinite (ST, I, 416).

49. W. Pannenberg, *Analogie und Offenbarung: Eine kritische Untersuchung der Geschichte des Analogiebegriffs in der Gotteserkenntnis* (Heidelberg Habilitationschrift, 1955).

50. In that context, we will explore other writings where Pannenberg articulates the philosophical conception of the true infinite and its relevance for theology. E.g., MIG, 35, 143ff.

51. W. Pannenberg, "Theta Phi Talkback Session," *The Asbury Theological Journal* 46, no. 2 (1991): 38.

does not help: ". . . the principle of ontological distinction in this differentiated intermingling remains unclear, leaving the basis for God's 'otherness' from creation in question."[52] In his response to Clayton's contribution to the American festschrift, Pannenberg explains that he sees the trinitarian conception of God as the answer:

> it provides a notion of created reality as different from but also united to God through the "economic" trinity, the "historical" aspect of the divine reality itself which nevertheless is one with the "immanent" trinity of God's eternal self-identity. . . . That God as economic trinity has a history is itself a facet of the abundance of the eternal life of the trinitarian God.[53]

For Pannenberg, then, the philosophical-anthropological problem of the true infinite is solved by the distinction-in-unity of the immanent and economic trinity. We will examine this in detail in ST below, but it is important to realize that this move is dominant in many of his writings. He notes Martin Luther's commitment to seeing the Christian God as the only explanation for the world. With reference to the creed, he asked why one should believe in God the Father Almighty. Pannenberg summarizes Luther's answer: "No one else could create the heavens and the earth. No one else could possibly be the origin of the world. No alternative explanation of its reality succeeds."[54] In the dialogue with other religions, Pannenberg argues that only the Christian view of the trinitarian God is consistently monotheistic. Religions that define God merely over

---

52. Philip Clayton, "The God of History and the Presence of the Future," p. 105. In Gary Culpepper's "Wolfhart Pannenberg's Proleptic Christology in Light of His Trinitarian Theology and Metaphysics" (Ph.D. diss., Catholic University of America, 1994), he accuses Pannenberg of "sacrificing the ontological difference between the being of God and the creation" (p. 11). Such a reading of Pannenberg misses the special nature of the "true infinite," and the particular kind of distinction it implies between God and the creation.

53. W. Pannenberg, "Response to American Friends," in *Theology of Wolfhart Pannenberg*, pp. 321, 323.

54. W. Pannenberg, "Theology and Science," *The Princeton Seminary Bulletin* (1992): 299.

against the world have inadvertently made God a correlate to the world. The trinitarian God, however, "without blotting out the *difference* between creator and creature, transcends while preserving [*hebt auf*] this opposition by means of the idea of the reconciliation of the world."[55] Here is perhaps his clearest statement:

> In the doctrine on the Trinity, the unity of the one God is conceived in terms of a differentiated unity. This enables the Christian teaching to do justice to the unity of transcendence and immanence with regard to God's relation to the world of His creation. God could not be conceived as *truly infinite* in distinction from His finite creatures, if He only were transcendent. In that case He would be limited by His being separate from the world and precisely by its distinction from God the world would then become constitutive of the very identity of His being God. Rather, the infinity of God has to be conceived in terms of being transcendent as well as immanent in the reality of the world. . . . The Christian trinitarian doctrine can be considered as determining the question of how these forms of God's presence in the world are related to His transcendent existence. The answer is that they cannot be different from God Himself, if the unity of the one God is to be preserved.[56]

In fact, this can be seen as the single argument of the entire three-volume ST: the biblical trinitarian God is the best explanation for the human experience of being in a historical relation to the true infinite. In 1981, Pannenberg indicated that when he did produce a systematic theology it "will be more thoroughly trinitarian than any example I know of."[57] Indeed, from §1 of volume I (p. 6) to the last sentence of volume III (p. 646), the relation of the immanent and

---

55. W. Pannenberg, "Problems of a Trinitarian Doctrine of God," *Dialog* 26, no. 4 (1987): 256. Emphasis added. For additional treatments of this issue see, e.g., BQT, II, 182, 249, and TKG, 71.

56. W. Pannenberg, "The Christian Vision of God: The New Discussion on the Trinitarian Doctrine," *The Asbury Theological Journal* 46, no. 2 (Fall 1991): 35.

57. W. Pannenberg, "God's Presence in History," *The Christian Century* (March 11, 1981): 263.

economic Trinity, their distinction and unity as a comprehensive explanation of the relation of all finite things to the infinite God *(sub ratione Dei)* is the key to Christian theology's claim to truth. It will be helpful to summarize the three volumes briefly in light of this Grundprinzip.

The first chapter of ST, I, begins by describing the task of systematic theology as the presentation of the inner coherence of the content of Christian doctrine and showing its coherence with all that is regarded as true. Of course, this task can never be fulfilled before the end of history, but we may argue proleptically and offer provisional confirmation of the Christian truth claims. Chapter 2 shows that the very concept of God itself requires this conception of truth, for philosophical reflection has provided a criterion for any concept of God: it must include the concept of an all-determining reality, which in turn guarantees the unity of truth. In the current experience of the conflict among the religions (chapter 3), it is debatable which conception of God is true. The argument for the truth of religion must be carried out on anthropological soil, with the aim of explaining the "religious relation" of finite humans to the infinite.

It is critical to recognize a major turn in the argument at this point. Pannenberg explains that after identifying anthropological elements of truth in the concept of religion, his task from chapter 4 onward will be "taking them up into ['Aufhebung'] the perspective of a theology that is oriented to the primacy of God and his revelation."[58] The first step in this task is clarifying the role and concept of revelation in Scripture and theology. The remaining doctrines then are "an explication of the self-revelation of God in Jesus Christ . . . [which claims] to reveal the one God who is the world's Creator, Reconciler, and Redeemer . . ." (257). Thus chapter 5 turns to a presentation of the Christian doctrine of the trinitarian God. Here he clarifies his well-known emphasis on the world as the "history of God," and the distinction of the divine persons revealed in the history of the man Jesus. Chapter 6 then attempts to make intelligible the unity and attributes of the divine essence. The key concept here

---

58. ST, I, 128. The original German has "Aufhebung" in quotation marks. The English translation does not capture this emphasis. See also ST, I, 61.

is the human intuition of the "true infinite" which transcends yet embraces the distinction between finite and infinite. For Pannenberg, this formal criterion for understanding the divine essence leads to a discussion of God as "spirit" and "love," the concrete material unity of the attributes.

Volume II begins with "The Creation of the World" (chapter 7) and ends with "The Reconciliation of the World" (chapter 11). The middle three chapters are an integration of the main themes of anthropology and christology, which Pannenberg sees as reciprocally related. He emphasizes that creation is a trinitarian act, oriented to the differentiation of creatures, which is a condition for the linking of creatures to God at the eschaton. Referring back to his discussions of Trinity and the divine essence in volume I, he insists:

> We cannot set God's relations to the world in antithesis to his essence, as though this were unaffected by the relations. We have seen already that essence itself is a relational concept (vol. I, 359ff.). But the relations of God to his creatures must be thought of as an expression of the freedom of his essence and therefore must be depicted as grounded in it. (ST, II, 85)

Chapter 8 treats the traditional loci of theological anthropology: the unity of body and soul, *imago Dei,* and sin. For Pannenberg, the definition and destiny *(Bestimmung)* of human beings is fellowship with God. The methodological discussion of "from below" versus "from above" is elevated to a new level in chapter 9, where Pannenberg argues that the two movements are mutually conditioning. The arguments from JGM (1964) are strengthened and placed in the larger context of a presentation of the trinitarian God in chapter 10. The unity of Jesus with God, a claim justified by his resurrection, is the basis for affirming his deity. The eleventh chapter treats the doctrine of reconciliation; here, too, it is seen as an act of the triune God. The Son differentiates himself from the Father in the incarnation and ultimately on the cross, making room for us alongside God; the Spirit completes our salvation by elevating us beyond ourselves into a relation with the Father. This is the good news of the Gospel.

The third volume continues the development of many familiar themes. Chapter 12, "The Outpouring of the Spirit, the Kingdom of God, and the Church," relates the consummating work of the Spirit in the church and society to the trinitarian act of creation and reconciliation. His treatment here of the relation of Law to Gospel expands upon his comments in volume II that Jesus' interpretation of the divine law in Israel in terms of the love of God (the great commandment) was at the core of his eschatological message. The existence of states and their laws shows the imperfection of the ability of humans to do right on their own, and points to the need for a basis for "right" that goes beyond humanity. The church is a sign of the eschatological in-breaking of the Kingdom of God, which already mediates the assurance of salvation to individuals, but also represents a not-yet-fulfilled hope in the ultimate future of God.

Chapter 13, "The Messianic Community and Individuals," dominates the third volume, representing nearly 340 of its 640 pages (in English translation). The chapter is divided into five major parts. The relation of the individual to God as mediated by Jesus Christ and the fellowship of believers is the subject of the first part. This work of the Holy Spirit is aimed at fulfilling our destiny, our true identity in relation to God. Next, Pannenberg treats the saving work of the Holy Spirit in the lives of individual Christians, examining the traditional themes of faith, hope, and love; these themes are aspects of our adoption as God's children, in which we are lifted up above our corrupt self-relatedness. The doctrine of justification is integrated into the concept of "adoption" by God, which Pannenberg takes as the ultimate form of fellowship, the goal of our creation. Part 3 explores the sacraments of baptism and the Lord's Supper, as well as the broader question of the nature of "sacraments," and the special case of marriage. In line with his long-standing ecumenical interests, Pannenberg urges that we not insist on too narrow a usage of the term "sacrament"; however, it should only be applied to things or actions that are demonstrably related to Jesus Christ as the mystery of salvation. He turns next to a treatment of ministry (and ordination) as a sign and instrument of the unity of the church, again calling for ecumenicity in the whole Christian church. The fifth (and shortest) part of the chapter posits "the Body of Christ" as the most basic and specific description of the church, but also proposes that it is a provisional representation of the "people of God," an anticipatory sign of the future of humanity reconciled to God under his reign.

In the fourteenth chapter, Pannenberg links the doctrine of "election" to history, noting that Israel's sense of election arose out of its experience of the free historical action of God, an awareness of a calling that oriented them to the future reign of God. This sense of election is continued in Christianity, but individuals are linked to the living eschatological reality of the risen Christ by the sacraments. In discussing the election of both individuals and the people of God as a whole, Pannenberg emphasizes that election has to do with "calling," and argues that this involves a participation in (but not a possession of) the consummation of human destiny for fellowship with God. He attempts to solve the problem of the particularity of election by arguing that the participation of those who are called in God's historical salvation does not imply exclusion of others, but is a movement toward their inclusion. Salvation and participation in the fellowship of the people of God is open to all; yet, all may not respond to the invitation.

Chapter 15 concludes Pannenberg's ST with a discussion of "The Consummation of Creation in the Kingdom of God," in which his interest in eschatological themes finds a careful systematic presentation. Emphasizing again that the unifying theme of theology is God, Pannenberg insists that eschatology, too (like all doctrines), must be grounded in the knowledge of God, the truth of which is debatable until the consummation of creation. The idea of the resurrection of the individual person is central for Pannenberg, because it is a condition for the fulfillment of our anticipated totality and identity; this, too, is the work of the Spirit. Human society, the human race as a whole and not merely individuals, is fulfilled and reaches its goal in the kingdom of God. Pannenberg conceives of the end of time as God's very being (rather than "nothing"); God's reign is the coming of eternity into time. Individuals continue to have their own identity in God's eternal present because "room" is made for them by the Son's self-distinction from the Father through the Spirit. With the consummation of the world, the biblical God will prove to be the all-determining reality. Pannenberg suggests that rational theodicies that attempt to justify God by argument are expressions of unbelief. It is God himself who will overcome wickedness and evil in the final perfection of the world, thereby revealing the ultimate manifestation of the divine love, which will encompass the whole world of creatures. His concluding paragraph:

> On the whole path from the beginning of creation by way of reconciliation to the eschatological future of salvation, the march of the divine economy of salvation is an expression of the incursion of the eternal future of God to the salvation of creatures and thus a manifestation of the divine love. Here is the eternal basis of God's coming forth from the immanence of the divine life as the economic Trinity and of the incorporation of creatures, mediated thereby, into the unity of the trinitarian life. The *distinction and unity of the immanent and economic Trinity* constitute the heartbeat of the divine love, and with a single such heartbeat this love encompasses the whole world of creatures.[59]

Clearly the theme of "relation to God" is central in Pannenberg's thought. At this point, we can see how this interpretation of his Grundprinzip subtends the common readings of reason, history, and anticipation. His view of the relation between God as all-determining reality and the totality of all finite reality informs his understanding of human **reason** as operating in such a way that it aims at a unity of truth. Human reason participates in the differentiation of the Logos; rational logical argumentation should be embraced in theological method because it offers provisional explanations of the conditions of our religious experience of the true infinite. Only because God is thus related to all things may we view **history** as the self-revelation of the all-determining reality. History is reconceived in terms of the ontological priority of the future, as the heuristic horizon of the relation of all things to God. All of our rational reconstructions and our interpretations of history are provisional, however, because human knowledge is **proleptic**; we perceive parts in relation to larger wholes, and the ultimate whole or to-

---

59. ST, III, 646. Emphasis added.

tality lies in the future, in the being of God. Anticipation is a constitutive aspect of our existence because our identity is determined by this relation to God as the future. Thus the principle of *sub ratione Dei* subtends the key concepts of reason, history, and prolepsis, and drives his interdisciplinary theological method.[60]

We have attempted to clarify the relational character of Pannenberg's method. It is precisely this relational dynamic that helps overcome reading him as a foundationalist. It is the movement back and forth between the "true infinite" and the Trinity that constitutes the driving force of his method. This would only be foundationalism if he started with one as immediately self-justifying, and then argued to the other. But Pannenberg wants to start "between" them, in the thought processes that are mutually conditioned by an understanding of humanity and a concept of God. This interpretation of his Grundprinzip opens up a new way of bringing him into dialogue with the emerging postfoundationalist model of theological rationality.

Pannenberg and the Postfoundationalist Couplets

The purpose of the following four subsections is to bring Pannenberg into explicit dialogue with the postfoundationalist couplets. My argument is that he holds more in common with the emerging postfoundationalist model than either of its rivals: foundationalism or nonfoundationalism. Several postfoundation-

---

60. This could be further demonstrated with reference to some of Pannenberg's other recent writings. For the sake of brevity, I will mention only one example for each of the common interpretations. For an example of the way in which the key concept of "reason" is incorporated within the basic principle of the "relation to God" (disclosed through true infinite and Trinity), see Pannenberg's "Die Rationalität der Theologie," in *Fides quaerens Intellectum: Beiträge zur Fundamentaltheologie,* ed. M. Kessler, W. Pannenberg, and H. J. Pottmeyer (Tübingen: Francke, 1992), pp. 536, 543. For the incorporation of "history," see "Offenbarung und 'Offenbarungen' im Zeugnis der Geschichte," in *Handbuch der Fundamentaltheologie: Vol. 2 — Traktat Offenbarung,* ed. W. Kern et al. (Freiburg: Herder, 1985), pp. 84-107. For "prolepsis," see "Die Aufgabe christlicher Eschatologie," *Zeitschrift für Theologie und Kirche* 92, no. 1 (1995): 71-82, especially 81f.

alist thinkers, including van Huyssteen and Clayton, were deeply influenced by Pannenberg's thought early in their careers. However, I do not want to argue the strong thesis that Pannenberg was a proto-postfoundationalist, or even the more moderate thesis that he *is* a postfoundationalist now. Rather, I simply want to point to areas of consonance that allow him into the discussion; even though we must move beyond him, his work offers resources for the contemporary constructive task of theology.

An important potential objection to this dialogue was alluded to in Chapters One and Two. It might be suggested (on a *prima facie* reading of Pannenberg) that he uses the language of "foundations" and this implicates him as still embedded in modernist epistemology. Indeed, Pannenberg uses a variety of terms that suggest foundationalism, including "fundamental" theology, which might be vulnerable to the same critique that nonfoundationalists bring against "revisionist" theological methods (e.g., David Tracy). Pannenberg's titles over the years, with the many uses of variants of "Grund," might also lend credence to his putative foundationalism.[61] However, the mere use of these terms does not necessitate foundational*ism* as defined in Chapter Two. As we also noted there, even nonfoundationalists have to start somewhere. The real question is how we *hold onto* our starting places.[62] I hope to show that

---

61. E.g., *Grundzüge der Christologie, Grundfragen systematischer Theologie,* and *Grundlagen der Theologie,* with Sauter, Daecke, and Janowski (Stuttgart: Kohlhammer, 1974). Another factor that lends to the appearance of foundationalism is his frequent use of the term *"vorausgesetzt,"* which is usually translated "presupposed," e.g., ST, II, 225; JGM, 405. But Pannenberg often simply means that logically, if B is the case, then A is "pre-required." This is not always clear in translation and adds to the appearance of foundationalism. This is especially true in ST, I, 7: "In the concept of theology the truth of theological discourse as discourse about God that God himself has authorized is always presupposed." He means that for such discourse to be true, it is required that such discourse is authorized by God. It is another question entirely how we *know* whether it is thus authorized.

62. Elsewhere I have described the important role that the *individual's* developmental stage plays in "holding on" (mentally subtending) the various disciplines that shape a particular methodology. See my "*Holding On* to the Theology-Psychology Relationship: The Underlying Fiduciary Structures of Interdisciplinary Method," *Journal of Psychology and Theology* 25, no. 3 (1997): 329-39.

both in his explicit statements about method, and in his actual theological argumentation, Pannenberg does not fall into foundationalism, either epistemologically or hermeneutically. Bringing him into dialogue with the postfoundationalist couplets, however, may suggest a refiguring of his language about method that would be clearer for those immersed in Anglo-American discussions about rationality.

For each of the couplets, the goal is to show the extent to which Pannenberg's solutions have points of contact with the postfoundationalist way of holding these pairs of concepts together. This dialogue will show how he contributes, but also how he needs to be critiqued. A secondary aim will be to illustrate how Pannenberg's attempts to resolve these tensions are couched in the back-and-forth movements of "true infinite" and trinity; this buttresses my interpretation of his Grundprinzip. His resolution of these tensions does occur on the soil of anthropology, but anthropology understood *sub ratione Dei*. In the following analysis, both his "fundamental" and his "systematic" movements will be noted, anticipating the development of my exposition of his theological anthropology in Chapter Four.

1. Experience and Belief

The postfoundationalist attempt to express the relation between experience and belief was expressed in Chapter Two as

> (PF1): interpreted experience engenders and nourishes all beliefs, and a network of beliefs informs the interpretation of experience.

In bringing Pannenberg into dialogue with this couplet, we will take the following steps. First, in order to make the initial case that Pannenberg meets the criteria of the postfoundationalist model we will examine his writings in light of Haack's definitions, showing the extent to which he avoids both foundationalism and coherentism and fits into a middle way. Second, we will respond to the most important objection to Pannenberg's inclusion in the post-

112

foundationalist camp, viz., the charge that his method has not escaped its roots in Popperian critical rationalism with its search for neutrality. Third, we will briefly illustrate the relation of this couplet to his basic principle of *sub ratione Dei*, which shapes his view of belief and experience. For Pannenberg, the latter are already embedded in the constitution of human existence by the true infinite, the best explanation for which is the trinitarian concept of God.

Where does Pannenberg fit in Susan Haack's taxonomy of models of rationality? We remember that she defines foundationalism as involving two theses:

> (FD1) Some justified beliefs are basic; a basic belief is justified independently of the support of any other belief; and
>
> (FD2) All other justified beliefs are derived; a derived belief is justified via the support, direct or indirect, of a basic belief or beliefs.[63]

While foundationalists may argue about the criteria for deciding which beliefs are basic, they agree that one does not have to argue *to* such beliefs; basic beliefs are immediately self-justified. In ST, I, Pannenberg explicitly insists that theological statements "are not self-evident and . . . do not follow with logical necessity from self-evident propositions. . . . Their truth depends on conditions that are not posited along with them" (ST, I, 56). As we will see in the next subsection, Pannenberg holds beliefs to be justified (in part) by their coherence with other beliefs. If Pannenberg is not a foundationalist in Haack's general sense, then *a fortiori* he is not a "classical" foundationalist. Although the conclusion that he does not embrace this modernist Enlightenment epistemology follows logically, it will be helpful to show from his writings that Pannenberg denies the possibility of using either (1) empirical experience, (2) rational intuition, or especially (3) "posited" revelational assumptions as underived and immediately justified starting points for Christian theology.

---

63. Susan Haack, *Evidence and Inquiry: Towards Reconstruction in Epistemology* (Oxford: Basil Blackwell, 1993), p. 14.

Regarding empirical foundations, Pannenberg is explicit: "Individual experience can never mediate absolute, unconditional certainty."[64] In his polemic against Lessing, he emphasizes that it is an illusion to think one can find truths in the source of "reason" that are somehow immune from historical conditioning.[65] In his early *Revelation as History,* Pannenberg did speak of the meaning of redemptive events as "self-evident,"[66] which makes him sound like a foundationalist. However, he himself notes that in his later development he came to assess "theoretical certainty . . . more subtly than earlier formulations."[67] He speaks of the "element of truth" in the idea of grounding religious experiences in their "self-evidence," but immediately adds: "religious experiences do not possess such self-evidence as isolated events, but by their reference to the whole current experience of existence" (BQT, II, 104). Clearly he is not affirming the linearity of argument in Haack's (FD1) and (FD2), nor the division of basic and derived beliefs which they assume.

If not an empiricist, might Pannenberg be a "rationalist" foundationalist? He does want to reintroduce metaphysical discussions into theology, but insists that

. . . one cannot let the philosophical concept transcend its own starting point in experiential knowledge, a limitation that applies equally to the religious consciousness. The implication is clear: Any metaphysics, if it is to be taken seriously, can *no longer claim the character of a definitive foundation* [emphasis added], constructed of concepts, for being and knowledge. Metaphysical reflection must instead take on the form of a *conjectural reconstruction* in relation to its object, one which distinguishes itself from

64. ST, I, 47. For a more recent treatment of the founder of modern empiricism, see Pannenberg on John Locke in *Theologie und Philosophie* (Göttingen: Vandenhoeck & Ruprecht, 1996): 170f.

65. BQT, I, 58n. In another essay, Pannenberg suggests that Lessing and his peers did not notice that the convictions of their age, including the idea of a "nasty ditch," were "themselves also historically conditioned, and were bound to lose their self-evidence and appearance of *a priori* validity in a later age," BQT, I, 142.

66. *Revelation as History,* p. 155. See also *Theology as History,* pp. 114, 127.

67. W. Pannenberg, *Faith and Reality* (Philadelphia: Westminster, 1975), p. viii.

its intended truth while at the same time construing itself as a preliminary form of this truth. (MIG, 93-94)

That is, Pannenberg will not allow the idea of *a priori* concepts that are not mediated by experience. He speaks of a "reciprocal mediation" of worldly experience and self-consciousness (MIG, 62). He does not see the contents of self-consciousness as immediately justified.

Finally, Pannenberg is explicit in his rejection of another kind of foundationalism, viz., the revelational positivism he saw in the work of Karl Barth. Pannenberg's most detailed critique of Barth on this point is in the sixth part ("Karl Barth and the Positivity of Revelation") of chapter 4 in TPS. Already in a 1965 article he had chastised Barth for withdrawing from the debate with Feuerbach, and for placing theology in "self-inflicted isolation" with his call to do theology only "from above."

> Is that not senseless renunciation of all critical discussion, and thus an act of spiritual capitulation to Feuerbach? Theology has to learn that after Feuerbach it can no longer mouth the word "God" without offering any explanation; that it can no longer speak as if the meaning of this word were self-evident.[68]

In the introduction to ATP, Pannenberg emphasized the "sad fate" of dialectical theology that became inevitable when Barth, "instead of justifying his position, simply decided to begin with God himself [and] unwittingly adopted the most extreme form of theological subjectivism" (ATP, 16). Precisely his refusal to allow immediately self-authenticating foundations is what exculpates Pannenberg from the charge of "foundationalism."

Is Pannenberg then perhaps a "coherentist"? Haack defined coherentism as asserting: (CH) A belief is justified if and only if it belongs to a coherent set of beliefs. As we will see in the next subsection, Pannenberg does accept coherence with other beliefs as a nec-

---

68. BQT, II, 189. Cf. Pannenberg's earlier call for the "depositivization" of the Christian tradition in *Theology as History,* pp. 228-29.

essary condition for justifying the truth of an assertion, but he clearly does not see it as a sufficient condition, which the use of the biconditional in (CH) entails. While he does occasionally use language reminiscent of nonfoundationalism, such as the "web of life" in which humans exist (e.g., ATP, 512), Pannenberg also requires criteria for justification that are external to the set of beliefs; e.g., adequacy to experience.

How does Pannenberg compare, then, to Haack's "foundherentism?" She defined her middle approach as involving two theses:

(FH1)   A subject's experience is relevant to the justification of his or her empirical beliefs, but there need be no privileged class of empirical beliefs justified exclusively by the support of experience, independently of the support of other beliefs, and

(FH2)   Justification is not exclusively one-directional, but involves pervasive relations of mutual support.[69]

Pannenberg's embrace of the coherence criterion for truth affirms (FH2), and the quotes above concerning the relevance of experience as well as its mediated character indicate his agreement with (FH1) as well.

We saw above that van Huyssteen emphasized the need for both "experiential adequacy" and "epistemological adequacy" as criteria for justifying our beliefs. These complementary demands express the postfoundationalist goal of showing not only that our beliefs do adequately account for our experience, but also that our beliefs are justified by their explanatory power relative to criteria external to the system. Would Pannenberg agree? In ST, I, he makes a very important concession that is relevant to this question. He points to an early article in which he had

> . . . referred to the reality of the divine mystery which is presupposed already in our dealings with the structure of existence. After studying the philosophy of science I have stressed more

69. Haack, *Evidence and Inquiry*, p. 19.

strongly that these dealings take place in experience of the world and wrestling with its implications, which tie in with an inexpressible knowledge of God that becomes an expressed knowledge only with experience of the powers that determine the world's reality. (ST, I, 159n.)

This suggests that, even for his concept of God, Pannenberg recognizes the need for his statements to be both experientially and epistemologically adequate.

The other aspect of the postfoundationalist model expressed by (PF1) was an emphasis on the fact that all experience is already interpreted. Here, too, we find Pannenberg in agreement, even if not in exactly the same words. In 1967, he insisted that all direct experience (even of God) "is itself mediated through the previous history of individuals within their environment."[70] And in a later work, he asserts,

As long as self-consciousness is conceived as the ground and truth of all the contents of consciousness, it falls unavoidably to such suspicion. If, however, the development and stabilization of the ego's identity are themselves already mediated through the process of worldly experience, the themes of philosophical theology can no longer be quite so casually dismissed. (MIG, 62)

In ST he explicitly recognizes the influence of interpretation on different understandings of the world (ST, II, 162). More importantly, he insists that all interpretations are "always mediated by the context of the experience" (ST, I, 234).

Before concluding that Pannenberg does indeed share a "family resemblance" with the postfoundationalists in articulating the relation of experience to belief, it is necessary to identify and respond to an important potential objection. One problem with appropriating Pannenberg has been raised by van Huyssteen.

Although [Pannenberg] shares Thomas S. Kuhn's view of the paradigmatic determination of our thought, he seems to remain

---

70. *Theology as History*, p. 238.

caught up on the critical rationalist demand for a specific noncommitment in the evaluation of theories in the so-called context of justification. Ultimately, this provides no means of thematizing, and even less of resolving, the problem of the role of the theologian's subjective religious commitment in the construction of his or her theories.[71]

The main problem he sees with appropriating Pannenberg is the carryover rationalism in his thought. Although Pannenberg followed the contextualism of Kuhn a long way, there are still elements of Popperian philosophy of science in his methodology. Van Huyssteen had pointed this out in more detail in his 1987 book: "We have seen repeatedly that Pannenberg clearly defined but failed to resolve the problem of a fideistic axiomatic theology, because he failed to face the crucial question of the theologian's personal commitment and the theorizing implicit in it."[72] As van Huyssteen observes, Pannenberg sees the problems with critical rationalism, but at times seems unwittingly to be holding himself to its criterion of neutrality.

Although Pannenberg rejects the idea of starting with self-evident foundations, and emphasizes a mode of argument that is much more coherentist in nature, he still has not sufficiently dealt with the role of personal, historically conditioned commitment at the level of "testing." For him, commitment has primarily a negative role (in the task of justification). Interestingly, Popper's conception of the two "contexts" of discovery and justification has not played a

---

71. van Huyssteen, "Truth and Commitment in Theology and Science: An Appraisal of Wolfhart Pannenberg's Perspective," in *Essays*, 66. It is important to note that van Huyssteen's charge is much more nuanced than David Polk's suggestion that Pannenberg tries to develop a theology "with no borrowed philosophical presuppositions" (*On the Way to God*, 48). In view of Pannenberg's exhaustive treatment of the relation between philosophy and theology, Polk's charge is difficult to understand. Clearly Pannenberg does not think his own use of reason is exempt from the influences of his own context. Van Huyssteen's critique makes a finer distinction, and focuses on Pannenberg's failure to thematize commitment adequately.

72. van Huyssteen, *Theology and the Justification of Faith: Constructing Theories in Systematic Theology*, trans. H. F. Snijders (Grand Rapids: Eerdmans, 1989), p. 98.

major role in Pannenberg's methodological discussions since his TPS. Yet, the idea of a neutral context of justification, somewhat watered down, is still present in ST.

> Christian theology has developed in the service of this truth claim, seeking to clarify it, to strengthen it by a systematic presentation of Christian teaching, but also again and again to test how far it may be made. Theologians can do justice to this task only if they examine the Christian truth claim *as impartially as possible.*[73]

This "as possible" suggests that Pannenberg recognizes the impossibility of total neutrality or impartiality. Rather, it seems that this has become for him an ideal, a kind of *focus imaginarius.* Yet even as an ideal, toward which we ought to aim, this would still be problematic, for van Huyssteen's point is that we cannot, and so should not try to be, *wholly* impartial.

The criticism of van Huyssteen still holds. Pannenberg has not shown how to bring theological commitment positively into interdisciplinary discussion. His statements are only "negative." Yet if we read Pannenberg's call for impartiality in a weak, rather than a strong, sense, we can at least remove this objection to incorporating his approach into the postfoundationalist model. In its strong sense, it would suggest that the theologian can (and ought to) stand neutrally in the context of justification and make universal rational judgments unconditioned by his or her historical embeddedness. If this is what he means, then he is certainly inconsistent, for van Huyssteen's analysis has shown the impossibility of consistently holding together divergent Popperian and Kuhnian themes.

A "weak" reading of this call would be that Pannenberg wants theologians not to use their commitments as premises in the inferential structure of their arguments. This reading is suggested by several of the quotes by Pannenberg above in ST. However, even in TPS, he shows a sensitivity to the issue.

---

73. ST, II, xiii. Emphasis added.

It is of course *inevitable* that every investigator should bring a subjective position to his work, *nor would it be desirable to eliminate this,* since the different interests and approaches can open up different aspects of the subject. The science of religion is no different from any other discipline in this respect.[74]

If this weakened version of impartiality is what he is after, this is surely compatible with the postfoundationalist model. We saw above in Chapter One that for Pannenberg, "Everybody's thought is historically and culturally conditioned, but it is something else to argue explicitly on the basis of partisan commitments."[75] My "weaker" reading of his intentions is also suggested by the following quote: "[the] anticipation of truth [in theology] is normally found in the *Interest* in the theme of theology, but it is not a premise or a principle of argumentation . . . theological thought has the character of conjecture . . . it is already conscious of its fundamental improvability and correctability. . . ."[76]

However, the postfoundationalist will want to go further, aiming for a model that recognizes a positive explanatory role for commitment in theological argumentation. Here is where Pannenberg is weakest from the point of view of the postfoundationalist model. Perhaps this is because the debate about the relation of experience to belief is at the center of the Anglo-American discussion, which Pannenberg's writings have not deeply engaged. As postfoundationalism tries to locate the explanatory role of commitment in the theological task, it will insist that such commitment should not be immune from critique in the argumentation. Here Pannenberg is surely right; the surety of faith or the reliance on the Holy Spirit cannot be used as a stopgap for weak arguments.[77]

Before moving to the next couplet, let us point briefly to the function of his Grundprinzip here. How is his view of the relation between experience and belief influenced by the true infinite and

74. TPS, 366. Emphasis added.
75. "Response to American Friends," in *Theology of Wolfhart Pannenberg,* 330.
76. W. Pannenberg, "Die Rationalität der Theologie," 542-43. My translation.
77. TKG, 87.

the Trinity? First, Pannenberg sees belief and experience as already embedded in the constitution of human existence by the true infinite. This will be shown in detail in Chapter Four as we explore Pannenberg's use of the anthropological concept of "exocentricity," which he interprets ultimately as openness to the infinite. The key here is that this relation to the infinite, which is expressed in the religious thematic in all human life, is constitutive of human nature. This means that all of our interpreted experience, as well as our emergent networks of belief, are mediated through this relation to the infinite. ATP is an attempt to demonstrate this thesis.

Second, this experience of openness to the infinite is best explained, Pannenberg argues, by the Christian concept of the Trinity. Only the trinitarian God can be thus related to the world. Human experience and belief are already participations in the trinitarian life, insofar as all existing things have their existence through this participation. For humans, who are aware of their finite differentiation and their dependence on the infinite, this participation involves a special relation to the Logos and the Spirit. The Logos is the creative principle of differentiation within which reason (and belief) operates, and the Spirit is the creative source of transcendence that raises humans above themselves, a source that is already present in the "feeling" of experience.[78] This interplay between the "fundamental" (true infinite) moment and the "systematic" (trinitarian) moment in Pannenberg's view of human nature will be synchronically presented below in Chapter Four.

2. Truth and Knowledge

The postfoundationalist attempt to express the relation between truth and knowledge was stated in Chapter Two as

(PF2): the objective unity of truth is a necessary condition for the intelligible search for knowledge, and the subjective multiplicity of knowledge indicates the fallibility of truth claims.

78. Cf. ST, III, 166-72 and ST, II, 193-94n.

121

In bringing Pannenberg into dialogue with this couplet, we will take the following steps. First, we will illustrate from his writings a commitment to the postfoundationalist themes of fallibility and intelligibility. Second, we will examine his emphasis on the unity of truth as well as his acceptance of the subjective conditioning of truth claims. Finally, as a parallel to our critique of the postliberal view of theological language in Chapter Two, we will explore how one of the most important contributions Pannenberg can make to the emerging postfoundationalist model may be found in his view of theological language and its implications for true knowledge of God.

We have observed that one of the hallmarks of classical foundationalist epistemology is the search for certainty. The contemporary nonfoundationalist, on the other hand, denying the possible success of such a search, gives up the quest for intersubjectively and transcommunally justifiable knowledge. The *post*foundationalist agrees we cannot achieve certainty, but continues the quest for truth, holding intelligibility rather than certainty as the ideal. At the same time, the postfoundationalist recognizes the fallibility of all truth claims, and so will never claim to have total or complete knowledge.

Does Pannenberg have these postfoundationalist characteristics? It will be quite easy to show that he does. We see permeating his works an admission of the provisionality of all theological statements: ". . . we can attain only provisional knowledge, which is subject to constant revision."[79] In an early interview, he insisted "I have a rather modest interpretation of knowledge and of reason. There is hardly knowledge of any ultimate character."[80] In his 1973 TPS, he explicitly said that "theological testing and reformulation of traditional religious statements can never attain theoretical certainty" (TPS, 344). More recently, he discussed the issue of truth claims in the context of religious pluralism. Noting that simply *relativizing* the truth claim of Christianity (or that of any religion) would precipitate its end, he nevertheless suggests that the current contestability of truth claims prior to the eschatological consummation should

79. *Theology as History*, 242.
80. "A Theological Conversation with Wolfhart Pannenberg," p. 295.

122

make Christians aware of the "provisional character" of their experience and knowledge.[81]

Pannenberg's well-known emphasis on "universal history" and the anticipation of "totality" in human knowledge can make him appear to hold the goal of modernist certainty. However, even in these formulations, Pannenberg is clear that while we "presuppose" the "thought" of the whole of reality in our experience of meaning, we do not "control" that whole and cannot claim that our assertions capture the totality. This is the case in his early formulations[82] as well as in the last volume of ST:

> Naturally, knowledge of the historical data in which God has revealed himself according to the church's proclamation is at best, like all human knowledge, *a matter of probability* . . . [we must accept] the involved relativity of historico-exegetical knowledge . . . [and recognize] that historical knowledge is limited and provisional.[83]

This acceptance of fallibility is also seen in Pannenberg's well-known description of theological assertions as "hypotheses." In fact, they are "third-order hypotheses: hypotheses about hypotheses about hypotheses" (TPS, 333). This can be seen as corresponding to the suggestions of philosophers we included as postfoundationalists in Chapter Two, especially Mikael Stenmark who argues for conceptualizing religious beliefs as "hypotheses," even if stable ones.[84]

81. W. Pannenberg, "Religious Pluralism and Conflicting Truth Claims," in *Christian Uniqueness Reconsidered: The Myth of a Pluralistic Theology of Religions,* ed. G. D'Costa (Maryknoll, N.Y.: Orbis, 1990), p. 103.

82. E.g., "Hermeneutic and Universal History" [1963], in BQT, I, 135. In TPS, Pannenberg explicitly says that the idea of anticipated totality is not "an arrogant claim to total knowledge, not a myth of total reason, but merely a matter of explicitly recognizing a process which takes place implicitly in all perception of meaning," 196.

83. ST, III, 153-54. Emphasis added. See also, "Eine philosophisch-historische Hermeneutik des Christentums," in *Verantwortung für den Glauben: Beiträge zur fundamentaltheologie und Ökumenik,* ed. P. Neuner and H. Wagner (Freiburg: Herder, 1992), p. 46.

84. M. Stenmark, *Rationality in Science, Religion, and Everyday Life* (Notre Dame: University of Notre Dame Press, 1995), pp. 324ff.

After a brief history of hermeneutics from ancient Greece through Schleiermacher, Pannenberg engages the proposal of H. G. Gadamer, who aimed in his *Truth and Method* to rid hermeneutics of all "objectifying" procedures, opting instead for a "fusion of horizons." His attack on objectivity is driven by his desire to affirm that all understanding is relative to one's tradition.

> Gadamer's critical view of the statement is directed, and rightly, against attempts to detach or isolate what is said from its unexpressed associations, but in taking this position he nevertheless seems not to allow the element of *objectification* in the statement its full theoretical legitimacy, not to recognize it as a fundamental structural element of language itself. (TPS, 168)

The problem is that Gadamer does not recognize that his own theory of interpretation inevitably involves objectification. Pannenberg is arguing that we can have the ideal of "objectivity" and still recognize our historical and linguistic situatedness.

For Pannenberg, an insistence on provisionality is connected to a drive for intelligibility: ". . . a provisional corroboration of theological hypotheses seems to be within reach and will be possible to the same degree that they illuminate the problems of the religious traditions and the implications of meaning in present experience."[85] Pannenberg has long been concerned with the lack of credibility of the Christian faith, because it has lost its connection to secular experience. He argues that theology must show how its idea of God has a "power which emanates from it to illumine and elucidate the whole of man's experience of reality."[86] To the extent that it renders experience intelligible, theological statements are "verified" or "proved." It is important to emphasize that Pannenberg does not mean "proved" in an absolute, modernist, or positivist sense. Rather, the sense of the German term "Bewährung," which he uses

---

85. W. Pannenberg, "The Nature of a Theological Statement," *Zygon* 7 (1972): 19.

86. W. Pannenberg, *The Apostles' Creed,* trans. Margaret Kohl (Philadelphia: Westminster, 1972), p. 25.

often, is "putting to the test." Commonly translated "validate," the verb "gelten" in Pannenberg's usage suggests showing the value or demonstrating the worth of an assertion. His use of the verb "beweisen" generally means to establish, to show, to substantiate; none of these necessarily entails finality or certainty.[87]

Pannenberg's commitment to the value of "intelligibility" is built right into his definition of theology: "The task is this: how can theology make the primacy of God and his revelation in Jesus Christ intelligible [*verständlich*], and validate [*geltend machen*] its truth claim, in an age when all talk about God is reduced to subjectivity?"[88] We can also see this commitment to the search for intelligibility in his many treatments of the concept of "meaning." In his discussion of Bernard Lonergan, Pannenberg says that although our anticipation of the universe of meaning is still incomplete as we move through our historical experience, "as we live on with it, it may prove itself by constantly illuminating and integrating the changing world of our experience."[89] The concept of meaning will be treated in more detail in our discussion of the couplet "explanation and understanding," where we will examine his use of the concepts of whole and part in hermeneutics. If Pannenberg's arguments about the provisional anticipation of a totality as a precondition for the search for meaning (intelligibility) are to be appropriated for the postfoundationalist task of linking truth and knowledge, we must show how he holds together the objective unity of truth and the subjective multiplicity of knowledge.

---

87. For a well-balanced treatment of Pannenberg's view of truth and his use of "validation," see D. W. Hackman, "Validation and Truth: Wolfhart Pannenberg and the Scientific Status of Theology" (Ph.D. diss., University of Iowa, 1989). Hackman interprets Pannenberg as opening the doors for ongoing interdisciplinary dialogue, not as closing them with absolutist claims (261). Ted Peters is sensitive to Pannenberg's intentions in "Truth in History: Gadamer's Hermeneutics and Pannenberg's Apologetic Method," *Journal of Religion* 55 (1975): 36-56. John M. Russell, on the other hand, seems to read Pannenberg as seeking proof in the sense of finality; "Pannenberg on Verification in Theology: An Epistemic Response," *The Iliff Review* (Winter 1986): 37-55.

88. ST, I, 128.

89. W. Pannenberg, "History and Meaning in Lonergan's Approach to Theological Meaning," *Irish Theological Quarterly* 40, no. 2 (1973): 114.

In his discussions of truth, Pannenberg so emphasizes "coherence" that (ironically) he might be mistaken for a *nonfoundationalist*. Although he treats the coherence theory of truth in earlier writings,[90] we may take his comments in the first chapter of ST, I, as the *locus classicus* of his view of truth. "Systematic theology ascertains the truth of Christian doctrine by investigation and presentation of its coherence as regards both the interrelation of the parts and the relation to other knowledge" (ST, I, 21-22). However, here the similarity with nonfoundationalism ends, for Pannenberg includes the criteria of correspondence to "what is" within the concept of truth. "The concept itself, if truth is understood in terms of coherence, unavoidably becomes ontological. Coherence in the things themselves, not in judgments about them, is constitutive for the truth of our judgments."[91]

This brings us to his affirmation of the unity of truth as part of the concept of truth, which we must emphasize again does not entail that our subjective knowledge has grasped the final content of that unity. In his early "What Is Truth?," Pannenberg is explicit in affirming that the concept of truth requires that in essence it can only be one (BQT, II, 1). He concludes that essay by arguing that "subjectivity" cannot understand itself without presupposing the unity of truth, and God as the "one origin of everything that is real." But since the emergence of historical consciousness, the unity of everything must be conceived as a history. Pannenberg then makes the explicitly Christian claim: "the unity of truth is constituted only by the proleptic revelation of God in Jesus Christ" (BQT, I, 27). *That* the truth is one is the case regardless of the decision about who (or whether anyone) "knows" the truth. "*My* truth cannot be mine alone. If I cannot in principle declare it to be truth for all — though perhaps hardly anyone else sees this — then it pitilessly ceases to be truth for me also" (ST, I, 51). This presup-

90. E.g., "Wahrheit, Gewissheit und Glaube," in *Grundfragen, II*, 236.

91. ST, I, 53. Cf. ST, I, 24, where Pannenberg speaks of the "element of 'correspondence' to the object, the actual truth, which is basic to the epistemological aspect of the concept of truth." For this reason, we must disagree with the assessment of Richard Viladesau that Pannenberg locates truth in "the coherence of ideas rather than in judgments of being," review of *ST, I*, by W. Pannenberg in *Theological Studies* 54 (March, 1993): 172.

position about the unity of truth (though not an insistence that one "knows" it) should be brought into the pluralist discussion, even (and especially) among religions.[92]

Pannenberg recognizes that we do not have this truth at our disposal (ST, I, 58). On the contrary, our knowledge and our judgments are always "subjectively conditioned" (52). The key here, as we have seen, is Pannenberg's understanding of the structure of anticipation. This is how he tries to hold together the unity of truth *and* the subjectivity of knowledge. Jim Halsey has noted that Pannenberg's goal is to "construct a system which allows for *both* relativism in interpretation (the historical character of human understanding), *and* an absolute supra-temporal standpoint from which the meaning of history can ultimately be discerned."[93]

Note that this search for a middle way between relativism and absolutism is precisely the goal of the postfoundationalist model of rationality. In order to understand the potential contribution of Pannenberg here, it will be helpful to show how his view of theological language shapes his attempted solution. Here we find ourselves close to the critique of the postliberal conception of truth and its relation to language as used in communities of faith. George Sumner, in his dissertation at Yale (under Lindbeck), notes that Pannenberg wants to accept the universality of truth claims without falling into relativism. Sumner sees this as a failure and proposes to reconstruct Pannenberg to fit more into the nonfoundationalist approach.[94] My task in what follows is to help Pannenberg off the Procrustean

---

92. See especially Pannenberg's "The Religions from the Perspective of Christian Theology and the Self-Interpretation of Christianity in Relation to the Non-Christian Religions," *Modern Theology* 9, no. 3 (July 1993): 297.

93. Jim S. Halsey, "History, Language, and Hermeneutic: The Synthesis of Wolfhart Pannenberg," *Westminster Theological Journal* 41 (Spring 1979): 289. Halsey deems Pannenberg's attempt a failure; this misinterpretation assumes that Pannenberg thinks that *we* have access to a "supra-temporal" standpoint from which we discern truth.

94. George Sumner, "Pannenberg and the Religions: Conflictuality and the Demonstration of Power in a Christian Theology of the Religions" (Ph.D. diss., Yale, 1994), pp. 310ff. Reconstructing Pannenberg into a nonfoundationalist was also Nancey Murphy's goal in the last chapter of her *Theology in the Age of Scientific Reasoning* (Ithaca: Cornell University Press, 1990).

bed of postliberalism, and show that he already fits nicely with the emerging postfoundationalist model.

M. Fraijó has argued that the issue of speech about God is the central theme of Pannenberg's theological approach. After tracing the way in which the concept of "prolepsis" plays a role in theological language for Pannenberg, Fraijó finds himself in basic agreement with him.[95] Clearly, this has been a dominant theme in Pannenberg's work, and in his recent *Theologie und Philosophie* he again emphasizes the central significance of speech about God in understanding the relation between philosophy and theology.[96]

Pannenberg's rejection of "analogy" in theological language about God at first appears to be one of the most perplexing aspects of his method. An understanding of the relation of all things to God, however, and the way it shapes his proposal for viewing theological language as "doxology," discloses the rationale for his view. Let us provide a brief summary of Pannenberg's view of the issue.[97] His polemic against analogy in theological language goes back to an article on Barth in 1953[98] and was the subject of his 1955 Habilitationschrift, *Analogie und Offenbarung*, where he traced the concept of analogy as it has to do with knowledge of God, from the Old Testament to the present, with special attention to neo-Platonic high scholasticism and the particular development of the idea in Albert and Thomas.

He summarized his critique of the concept in an article on "Analogie" two years later. His basic point there was that the concept of analogy demands an element of univocity, and this holds not only for the *analogia entis,* but also for Barth's *analogia fidei.* In the lat-

---

95. Manuel Fraijó, *Das Sprechen von Gott bei W. Pannenberg* (Tübingen: B. V. Spangenberg, 1976), p. 219.

96. Pannenberg, *Theologie und Philosophie,* pp. 12-15.

97. For a fuller treatment, see Nnamdi, *Offenbarung und Geschichte,* pp. 176-84.

98. W. Pannenberg, "Zur Bedeutung des Analogiegedankens bei Karl Barth: Eine Auseinandersetzung mit Hans Urs von Balthasar," *Theologische Literaturzeitung* 78 (1953): 18-24. See also his "Möglichkeiten und Grenzen der Anwendung des Analogieprinzips in der evangelischen Theologie," *Theologische Literaturzeitung* 85 (1960): 225-28, where he makes clear that the problem is with seeing human and divine action as having a common logos.

ter, the relation between God and the world is not accessible to natural knowledge or available as a neutral philosophical construction-principle, but is upheld as a gift by God and can only be known in faith. Nevertheless, there is an analogy and it includes an analogy of proportionality (in spite of Barth's denial) as well as an analogy of attribution.[99]

In an important 1963 article, Pannenberg emphasized once again the problems with analogy and proposed instead that theological language is "doxology." He sees this as one of the most basic questions of theology, and argues that "one speaks of God by speaking about something else, but in such a way that this other being is viewed in its relation to the reality of God."[100] Clearly, we have to do here with an issue that is closely connected to his basic principle of *sub ratione Dei*. The problem with analogy is that it fails to uphold what Pannenberg would later call the criterion of the true infinite.

> It is decisive for the analogical inference from the creation back to the divine origin that despite all dissimilarity between God and the realm of finitude, there nevertheless still exists a common logos which permits the attributes in question in any given instance to be ascribed to God himself.[101]

One possible objection to Pannenberg on this point might be that his claims about theological language commit a "self-

---

99. W. Pannenberg, "Analogie," in *Die Religion in Geschichte und Gegenwart*, vol. 1 (Tübingen: J. C. B. Mohr, 1957): 350-53. This reading of Barth seems to be confirmed in the fact that in *Church Dogmatics*, III/2, ed. G. W. Bromiley and T. F. Torrance (Edinburgh: T. & T. Clark, 1960), p. 323, he finally admitted that "the statement is unavoidable that it [the being of man] is a being in correspondence to God Himself, to the being of His Creator."

100. W. Pannenberg, "Analogy and Doxology," in BQT, I, 212. For Pannenberg, the pointing out of analogies always comes "from below" (BQT, I, 51-52). But the biblical God is completely without analogy (BQT, I, 83). Because God is the power of the future, he is beyond all analogy (BQT, II, 242). Although human use of analogy infringes on God's transcendence (*Theology as History*, 251), it must be possible to "think" an all-determining reality (*Theology as History*, 232). The critique of analogy also played a role in the christology of JGM (e.g., 184).

101. BQT, I, 216-17.

exempting" fallacy. That is, take the predicate "is not susceptible to predication by analogous language" and call it *A*. Pannenberg seems to want to predicate *A* of God. The problem arises when we ask: Does this predication succeed? If it *does not* succeed (and such predication is the intent of Pannenberg's claims against analogy), then his claim fails. On the other hand, if this predication *does* succeed, then we are caught in a self-contradiction. This objection would assume that *A* involves some element of "analogical language" and would reject any rationale for exempting this predicate from the claim made about other predicates. In this case, if "God is *A*" is true (i.e., if *A* may be predicated of God) then "God is *A*" is false, for then God *would* be susceptible of analogical predication.

I think Pannenberg is aware of the self-reference issue; he notes that when we call God Father, the "metaphorical character of our speech about God is not thereby overcome. Only it is one thing whether our speech about God leads to emptiness, and quite another if God himself acknowledges the metaphors of our devotional speech about him — even if this statement again has a metaphorical character" (BQT, I, 235). Further, Pannenberg clearly does not want to predicate *A* of God analogically, but rather "doxologically." Whether this distinction works without the latter somehow collapsing into the former is another question; answering it would require a more detailed discussion of the tradition of *via negativa*.

To my knowledge, this objection has not been raised and so Pannenberg has not responded explicitly. He might respond to the self-exempting criticism by asserting that such a criticism has not taken seriously the uniqueness of the Christian distinction between the infinite God and finite creation. God (understood as "true infinite") cannot be grasped in any predicative structures, for the latter apply only to finite objects and assume finite distinctions. Predication involves the inclusion of a subject or entity within a "set." But God does not fit into any "set" as finite entities do. In other words, one could respond to the objection of self-reference by pointing out that the problem is not in the nature of the predicate itself, but in the failure to recognize the unique nature of the subject and its resistance to finite predication. Here we might suggest that idolatry can also take the form of a graven *linguistic* image that attempts to capture and "name" the One whose name is above all names. The criterion of the true infinite insists that only God can name God.

In discussing his treatment of eschatology, Pannenberg notes that the predominance of metaphorical language is

> an expression of the fact that in a special way the themes under discussion are all beyond human comprehension. The eschatological statements of theology deal with an event that does not lie in the sphere of our present experience. This does not mean they are unfounded or bear no relation to present experience. On the contrary, what they express is a sense of the defectiveness of our human reality and destiny as we now experience it. But this kind of indirect relation to the reality of human experience as it now is expresses itself linguistically in the adoption of metaphorical language. In so doing it does not simply give free rein to poetic fancy. The statements are as precise as human speech about these matters can be on the basis of our present experience. (ST, III, 621)

In our statements about the nature of God human language simply breaks down (which is what contemplatives have been telling us for centuries). This does not excuse us from the requirement to speak about God, but it does radically qualify such speech and may encourage more humility in theological discussions.

The most detailed treatment in English of the issue of analogy in Pannenberg is by Elizabeth Johnson, who summarizes Pannenberg's view of the task of theology as thinking about the difference the Christ event makes in human history. His goal is "to think christology in connection with God's relation to the world in such a way that the history of Jesus is seen as providing the key to that relation and therefore to reality as a whole."[102] In another article, she em-

---

102. Elizabeth Johnson, "Analogy/Doxology and Their Connection with Christology in the Thought of Wolfhart Pannenberg" (Ph.D. diss., Catholic University of America, 1981), p. 106. She provides an excellent and fair summary of Pannenberg's arguments, but suggests three areas in which his understanding might be challenged or expanded. First, advocates of the classical view might argue that he has not seen that being *(esse)* is not a genus and cannot be predicated. Second, the idea

phasizes that this involves the attempt to find a third way between the alternatives "from above" and "from below."[103] Her insight that the issue of analogy/doxology is linked to christology indicates the fact that Pannenberg's view of theological language, too, must be brought into the dual move, the reciprocal relation between "fundamental" and "systematic" theology.

The fact that the issue of "analogy" has played a less central role in Pannenberg's later discussions of theological language can best be explained by noting his own very early turn to anthropology. In his contribution to the series "How My Mind Has Changed," Pannenberg notes that his new view of history "meant that there is no direct conceptual approach to God, nor from God to human reality, by analogical reasoning, but God's presence is hidden in the particulars of history."[104] His view of religious language had been broadened; he recognized that one of the irreducible roots of human language is the religious dimension of life. In a German interview the same year, Pannenberg argued that the question of religion can become the starting point for a renewal of Christian speech about God.[105]

The question of religion, of course, is precisely the starting point for Pannenberg's ATP. Interestingly, after this book the idea of analogy no longer has a central place in Pannenberg's discussion of theological language. Laurence Wood concludes that Pannenberg became convinced that human speech is essentially religious through his early research into the history of religious language. He rejected the Thomist doctrine of analogical language, which as-

---

of "judgment" in analogical operation might be construed by "transcendental" thinkers as an act of self-transcendence toward God, not as an assault. Third, Johnson thinks Pannenberg has not recognized that the "negative moment" in the classical doctrine of analogy may include the element he desires in theological language. She summarized her arguments in "The Right Way to Speak about God? Pannenberg on Analogy," *Theological Studies* 43 (1982): 673-92.

103. Elizabeth Johnson, "The Ongoing Christology of Wolfhart Pannenberg," *Horizons* 9, no. 2 (1982): 251-70.

104. Pannenberg, "God's Presence in History," 261.

105. W. Pannenberg, "'Wie von Gott reden?' Ein Gespräch mit Professor Wolfhart Pannenberg," *Herder Korrespondenz* 35, no. 4 (April 1981): 184.

sumed human words are secular by nature and need to be linked somehow to the supernatural. As Wood notes, Pannenberg follows Michael Polanyi's distinction between *tacit* and *explicit* knowledge, "along with his emphasis on the personal/religious nature of human language in general. . . . The theological task of developing a more *explicit* understanding of our *tacit* knowledge of God does not require an artificial linkage between the supernatural and the natural.[106]

In ST, Pannenberg revisits the issue of analogy and finds himself in basic agreement with his earlier concerns.

> The question of analogous predication achieved such fundamental importance in Aristotelian High Scholasticism because on the basis of Aristotelian epistemology it was assumed that all speech derives from sensory experience and has its source there, so that talk about God rests on a transferred use of words. Doubts are valid at this point if the rise and development of human speech are also influenced from the very first by religious themes (cf. my *Anthropology*, pp. 340ff., 361-62, 370-71). We then have to consider that human speech and experience of the world have a common original form in the mythical consciousness. . . . Thus the question of analogous transferring of words from what is thought to be purely secular experience of the world to talk about God loses its basic theological importance. (ST, I, 345n.14)

Although Pannenberg continues to critique the concept of analogy,[107] this polemic no longer has the importance for him it once had. This can be explained by pointing to the fact that he sees the emergence of language itself as already mediated by the relation to

---

106. Laurence W. Wood, "Above, Within or Ahead of? Pannenberg's Eschatologicalism as a Replacement for Supernaturalism," *The Asbury Theological Journal* 46, no. 2 (Fall 1991): 63. Although Pannenberg does not treat Polanyi extensively, others have identified commonalities in their thought. E.g., J. Apczynski, "Truth in Religion: A Polanyian Appraisal of Wolfhart Pannenberg's Theological Program," *Zygon* 17, no. 1 (1982): 49-79.

107. Pannenberg, *Theologie und Philosophie* (1996), pp. 13-14, 83.

the infinite. Unlike the postliberal conception of truth and language, which accepts the "linguistic turn" and its reduction of all philosophical issues to issues about language,[108] Pannenberg treats language as just one part of the world, a part that has its origin in the religious thematic of human existence.

This thematic is illustrated in terms of the openness to the infinite in his "fundamental-theological" movement in ATP. Already in TPS, Pannenberg had suggested that the twofold movement would help clarify the issue of truth. By privileging "history" over "concept" we can accommodate both the extant plurality of viewpoints and the struggle for the "one truth." A view of history that assimilates the "conditions of the plurality" is "the most comprehensive claim to truth that is justifiable in view of relativity and pluralism" (TPS, 421). With ST we see the correlated "systematic-theological" movement that aims to explain truth and knowledge (and not merely language) as already mediated by relation to the trinitarian God. As Grenz puts it, "This combination — doxological speech and knowledge of God's essence — which at first glance appears impossible, is accomplished by means of the eschatological *unity of the economic Trinity with the immanent Trinity.*"[109]

Clearly Pannenberg's views of truth and knowledge are influenced by an attempt to understand and explain all things *sub ratione Dei.* For Pannenberg, there do not seem to be any reasons to deny the traditional *definitions* of truth as correspondence to what is, and of knowledge as justified true belief. However, when it comes to the question of *justification* of our knowledge and our *claims* to truth, Pannenberg's approach lines up with the postfoundationalist criteria of fallibility and intelligibility.

108. For a critique of the common conflation of metaphysical and semantic issues in philosophers (and theologians) influenced by the "linguistic turn," see Michael Devitt, *Realism and Truth,* 2nd ed. (Oxford: Basil Blackwell, 1991), pp. 47ff.

109. Stanley Grenz, "Pannenberg and Evangelical Theology: Sympathy and Caution," *Christian Scholar's Review* 20, no. 3 (1991): 282. Emphasis added.

3. Individual and Community

As we noted in Chapter Two, the third and fourth of the post-foundationalist couplets are more focused on hermeneutic issues rather than epistemological ones, although inevitably they interact. Our task in this subsection will be to examine Pannenberg's approach to hermeneutics, interpretation, and rationality, in light of the postfoundationalist attempt to connect the individual and communal factors in rationality.

> (PF3): rational judgment is the activity of socially situated individuals, and the cultural community indeterminately mediates the criteria of rationality.

In bringing Pannenberg into dialogue with this couplet, we will take the following steps. First, to make the initial case that Pannenberg affirms the postfoundationalist way of acknowledging individual and communal elements in shaping hermeneutical decisions, we will examine his approach in light of Calvin Schrag's dialectic between participation and distanciation. Second, we will point to potential contributions Pannenberg might make to the postfoundationalist model in both his "fundamental" and "systematic" theological moves, illustrating the operation of his basic principle of *sub ratione Dei* in his solution of this hermeneutical tension. Because the last section of Chapter Four will deal with the material anthropological issue of the relation of the individual to society, but not with ecclesiology and eschatology proper, we will focus on the role of the latter in what follows. Finally, we will emphasize Pannenberg's acceptance of the search for intersubjective and transcommunal criteria by contrasting his approach to that of Nancey Murphy, who has criticized him on this point.

What is the relation between the operation of reason in each individual and the communal practices and traditions through which that operation is mediated? In articulating the dialectic between these two, Calvin Schrag has argued against either a linear or a hierarchical model. The first "simply juxtaposes rationality and community within a serial succession and ends up in an aporia of origins," while the latter subsumes one under the other, resulting in an "aporia of ultimate grounding."[110] Schrag rejects both of these models and argues for a "transversal interplay" between individual judgment and communal praxis. As we saw above, he sees this in the dialectical play of participation and distanciation in the hermeneutic task. Schrag wants to respond to the postmodern challenge to absolute reason in the individual, but without collapsing into a relativism that absorbs the subject into the community.

> The grammar of dialectics thus falls out as an articulation of the entwined moments of participation and distanciation as they configure our discourse and action in the public world. . . . Within the interstices of this socio-pragmatic dialectic of participation and distanciation, the voice of the subject continues to be heard, and its actions continue to be registered. A displacement of the centripetal, subject-centered reason does not entail a jettisoning of rationality.[111]

Like Schrag, Pannenberg deals with these issues (in TPS) by engaging the debates between Habermas and Gadamer within the context of the hermeneutic tradition. He, too, wants to avoid the jettisoning of objectivity by Gadamer and to critique Habermas's grounding of hermeneutics in communicative practice. They also hold in common a desire to hold onto the concept of "subjectivity," even seeing the drive toward objectivity as a constitutive moment for the former.[112] Also like Schrag, Pannenberg wants to reclaim "dialectic" and not be satisfied with "hermeneutic" alone. In neither case, however, is this merely an acceptance of Hegelian or Platonic dialectic, but a refigured understanding of dialectic as including the historical particularity of human existence.

The major difference between Schrag and Pannenberg seems to be not a structural or hermeneutic one, but rather one of emphasis.

---

110. Calvin Schrag, *The Resources of Rationality: A Response to the Postmodern Challenge.* (Bloomington: Indiana University Press, 1992), p. 63.

111. Schrag, *Resources of Rationality,* p. 66.

112. Pannenberg, TPS, 205. Cf. Schrag, *Resources of Rationality,* p. 66.

Pannenberg simply has not engaged the postmodern literature with its emphasis on the effect of participation within a community on the standards of rationality held by the individual. This is certainly a lack that should be remedied, and a central goal of the post-foundationalist model. However, Pannenberg's lack of engagement should not obscure the fact that his way of understanding the relation between individual and community is structurally compatible with postfoundationalism.

In ATP, Pannenberg deals with these issues in great detail, especially in chapters 4–6. I will look at these texts in more detail in the next chapter, but suffice it to say here that Pannenberg recognizes the conditioning influence of society, not only for the rationality of the individual, but for the formation of the ego itself. However, this is not a one-way street. "While the identity of individuals is not to be conceived as the product of a subject that already exists with its own identity, neither is it to be understood as a simple internalization of social appraisals and expectations" (ATP, 225). Pannenberg argues for an idea of the self

> which, on the one hand, is mediated through the dialogically structured social sphere and therefore shows itself to be constituted by the symbiotic exocentricity of the individual, and with which, on the other hand, the ego knows itself to be identical in the for-itselfness of its self-consciousness. Here the peculiarly temporal structure of the person's wholeness is important for its relation both to its social context and to the ego. (ATP, 237)

In line with the overall concern of ATP, Pannenberg argues that the religious thematic has been left out of these discussions. Bringing it back into the dialogue opens up new ways of thinking about the relation between individual and society. For Pannenberg, "the totality of meaning as the universe of meaning experienced and implicit in experience also transcends society" (TPS, 203). This is also suggested by his dialogue with the sciences, especially physics and cosmology. Here we can see that he is addressing the issue of rationality in a context that is even broader than Schrag's analysis. For Pannenberg, the concept of the individual's anticipation of his or her identity arises during reflection on the constitutive relation of humans to the infinite, to which they find themselves "open." This focus on the illuminative power of the human relation to the infinite illustrates how his Grundprinzip of *sub ratione Dei* is functioning in the "fundamental" theological move of ATP.

As a segue into his "systematic" move it will be helpful to point out the connection between his emphasis on anticipation in hermeneutics and the idea of the individual's "self-conception," which we saw in Clayton and Knapp above. They argue that

> a necessary condition for my claiming that a belief is rational is that it has been subjected to (or is genuinely open to) criticism by what I take to be the relevant community of inquiry. Similarly, a necessary condition for my claiming that an *action* is rational is that it has been subjected to assessment by the relevant community . . . [but] there is no reason to hold that any *presently existing* community fully instantiates the agent's sense of what the relevant community is . . . it would seem that a rational agent has to have in mind not just some criterion for identifying what she takes to be a relevant existing community but at least a partial image of that community's normative *future* state — which is to say, and *ideal* of what that community will become if it goes on properly pursuing its course of inquiry.[113]

With this understanding of the relation of the concept of an ideal community and its shaping of the rationality of the individual, we can move into Pannenberg's understanding of how the Christian view of the coming kingdom of the trinitarian God clarifies the way in which the hope for salvation is mediated to the individual through the community.

The hope for an ideal society beyond the forms of society in the world order has long been for Pannenberg a way of distinguishing between the church and society.[114] This finds full expression in the

---

113. Philip Clayton and Steven Knapp, "Ethics and Rationality," *American Philosophical Quarterly* 30, no. 2 (April 1993): 152.

114. See, e.g., W. Pannenberg, "The Church and the Eschatological Kingdom,"

third volume of ST, where Pannenberg treats the overcoming of the antagonism between individuals and society by the fulfilling of human destiny in fellowship with the trinitarian God. This plays itself out in a number of themes, including the mediation of salvation (ST, III, 24), the Christian view of law and gospel (75), the fellowship of believers (97ff.), the sacraments (237), election of individuals and the people of God (463), and finally in individual and general resurrection.

> Because God is the Creator of the world, where he reigns his creatures attain to the goal of the destiny that is constitutive of their nature. This is true of individuals, whose restless demands first find peace in fellowship with God. But it is also true of human society, in which the common destiny of individuals take shape. (ST, III, 580; cf. 584, 607)

In an earlier article, he made the claim very strongly: "It is only in biblical eschatology that the destiny of each individual is taken equally seriously with that of the society."[115] In ST, it is clear that the Trinity is central to this conclusion. The divine love is "the eternal basis of God's coming forth from the immanence of the divine life as the economic Trinity and of the incorporation of creatures, mediated thereby, into the unity of the trinitarian life" (ST, III, 646). Whether or not one follows Pannenberg in his particular material decisions, the point is that his methodology squares with the postfoundationalist model, which avoids the absolutism of foundationalism on the one hand and the relativism of nonfoundationalism on the other.

Third and finally, I want to examine the extent to which Pannenberg can be differentiated from the nonfoundationalist model by his affirmation of the search for transcommunal and intersubjective criteria. Comparing his approach to that of Murphy

---

in *Spirit, Faith and Church,* by W. Pannenberg, Avery Dulles, S.J., and Carl E. Braaten (Philadelphia: Westminster, 1970), pp. 108-23; WIM, 94; and "The Future and the Unity of Mankind," in *Ethics,* trans. Keith Crim (Philadelphia: Westminster, 1981).

115. "Constructive and Critical Functions of Christian Eschatology," *Harvard Theological Review* 77, no. 2 (1984): 127.

will help us here, and provide a segue into the next couplet which is concerned with the interdisciplinary location of theology. Murphy notes that "recent epistemology recognizes that systems of belief are the property (and responsibility) of communities."[116] She argues that it is the *community* that has the responsibility "to give an account of its beliefs to all comers." This explains her resorting to "research programs," which are also the property of communities of faith. We must ask at this point whether this even makes sense. How does a community "hold a belief" or "argue" or "give an account"? Is it not an individual within a community who does all of these things? Here we see the Achilles' heel of the nonfoundationalist privileging of communities at the expense of the individual. The postfoundationalist, on the other hand, recognizes that communities inform the criteria of rationality for any particular agent, but insists that it is individuals who actually make rational judgments.

It is precisely the immunization strategy of appealing to one's confessional community that Pannenberg wants to avoid, a theme we have seen dominating his work. In *An Introduction to Systematic Theology* he made explicit the role of the individual theologian; he or she has a critical task as well as a systematic task in relation to the traditional language of Christian teaching.[117] Because the individual theologian has these tasks over against (but also as part of) the Christian community, which in turn is historically situated in the nexus of the wider multicultural arena, he or she cannot sidestep the interdisciplinary aspect of the theological enterprise in relation to all the various modes of human inquiry. This interdisciplinary location is further illuminated in our next couplet.

4. Explanation and Understanding

Analysis of this couplet will reveal some of the most obvious points of contact between Pannenberg's view of hermeneutics and the emerging postfoundationalist model of rationality. In Chapter Two,

116. Murphy, *Theology in the Age of Scientific Reasoning*, p. 195.
117. Pannenberg, *An Introduction*, p. 7.

we expressed this model's way of connecting explanation and understanding as

(PF4): explanation aims for universal, transcontextual understanding, and understanding derives from particular contextualized explanations.

Our overall concern is to demonstrate that the way in which Pannenberg treats this pair of concepts is the key to his view of the interdisciplinary location of theology. The majority of what follows is a summary and analysis of Pannenberg's emphasis on the importance of the categories of whole and part in theology, and an exploration of the extent to which this shows his affinity to postfoundationalism. Our primary focus will be on expositing these themes in his TPS (1973) and MIG (1988), which will clarify the "true infinite" moment of his basic principle. Finally, we will briefly explore the "trinitarian" moment in Pannenberg's method, through which he hopes to illuminate the nature and function of human knowledge.

Discussion of the interdisciplinary location of theology is a central theme for postfoundationalists. Clayton's definition of theology as a "science" (which includes explanation) illustrates this emphasis:

(a) As an academic discipline, theology formulates explanations that should be intersubjectively criticizable. (b) The results of research in other disciplines are relevant; as part of her task the theologian will be concerned with objections from natural scientist, social scientist, historians, philosophers. (c) Where basic theological beliefs are disputed by others in the discussion, some warrant must be given for assuming their truth in arguments in the intersubjective explanatory context . . . (d) theology's claims must be taken as hypothetical in the academic context.[118]

118. Philip Clayton, *Explanation from Physics to Theology* (New Haven: Yale University Press, 1989), p. 62.

We also saw how Calvin Schrag tries to overcome the explanation/understanding dichotomy by refiguring the interplay between "whole" and "part" in the operation of rationality across disciplines.

Perhaps the most important contribution Pannenberg can make to the postfoundationalist concern for interdisciplinary dialogue is his dual emphasis, on the one hand, on the similarity of theology to the other sciences due to the fact that they all must interpret reality with the categories of whole and part and, on the other hand, on the uniqueness of theology among the sciences due to its special relation to the concept of "whole." The main point of this subsection is that the relation of part and whole is key to Pannenberg's view of hermeneutics, and to his claim that theology involves both explanation and understanding. The full significance of this relation can only be understood under the aspect of the relation to God, qualified as "true infinite." This means that the "whole" (as an object of theology) is beyond the distinction between the whole and the parts. Thus, Pannenberg's hermeneutical approach is dependent on his view of the task of theology as understanding and explaining all things *sub ratione Dei*.

In a 1964 article "On Historical and Theological Hermeneutic," Pannenberg attempted to show the connection between these two modes of interpretation. He gave special attention to the impact of Dilthey's work in the formulation of these same issues that were still shaping hermeneutical discussions in the sixties. The concept of "universal history" was central for Pannenberg. This theme

> . . . is intimately related to the old hermeneutical principle that in the process of interpreting the text, the whole and its parts reciprocally illumine each other . . . [for Dilthey] there can be no other history than universal history because the meaning of the individual itself is determined only from the standpoint of the "whole." The fundamental point here is that Dilthey defines the key hermeneutical concept of meaning by means of the relationship between part and whole: "the category of meaning designates the relation rooted in life itself, of parts to the whole." . . . [For Dilthey] "the relationship between whole and parts" exists everywhere in society and in history. And it is only this conclu-

sion, as Dilthey explicitly pointed out, that justifies "the application of the concept of meaning to the whole breadth of reality." (BQT, I, 162)

The concept of the "whole" is required for the "parts" to have meaning; this requirement applies not only to the science of history, but to all human inquiry. For Pannenberg, of course, it is the history of Jesus that discloses the proleptic nature of reality (as a whole) and answers the post-Hegelian problem of how to conceive the whole as a totality, while still affirming particularity (BQT, I, 181). His 1967 article "Appearance and the Arrival of the Future" worked out this claim in much greater philosophical detail.[119]

The part/whole interplay is operative in both faith and reason. These are not two absolutely separated processes, but they are differently oriented; faith focuses on the whole (anticipated in the future), and reason emphasizes the part (concerned with the present). Pannenberg's view of the part/whole interplay is an excellent example of the intercalation of the key concepts of reason, history, and prolepsis. I argue that the entire enterprise is driven by his Grundprinzip; Pannenberg examines hermeneutics itself *sub ratione Dei*, disclosing the need to explain its operation in light of the "true infinite." In this case, the latter is described in temporal rather than spatial terms.

> Faith is explicitly directed toward that eschatological future and consummation which reason anticipates while at the same time keeping behind it when it says what those things are whose essences it names. Reason is indeed not confined to such naming of present things. As a movement of reflection, it returns to its absolute presupposition, which has been shown to us to be the anticipation of a final future constituting the wholeness of reality. But reason is always concerned with present things in the first instance. (BQT, II, 63)

For Pannenberg, even reason presupposes that there must be an ultimate condition for the operation of reason. "Faith is directed to

119. TKG, 127-43.

this future which constitutes reality as a whole and thereby brings everything individual to its essential perfection. However, because this future is not alien to reason, but is rather its origin from which it implicitly always derives, faith cannot stand in opposition to reason" (BQT, II, 64). In a way, this makes faith the criterion for the rationality of reason; such a move should seem shocking for those who see him as a "rational" foundationalist. The critical point for the present argument is that both faith and reason, which are two moments in the hermeneutical task, must presuppose a final, eschatological future as the unifying basis for the anticipation of the *whole* in the knowledge of the *parts*. This "future" is for Pannenberg the coming Kingdom of God; yet such assertions are provisional and depend on the future for their confirmation. So his view of the part/whole interplay (the core of hermeneutics) is dependent on his time/eternity conception, which in turn is connected to the "true infinite."

The *locus classicus* of Pannenberg's treatment of hermeneutics is TPS. He develops his own view of the part/whole relationality by critically appropriating and refiguring various thinkers. So in the following exposition, we will examine how he reacts to those authors who have most deeply influenced (positively and negatively) his own constructive work. Chapter 2 of TPS is titled "The Emancipation of the Human Sciences from the Natural Sciences," and this is the background against which Pannenberg carves out his argument for part/whole relationality. Pannenberg traces the roots of the "so-called" *Geisteswissenschaften* through German idealism (which strongly distinguished spirit and nature) back to the basic dualism in Descartes (between mind and body).

The key figure for the solidification of this terminology was Dilthey, who made it a bifurcation of method, rather than substance, so that he could affirm the psycho-physical unity of human being. Dilthey also moved beyond Hegel by replacing the absolute mind with "the unity of (intelligent) life which links all individuals" (TPS, 75). Although the early Dilthey applied the concepts of whole and part only to explain the experienced unity of life in the *individual*, in his latter writings he recognized that individuals, too, are parts of a larger whole (society), which indicates the idea of a totality of historical and social life. This required him to "develop the logic of the mutual relationship between whole and part — a logic which determined the psychic structure — as a *historical* relationship and extend it beyond the individual to his social environment in its historical development" (77). A tension remained in Dilthey, however, between his hermeneutical and logical insistence that parts can only be intelligible if a whole can be (at least implicitly) presupposed, on the one hand, and his refusal to accept a "metaphysical" reality that could ground the possible "objectivity" of experience beyond the individual, on the other hand. Pannenberg wants to move toward the latter, affirming the idea of an ultimate "totality" as the presupposition of the possibility for any experience of meaning whatsoever. This "totality" would be explicated in terms of the "true infinite."

Pannenberg critiques Habermas for his suggestion that human *interests* are the "natural basis" of the mind, such "instinctual energies" being transcendental conditions and knowledge-constitutive. Pannenberg argues that such an approach, which is bound up with Habermas's conception of consensus, cannot exclude the possibility that all reflection may be simply distorted forms of communication. To use the parlance of the Anglo-American debate: this approach cannot protect against nonfoundationalist relativism. Instead, Pannenberg follows N. Luhmann, who insists that a theory of action is an insufficient basis for sociology; all experiences of meaning presuppose an element of universality, an ability to "apprehend the universal" through the negation of the particular.

Pannenberg points out a weakness in both Habermas and Luhmann, who failed to note that this negation, as a logical factor, precedes language in early childhood development. This means that they "have still not completely overcome the limitations of a view of 'meaning' as intentional . . . derived from the prior concept of subject" (TPS, 99). In their revisions of Dilthey, they failed to retain the latter's insight that the categories of whole and part have already defined the concept of meaning. Pannenberg suggests that one implication of this part/whole structure is that

the self-givenness of the totality of the individual person who *experiences* himself as a totality has to be recognized as a modification of the general systematic structure of the relation between parts and wholes. This would entail investigation of the origin of this peculiarity in the self-transcendence of man. (TPS, 131)

This investigation is central to the task of ATP as we will see. Pannenberg insists that "it is impossible to escape from the reciprocal nature of experiences of anticipation; these may be conditioned by a prior totality of meaning, but of its nature that totality can never be finally and unequivocally captured in a particular form" (TPS, 103, translation emended). Notice that last (postmodern-like) phrase is a recognition of the inevitable contextuality of all particular forms of rational knowledge. But the fact that knowledge is particular all the way down and all the way back up does not mean that there is nothing beyond the particular.

A critique of the strong division of the human and natural sciences, and the related dichotomy between "understanding" and "explanation," forms the last two subsections of chapter 2 in TPS. Pannenberg's solution to these issues is linked to his view of the part/whole relationality. He argues that

> . . . the association of nomothetical and ideographic methods with the areas of "nature" and "mind" or "culture" respectively contains an element of truth in so far as ideographic methods have many more applications to the study of man because of the greater complexity and individualisation of human beings. But this is not a reason for maintaining a dualism of nature and mind. Today this dualism is unsatisfactory both in itself and as a principle of classification in the sciences. (TPS, 124)

At this point in the discussion, Pannenberg reintroduces Dilthey, whose emphasis on a totality of meaning supports the contention of general systems-theory that the relation of whole and part is a fundamental hermeneutical consideration, and that this applies to the natural as well as the human sciences. We can only speak of "meaning" wherever the relations of part and whole are perceived. Pannenberg agrees that this is the basic method of the human sciences; however,

... this also means that the study of meaning cannot in itself be the private reserve of the human sciences and cannot justify a theoretical opposition between human and natural science. The uniqueness of the human sciences can be described only in terms of their special form of perception of this common object. This special form is a concentration on the historical character of the formation of meaning. . . . (TPS, 134-35)

"Explanation" *(Erklärung)* was originally associated with the nomothetic approach of the natural sciences in which an individual phenomenon was included under a general law or rule, while "Understanding" *(Verstehen)* was concerned with the place of the particular in the context of the relevant whole. However, this dichotomy has come under attack as a methodical expression of Cartesian dualism. Pannenberg joins the debate by suggesting that, on the one hand, explanation should be seen as always presupposing understanding. On the other hand, explanation always has the goal of understanding. Pannenberg wants to broaden the concept of "explanation" beyond its deductive-nomological sense, so that hermeneutical method, too (in the sense of interpreting parts in relation to a semantic horizon), is another form of explanation. In fact, Pannenberg shows that the deductive-nomological view of explanation cannot in itself provide explanations except in reference to subsumption under general laws, but that move itself requires a broader concept of explanation in order to be intelligible. Pannenberg affirms A. C. Danto's point that "bringing an individual event under a law does not explain its particularity" (TPS, p. 145).

Pannenberg believes a broader concept of explanation as "the fitting of particulars into a whole" (151) can be seen as operative in all the sciences, for this part/whole structure is built into the human perception of meaning. Whatever the field, an explanation is needed whenever a state of affairs does not seem to fit previous theoretical explanations. The new explanation must show the limits but also retain the valid aspects of the previous explanation. He redefines the relation between understanding and explanation with an example from physics. Newton's explanation of the cosmos provided an understanding of the world out of which scientists operated. As long as we understand, no new explanation is needed. The latter is needed only when one's general understanding of the world and its intelligibility breaks down. When this happens,

> . . . the explanation explicates the existing frame of reference used by the person who seeks understanding, and at the same time partly replaces it with an intellectual construction of the totality of meaning under question. It is not just the sciences which do this; the process also occurs in religion and art. (TPS, 153)

The natural sciences reconstruct the meaning of the world through explanatory hypotheses. But this is also true of the human sciences, and of theology. "Where there are differences between them, they relate not to the explanatory process itself but to the methods used in the different disciplines to produce explanations" (TPS, 154).

Pannenberg introduces chapter 3 on "Hermeneutic" by emphasizing that its aim is "the understanding of meaning, and meaning is to be understood in this context as the relation of parts to whole within a structure of life or experience" (156). In this chapter, too, we can see that Pannenberg is doing theology, in the sense of examining the problem of hermeneutics *sub ratione Dei*. Pannenberg critiques Habermas for his rejection of "dialectic," yet affirms Habermas's insistence on universal history and anticipatory expectations which "have first to create the 'whole' in the context of which the 'parts' of the historically given have their significance" (187). Noting Hans Albert's critique of Habermas's ambiguous attitude toward dialectic, Pannenberg argues that theologians must explicitly embrace the need for dialectic.

> Dialectic and hermeneutic share the fundamental feature of being concerned with the analysis of the interrelation of wholes and parts. However, whereas hermeneutic sees the whole only as a horizon which establishes the meaning of all the details and whose transformations initiate the continuing process of interpretation, and can therefore remain uncertain about the final form of this whole, dialectic considers the totality as such, with-

out which the individual element could have no definitive meaning. Because dialectic analyses the categories which hermeneutic applies in its practical work, it has to make explicit the totality which hermeneutic assumes only implicitly and for that reason can leave uncertain. This has always led to the accusation that dialectic claims a totality which goes beyond the limitations of human experience and human knowledge and therefore can only be ideological. (TPS, 189-90)

It is this "ideological" tendency that is so often attacked (and rightly so) by postmodernists. However, it may be possible to thematize "totality" as a concept without "ideologizing" one's thematization. For Pannenberg, philosophical analysis of the totality of meaning can never be more than an anticipation of that which is implicitly assumed as a condition for any particular experience of meaning. "It can demonstrate its truth only by its ability to integrate, and so illuminate, actual experiences of meaning. . . . Theology also deals with the totality of meaning of experience and must be aware of this if it is to know what it is saying when it talks about God" (TPS, 224). Notice here Pannenberg's proximity to the postfoundationalist valuation of experiential and epistemological adequacy. He aims to thematize the relationality between the tradition-mediated totality (participation, understanding) and the shaped-yet-free interpreter (distanciation, explanation). The fact that we perceive meaning requires a totality that must be made explicit in philosophy and, in a different way, in theology.

Thus far, our analysis has focused on TPS. This should not obscure the fact that the part/whole interplay is pervasive in Pannenberg's works. We have already alluded to the connection of universal and particular in the history of Jesus (see JGM, 406). In ST, II, the part/whole relationality underlies his discussions of human destiny (e.g., 272). In 1995 he utilized the concepts of totality or "whole" and the particularity of human existence in his dialogue with natural science in discussing "The Emergence of Creatures."[120]

---

120. "The Emergence of Creatures and Their Succession in a Developing Universe," *The Asbury Theological Journal* 50, no. 1 (Spring 1995): 23. Cf. ST, II, chapter 7.

His 1996 *Theologie und Philosophie* also emphasizes the conceptualization of the world as a whole (or totality) as a crucial move for theology in its relation to philosophy.[121]

But I would like to focus on a 1978 article, translated and published in MIG, "Theology and the Categories 'Part' and 'Whole.'"[122] This treatment best illustrates his thematization of theological hermeneutics under the aspect of its relation to God. Pannenberg reaffirms his belief that the concept of the whole "plays a fundamental role in the so-called human sciences similar to that of law in the natural sciences" (MIG, 136). But it has a special significance for the discipline of theology.

> The particular significance which the category of the whole holds for theology (and continues to hold, even when the individual theologian shies away from taking this fact into account) is conditioned by the idea of God. Whoever uses the word "God," particularly as a singular, makes a claim at the same time about the totality of what exists finitely. The Christian doctrine of God as the Creator of the world has this significance. . . . The concept of the whole as the all-inclusive whole of all finite reality, a notion that in the human sciences otherwise remains nebulously in the background, therefore becomes an explicit theme for theology whether one wishes it or not. (MIG, 142)

The critical point at this juncture of my argument is that Pannenberg's view of the regulative function of part/whole is a result of his thematization of hermeneutics under the aspect of its relation to God *(sub ratione Dei)*. Here we have an explicit reference to the doctrine of Creation, which entails the Christian distinction (between Creator and creature) that transcends finite distinctions. Neither historical analysis (Dilthey) nor philosophical assessment (Hegel) of the part/whole relationality made this move. "The cate-

---

121. W. Pannenberg, *Theologie und Philosophie: Ihr Verhältnis im Licht ihrer gemeinsamen Geschichte* (Göttingen: Vandenhoeck & Ruprecht, 1996), pp. 364-67.

122. MIG, 130-52. Original German essay: "Die Bedeutung der Kategorein 'Teil' und 'Ganzes' für die Wissenschaftstheorie der Theologie," *Theologie und Philosophie* 53 (1978): 481-97.

gory of the whole (and its relationship to the parts) therefore has its specific significance for theology in that it makes possible the conceptual mediation between the finite and the absolute reality of God" (MIG, 146). Thus theological treatment of the "whole" goes beyond philosophical treatment; this is what makes it "theology."

> In contradistinction to the metaphysical tradition within philosophy, however, the totality of the world is certainly not the real theme for theology, but only the correlate of its real theme, the idea of God. God is not the whole of what exists finitely, and the concept of the whole does not include God within it as one of its parts. Whatever is a part of the whole — a part alongside other such parts and in distinction to the whole — is for that reason finite (in the Hegelian definition of the finite as a something in distinction to an other) and thus cannot be God. But neither can the whole be absolute, and therefore it cannot be God — at least not if it, as the whole of its parts, not only itself constitutes the being-as-part of its parts, but conversely is also dependent on the parts whose whole it is. This means that the whole cannot be conceptualized as self-constitutive. As the whole of its parts, it is a unified unity that presupposes some ground of itself as *unifying unity*. As the unifying unity of the world, God is distinct from the totality of the finite, though again not absolutely distinct. If God were merely distinct in relation to the totality of the finite, then he himself would be finite and would consequently have to be conceived as a part of that totality of the finite that we think of as world. As the unifying unity of the totality of the finite, God is indeed necessarily distinct from it. Yet at the same time, he is just as necessarily immanent to the world of the finite (given that its existence is already presupposed) as the continuing condition of its unity. (MIG, 142-43)

At the end of this essay, we find a key section that illustrates the critical difference between Pannenberg and Hegel (as well as process theology). With his parallelism of the expressions "whole" and "totality" in the *Science of Logic*, Hegel allowed the "whole" itself to become dialectical. For Hegel, "each of the two sides [the two 'totali-

ties'] is in itself at the same time the 'whole' of the relationship."
Hegel aimed to go beyond the abstract concept of the whole and "to
think the concrete whole itself using the concept of the Idea, and to
do so on the basis of the principle that constitutes it, which in the
process of realizing simultaneously realizes itself." Unfortunately,
by using this concept of the Idea, "Hegel also eliminated the difference between God and world, thereby replacing the concept of God
with that of the absolute Idea" (MIG, 151-52).

In the following quote, we have the clearest statement (outside
ST) of the importance of the Christian distinction between the infinite Creator and the finite creation for the task of theological hermeneutics. Unlike Hegel, Pannenberg wants to insist

> . . . upon the abstractness of every concept of the whole or of the
> totality, an abstractness that results from the anticipatory na-
> ture of all knowledge of the whole in a world which has not yet
> been completed and reconciled to the whole. To this corre-
> sponds the consciousness of the difference of the world from
> God — a difference which, to be sure, must not be hardened into
> a dualism, since this would result in making God himself finite,
> yet one which also, as the condition of the unity of any creature
> with God, will not be transcended and eliminated even in the
> eschaton. (MIG, 152)

This is what the part/whole interplay in hermeneutics looks like for
Pannenberg when it is thematized *sub ratione Dei*. Here we see the
"true infinite" aspect of his Grundprinzip operative in his definition of theological hermeneutics.

The same may be said of the "trinitarian" aspect of his method.
In the human experience of meaning and interpretation, it is participation in the life of the trinitarian God that explains the philosophical problem of the true infinite.

> . . . always related to the thought of finitude is that of the Infi-
> nite. Hence our human awareness is essentially a transcendent
> awareness that rises above the finitude of objects. In grasping fi-
> nite objects in their distinction, we are also aware of the Infinite

152

as the condition of their knowledge and existence ... in this constitution of conscious life, the Logos is present in a special way. As the generative principle of differentiation, he establishes and permeates the distinctive existence of all creatures ... in our conscious life, then, we are especially within the Logos who permeates all creation. (ST, II, 292)

Not only the Logos, but also the Spirit is involved in the constitution of human life and especially the consciousness of meaning. We are able to make finite distinctions, and a distinction between ourselves and God, only "where we are already lifted above ourselves by the Spirit of God." The goal of human creation is being enabled by the Spirit to accept our own finitude, being "fashioned into the image of the Son, of his self-distinction from the Father" (ST, II, 230). We will examine this aspect of Pannenberg's theology in more detail in Chapter Four. Here we simply note that Pannenberg sees Christian theology as offering explanations of our experience, aimed at understanding the conditions behind all of our inquiry. We now turn to a summary of the dynamic intercalation of movements in Pannenberg's method that we hope to appropriate for the postfoundationalist task of theology.

Anthropology: Linking Philosophy and History

The central importance of anthropology for Pannenberg's method was discussed already in Chapter One. He does indeed see it as the methodological starting point for theology. However, this does not entail that he is privileging it in a "foundationalist" sense, because the nonfoundationalist, too, starts *somewhere* (discussion of webs of belief), as does the postfoundationalist (discussions of rationality). By placing Pannenberg into dialogue with the four couplets, we have made a case that his approach is much more compatible with the postfoundationalist model.

In the final part of Chapter Two, we saw that a distinctive feature of this model, particularly in its articulation by van Huyssteen, is its desire to define rationality in a way that recognizes an inherent link between epistemology and hermeneutics. We defined the post-foundationalist task of theology in this way:

> to engage in interdisciplinary dialogue within our postmodern culture while *both* maintaining a commitment to intersubjective, transcommunal theological argumentation for the truth of Christian faith, *and* recognizing the provisionality of our histori-cally embedded understandings and culturally conditioned ex-planations of the Christian tradition and religious experience.

I have tried to show how foundationalists tend to emphasize epistemology as the primary philosophical theme, while the nonfoundationalist sees hermeneutics as dominating (or solely oc-cupying) the philosopher's slate. The *post*foundationalist wants to refigure epistemology and hermeneutics as mutually conditioning moments in the definition of human rationality. This plays itself out in the resolution of the tensions inherent in the postfoun-dationalist couplets. Our goal thus far in Chapter Three has been to demonstrate that Pannenberg desires, like the postfoundationalist, to find a middle way.

Does Pannenberg also share the desire for a linking (or fusion) of a modernist valuation of epistemology (without absolutism) and a postmodern privileging of hermeneutics (without relativism)? While affirming the inherent connection between knowing and in-terpreting, Pannenberg has not rigorously dealt with radical post-modern hermeneutics. On this point, clearly the postfounda-tionalist model must go beyond Pannenberg. Nevertheless, as it moves beyond him, I believe there is an important point of contact here, and even a potential resource, that should not be ignored.

In a way structurally similar to the postfoundationalist linking of epistemology and hermeneutics through *rationality*, Pannenberg sees a linking of philosophy and history through *anthropology*. The similarity is not merely structural, for epistemology has long been seen as central to *philosophy*, and postmodern hermeneutics is shaped by its emphasis on the *historical* embeddedness of human knowing.

So, rather than causing a collapse into foundationalism, as his critics fear, Pannenberg's use of anthropology signals a distinctive attempt to find a way past foundationalism without adopting relativism. Pannenberg selects anthropology as the link because he sees it as shaping post-Renaissance thought in a way that makes it the proper field for argumentation about the nature of religion and all talk about God.[123] This decision to engage in anthropological debate is rooted in Pannenberg's commitment to interdisciplinary dialogue in the search for intelligibility, a commitment shared by the postfoundationalist. The problem here seems to be that Pannenberg has not recognized the impact of postmodern hermeneutics and the relativist challenge to human rationality on the field of interdisciplinary debate. The postfoundationalist will recognize the postmodern challenge to the whole enterprise of epistemology as now inextricably connected to broader anthropological concerns, and therefore inherently shaping views about the reasonableness of talk about God in contemporary culture.

In spite of his not going far enough materially, I believe Pannenberg's formal use of anthropology can make a valuable contribution to the emerging postfoundationalist model. By spelling out this usage of anthropology in detail, we can see it as illustrating the type of argumentation necessary for avoiding the extremes of absolutist foundationalism and relativist nonfoundationalism. In Chapter Four, we will explore these structural dynamics in more detail and try to demonstrate the operation of his method, focusing on the relationality per se. In this final section of Chapter Three on Pannenberg's method, however, I want to provide a very general outline of his use of anthropology to show, first, its basic similarity to the postfoundationalist use of rationality. Second, we will see how this reciprocal dynamic that is the undercurrent of his whole *corpus* is another (and perhaps the primary) confirmation of my interpretation of his basic principle as *sub ratione Dei*, spelled out in the mutual conditioning and relational unity of the "true infinite" and "trinitarian" moments.

123. See, e.g., "Types of Atheism and Their Theological Significance," BQT, I, 192; *The Idea of God and Human Freedom*, 90ff.; TPS, 42; ST, I, 61, 128; and of course the entirety of ATP.

First, how exactly does anthropology function as a "link"? This must be understood in the context of his call for a "theology of religions."[124] For Pannenberg, the proposed theology of religion would have two major disciplines: philosophy of religion and history of religion. The task of the first would be "constructing the general concept of religion and of introducing in the context of that the idea of God as the all-determining reality" (TPS, 367-68). The history of religion, in this approach, would then take the abstract concept of religion thus produced and translate it into *(hebt . . . auf)* the concrete "historic reality of religious life" (369). Because they operate "midway between empirical investigation and conceptual systematisation," the auxiliary disciplines of psychology, phenomenology, and sociology ("general anthropology") are able to function as a link between these two major disciplines of a theology of religion. Thus understood, Christian theology and all its subdisciplines "should be given a foundation in a general theology of religions" (417).

This surely sounds foundationalist, but a careful reading of these sections reveals that it is not foundational*ism*. Pannenberg does not intend to found the history of religion on the findings of philosophy of religion or vice versa. He explicitly states that "it cannot be the function of this fundamental theology to determine the truth of Christianity; all it can do is provide a provisional location of Christianity within the historical world of religions" (TPS, 417). On the one hand, Pannenberg does not want to allow a specific premise of Christian doctrine to form the foundation of his approach, but rather to test the eschatological consciousness of Chris-

---

124. This phrase has evoked much discussion. My goal is not to determine the validity of this approach, but to show how it shapes and is shaped by Pannenberg's use of anthropology in theological method. For detailed summaries and critiques of Pannenberg's "theology of religion," see M. W. Worthing, *Foundations and Functions of Theology as Universal Science: Theological Method and Apologetic Praxis in Wolfhart Pannenberg and Karl Rahner* (Frankfurt am Main: Peter Lang, 1996), pp. 290-312; George Augustin, *Gott eint-trennt Christus? Die Einmaligkeit und Universalität Jesu Christi als Grundlage einer christlichen Theologie der Religionen: ausgehend von Ansatz Wolfhart Pannenbergs* (Paderborn: Bonifatius, 1993), pp. 18-62; Carl Braaten, "The Place of Christianity among the World Religions," in Carl Braaten and Philip Clayton, eds., *The Theology of Wolfhart Pannenberg: Twelve American Critiques, with an Autobiographical Essay and Response* (Minneapolis: Augsburg, 1988), pp. 287ff.

tian faith in the context of the disputed nature of the reality of God as manifested in religious history (366n.). On the other hand, the philosophy of religion is not the foundation either, but has only the status of a "propaedeutic." This is because general concepts are always mediated in concrete historical experience. For Pannenberg, there is a redefinition of the relation of history and concept, so the former has priority over the latter; in this way he attempts to solve the problems of the relation of philosophy to theology, of plurality and unity of truth, and of theory and practice (421).

It is crucial to see that Pannenberg defines "theology" as an overlapping or transcending *(übergreifende)* category,[125] i.e., a discipline that moves between and holds together philosophy of religion and history of religion. "Theology" in this overlapping sense is like "anthropology" in its ability to move back and forth, thereby linking concrete and abstract. Already in 1962, Pannenberg was distinguishing between "theology" and "dogmatics" (BQT, II, 112). His "theology" of religions will find its basis in a "general" anthropology; even in the case of systematic theology, the most "general foundations" will have to come from anthropology (TPS, 422). But this means methodological starting point, not self-authenticating ground; theology does not simply accept the findings of anthropology and build upon them. Rather, "theology broaches the anthropological phenomena with a view to their religious and theological implications" (TPS, 422). In this context, we have a clear allusion to what Pannenberg will try to accomplish with ATP: sublating the abstract levels of anthropological inquiry (biology, psychology, sociology) into the concrete historical level of history, all in order to reintroduce the "religious thematic" as an essential aspect of human nature.

In a 1962 article, Pannenberg had expressed a similar dynamic between historical and dogmatic statements in the context of discussing the Christ event.

what people have become accustomed to separate as historical and dogmatic statements are *really [two] moments in a single cogni-*

---

125. TPS, 368n. The English translation renders "a category which bridges the gap."

tive process. . . . The point of departure for historical work is constituted by a spontaneous pre-projection of nexuses of meaning which then are tested against observation of all the available individual details, and confirmed or modified in accord with each of these. The dogmatician, however, inquires in the opposite direction, asking how a universal context of meaning arises out of a specific event, the history of Jesus Christ. Both aspects, the universal meaning and the specific individuality of Jesus' way, are *so intertwined that the process of acquiring knowledge of this always passes from one to the other.*[126]

This reference to Christology is important because Pannenberg makes explicit in this context his desire to avoid foundationalism. "It is not a matter of establishing a basis [*Begründung*], but of providing subsequent confirmation [*Bewährung*] of the deity of the God revealed in Jesus" (BQT, I, 202). Pannenberg is not interested in establishing universal ahistorical foundations, but in confirming the explanatory power of our understanding of the biblical trinitarian God.

We have seen that in Pannenberg's proposal for a theology of religion he sees anthropology (broadly conceived) as operative in both the (abstract) philosophy of religion and the (concrete) history of religion. These cannot be thought apart from each other; they are mutually conditioning. The point is that anthropology has a mediating role *between* dogmatic and historical statements (to use his earlier language). Our human self-understanding is operative on both sides, i.e., in philosophy of religion and in history of religion. But so is our idea of God, according to Pannenberg. So theology and anthropology are *not* two separate operations that one must work to bring together. Rather, they are mutually conditioning, unthinkable without the other. However, this unified thinking-together is a differentiated unity. The two tasks of fundamental and systematic theology are inseparable, though distinct, as are the two tasks of philosophy of religion and history of religion. Both anthropology and theology permeate both sides of the relation. However, we may still

126. BQT, I, 199. Emphasis added.

distinguish two tasks, one that starts with the anthropological data having the theological statements in the background, the other which presents the theological statements with the anthropological data in the background.

What does this mean for the actual *relation* between these two disciplines within an overall theology of religions? "In the detailed treatment of the phenomenon of religion the abstraction of the general concept of religion, which is unavoidable as a starting point, must be subsumed [*aufgehoben*] in the complexity of the historical reality of religions" (TPS, 419). A few pages later, Pannenberg explains that "on the basis of general anthropology the theology of religion first elaborates, as a propaedeutic, the concept of religion (philosophy of religion) and then subsumes [*aufzuheben*] it in the actual movement of the history of religion."[127]

The relation, then, is one of "Aufhebung" or "sublation."[128] One does not have to accept all of Hegel's conclusions to see the legitimacy of the dynamic of "aufheben" in human experience and thought.[129] We have here the idea of something being negated, yet preserved, as it is elevated into something else. This is not the founding of one concept or belief upon another, but a dialectical relation between them. Anthropology, then, is not a foundation, but the field within which the philosophy and history of religion interact, mutually influencing each other.

If we strip away any Hegelian overtones, this concept of sublation might be applied to the postfoundationalist attempt to relate epistemology and hermeneutics. We saw in Chapter Two that the postfoundationalist sees "postmodernity" as a constant interroga-

127. TPS, 423. Translation emended.

128. The term "sublation" will be used in what follows as the English equivalent to "Aufhebung."

129. It is crucial to distinguish here between the appropriation of an aspect of Hegel's analysis and an appropriation of Hegel's whole system. In the last twenty years, only the rare scholar has charged Pannenberg with "Hegelianism." Such a charge is very difficult to support in light of the significant number of Pannenberg's writings that criticize Hegel and clearly show that he moves beyond him. E.g., several articles in *Grundfragen, II*, MIG, *Theologie und Philosophie,* and of course ATP and ST, which we will analyze in detail below.

tion of modernist foundations, not as simply an end to modernity. That is, our historically conditioned hermeneutical concern to critique ideology sublates (elevates, brings into itself without annihilating) the epistemological concern to justify our knowledge as we search for truth. Rationality is seen as operative between the two, overlapping them and holding them together. The concept of "Aufhebung" does not exhaustively describe the relation between epistemology and hermeneutics, any more than it does the relation between philosophy and history for Pannenberg. Nevertheless, we have here one more metaphor for articulating a relationality that is neither foundationalist nor nonfoundationalist, and to that extent it may be appropriated by postfoundationalists.

Anthony Thiselton has reviewed Pannenberg's TPS (and other methodological works) and attempted to appropriate him. Interestingly, Thiselton uses language reminiscent of "aufheben," without the Hegelian metaphysical baggage:

> [Pannenberg's TPS] constitutes a careful *metacritical* argument for the *unity* of knowledge which *incorporates hermeneutics*. . . . Pannenberg agrees with Habermas that positivism can be challenged only by some paradigm of critical knowledge which will *embrace* and *include* it; not by that which attacks it "from without" or tries to by-pass it.[130]

It is precisely this kind of "embracing and including" that the postfoundationalist imagines in the to-and-fro movement between modernity and postmodernity.

This relationality will be discussed in more detail in Chapter Four, but let us first ask the question: does this analysis of the use of anthropology as a link between philosophy of religion and history of religion confirm our reading of Pannenberg's basic principle as *sub ratione Dei*? Here we are discussing the dynamic structural relation that will be filled out materially by the concepts of "true infinite" and "Trinity." The relation between TPS, ATP, and ST is cru-

---

130. Anthony Thiselton, *New Horizons in Hermeneutics* (Glasgow: HarperCollins, 1992), p. 334. Emphasis in the original.

cial here. TPS sets out the need for a special relation between the first moment (which is articulated most comprehensively in ATP) and the second moment (presented in ST). The connection between these two will be exhaustively outlined below; the point here is to show that "anthropology" as well as "theology" overlaps both moments and that in both moments the concepts of true infinite and trinity are both present (although with varying emphasis).

The first moment is driving Pannenberg's project in ATP. Echoing his TPS, Pannenberg explains that Christian theology "must provide itself with a foundation in general anthropological studies" (ATP, 15). He notes immediately that we are not dealing here with a "neutral foundation," for the terrain of modern anthropology has failed (because of the influence of atheism) to deal with any explicit religious thematic in human existence. By ignoring the religious thematic, however, anthropology has been unable to explain the human phenomena of openness to the world or "exocentricity." In dialogue with each discipline of anthropology, Pannenberg will argue that their findings presuppose or point toward the structure of human existence as defined by what he will later call the "true infinite." Even when humans move beyond all experience or ideas of perceptible objects, "they continue to be exocentric, related to something other than themselves, but now to an Other beyond all the objects of their world, an Other that at the same time embraces this entire world and thus ensures the possible unification of the life of human beings in their world . . ." (ATP, 69).

Pannenberg is careful to distinguish his task in ATP from *dogmatic* anthropology, which develops the concepts of sin and image of God on the basis of what the Bible says. In contrast,

> . . . the studies undertaken here may be summarily described as a *fundamental-theological* anthropology. This anthropology does not argue from dogmatic data and presuppositions. Rather, it turns its attention directly to the phenomena of human existence as investigated in human biology, psychology, cultural anthropology, or sociology and examines the findings of these disciplines with an eye to implications that may be relevant to religion and theology. (ATP, 21)

This fundamental-theological move in ATP does not presuppose the truth of a trinitarian conception of the reality of God, but aims to thematize human openness to the world, showing that it requires an infinite reality. It remains to be shown, however, what this reality is. As Pannenberg put it in an earlier work, "the messages of the religions are to be tested on the basis of whether they conceal the infinite openness of human existence or allow it to emerge."[131] This is not the task of ATP, but of ST.

"Theology" in the broad (overlapping) sense, however, is operative in ATP. The reality of God is "problematic" rather than presupposed here, as Pannenberg said (in TPS) that it should be. Nevertheless, it still fulfills the requirements of *Wissenschaft*, because "the idea of God is measured and verified *on its own implications;* in other words, the idea of God as, by definition, the reality which determines everything must be substantiated by the experienced reality of man and the world" (TPS, 300). Already in TPS, then, we can see the emergence of the concept of "true infinite" as driving the fundamental-theological moment, and clearly connected to *sub ratione Dei*. In theology,

> . . . things as a whole are the object of study only in relation to the reality of God, that is, only because God is conceived of as the reality which determines everything. . . . How can we conceive of a totality without conceiving of something outside it? It seems that every totality is constituted as a specific whole only by being separated from something else that it leaves outside it. It seems that even an infinite totality must have at least its unifying unity outside itself, and in that case what is the relation of the totality of "everything" that exists to the reality of the unity which unifies it, and what is its own reality? The totality which has its unifying unity outside itself cannot be the totality of everything that exists. . . . The problems raised by the concept of a totality of everything real — or even of everything finite — can be solved only by another category which transcends the opposition of whole and part. (TPS, 305)

131. WIM, 11.

ATP represents the first "moment" in a theology of religion, whereby Pannenberg aims to demonstrate that our experience of the world inherently points us to the concept of the true infinite, which calls for an explanation. However, this first moment is not wholly cut off from the second moment, which it anticipates. In fact, Pannenberg can even attempt to show that many of the themes in secular anthropology arose historically due in part to aspects of the Christian faith. One might argue with Pannenberg on specific points, but the relevant issue of interest here is his methodological sense of the mutual conditioning between the moments. Already in ATP we see Pannenberg alluding to the solution of the trinitarian conception of God (e.g., ATP, 484, 531f.).

The second moment is articulated in *Systematic Theology*. As we have seen, it is from beginning to end an argument for the explanatory power of the Christian concept of the distinction and unity of the immanent and economic Trinity. However, the second moment is not separable from the first moment. The latter is "sublated" into the former, just as Pannenberg argued (in TPS) that it should be. He had noted there that until the science of religion develops "into a theology of religions in the sense described here, and so becomes the basic discipline of theology in general, this basic theological work must be accommodated provisionally within systematic theology" (TPS, 369).

So ST sublates the work of ATP. For example, he identifies issues in the anthropological understanding of religion in chapter 3 of ST "in the interests of taking them up ["Aufhebung"] into the perspective of a theology that is oriented to the primacy of God and his revelation" (ST, I, 128). In this "systematic" context, he explicitly responds to critics; in TPS he had "accorded fundamental theological rank to anthropology as the basis of a theology of religion. I naturally have in view only a methodological priority and am not treating anthropology as materially the basis of theology" (ST, I, 157-58n.111). The findings of both TPS and ATP regarding the true infinite as a criterion for ideas of God are recapitulated and updated in the first few chapters of ST, and then "taken up into" the second moment of theology, which involves the systematic presentation of the biblical trinitarian God (chapter 4 onward) as the best explanation for the experience of the history of religions.

163

Interestingly, in a 1992 article Pannenberg states that the Trinity is the "central illustration of the linking of historical and philosophical elements in Christian theology."[132] It is the result of both moments, the demonstration of the relation of the history of Jesus to the Father confirmed in the resurrection, and the connection of the trinitarian God to the Creator of the world as all-determining reality. So we can see that the trinitarian concern is operative in both moments as well. Whether or not one agrees with Pannenberg's material conceptions of "true infinite" and "Trinity," we have attempted to show that his use of anthropology as a link between philosophy and history in the theological task is not intended by him to be foundationalist, for the inferential structure goes both ways. But neither is it nonfoundationalist, for his claims are not justified merely by "coherence" but reach out for intersubjectively criticizable criteria that may be tested against the multiplicity of human experiences of reality. Pannenberg's approach actually pushes us toward the concerns of the emerging postfoundationalist model, and the next chapter aims to outline the contours of his inherently relational method in order to illustrate its potential contributions to our contemporary understanding of the task of theology.

132. W. Pannenberg, "Eine philosophisch-historische Hermeneutik des Christentums," in P. Neuner and H. Wagner, eds., *Verantwortung für den Glauben: Beiträge zür fundamentaltheologie und Ökumenik* (Freiburg: Herder, 1992), p. 43. My translation.

CHAPTER FOUR

The Reciprocity of "Fundamental" and "Systematic" Theology

The last chapter confirmed our reading of Pannenberg's Grundprinzip, and pointed to a structural similarity between his method and the postfoundationalist model, insofar as both aim to identify a higher relational unity where previous models have seen dichotomies. The term "reciprocity" will be used here to emphasize the dynamic quality or "state" of the relational unity itself, rather than the focus on the material aspects of each pole. This chapter will examine the precise nature of Pannenberg's methodological relationality, showing that he views the "from below" and "from above" movements as complementary, not as conflicting or mutually exclusive.

On the basis of several uses of the term "aufheben" in TPS[1] to describe the relation between philosophy of religion and history of religion, we might anticipate that this conceptual "sublation" would be evident in his use of anthropology in other writings. The second major section of this chapter, a diachronic survey of his use of anthropology, will show that this is indeed the case, although the exact nature of his understanding of the term still needs to be determined. In fact, several characteristics of the "reciprocity" in

---

1. E.g., TPS, 313, 369, 419, 423. See the last section of Chapter Three for details.

Pannenberg's methodology will emerge that are not captured by the simple concept of sublation. These include *asymmetry* (material primacy of the "from above" movement), *bipolarity* (two clearly differentiated tasks), and a real relational *unity* (a single process with two moments).

An accurate picture of Pannenberg's method must capture these qualities. To accomplish this task, in the final major section of this chapter we will appropriate a model of relationality developed by James Loder and W. Jim Neidhardt. Their model is heuristically helpful in enhancing and clarifying the coinherence of the two movements in Pannenberg's work. Demonstrating the actual performance of the reciprocity will require a synchronic presentation of his two treatments (in ATP and ST) of the traditional loci of theological anthropology. This analysis and synthesis will fill in a gap in the scholarly literature on Pannenberg, and prepare us for a summarization of the connection between Pannenberg and the postfoundationalist model of rationality in Chapter Five.

The Mutual Conditioning of "from below" and "from above"

In this subsection, I will first outline Pannenberg's understanding of the relation between the movements "from below" and "from above" by pointing to specific key texts, including both recent treatments and some earlier methodological discussions. With this background, I will suggest that many interpreters of Pannenberg have missed this double movement in his theological method. I will then briefly examine three scholars who have seen this double movement and attempted to articulate models to describe its operation. In a form analogous to the critique of "key concept" interpretations in Chapter Three, I will argue that these models do not fully describe the mutual conditioning of the two moves in Pannenberg's thought.

Soon after the publication of his 1964 JGM, many theologians raised objections to Pannenberg's call for a christology "from below." Some saw it as an attempt to provide a foundation for theology (or faith) in historical research or human reason. These concerns continue to shape the reception of his theology even today, as we saw in Chapter One. Our purpose here is not to reconstruct this debate, but simply to point to the nuances in Pannenberg's methodology already present in his early works, but made more explicit in the later ST:

> Hence we cannot regard a christology from below as ruling out completely the classical christology of the incarnation. It is simply reconstructing the revelatory historical basis that classical christology has always in fact presupposed, though never properly explained. Only methodologically do we give precedence to arguing from below, presupposing, of course, that this procedure leads to the conclusion that the concept of incarnation is not a falsification but a pertinent development of the meaning implicit in the coming and history of Jesus. In truth, material primacy belongs to the eternal Son, who has become man by his incarnation in Jesus of Nazareth. Rightly understood, then, the two lines of argument from above and from below are *complementary.*[2]

He describes this as a "relation of *real mutual conditioning* between an idea of God and a human self-understanding" and refers to "the *actual reciprocal relation* of theology and anthropology that characterizes human self-understanding" (ST, II, 290, 291, emphasis added).

It might be thought that Pannenberg has changed his mind since the early christology monograph. However, he made clear in his 1976 "Afterword" to the fifth edition that "the alterations that appear to be necessary still do not mean any departure from the path engaged by this book, but rather a continuation of it."[3] The limitations of his book "are connected with the limitation within which the history of tradition approach 'from below' is carried

---

2. ST, II, 288-89. Emphasis added. Cf. *An Introduction to Systematic Theology*, p. 67: "the emerging synthesis is no more what I earlier called a 'christology from below.' But it *presupposes and integrates* that methodological approach." Emphasis added.

3. JGM, 399 (in the "Afterword").

through here by treating the reality of God as a *presupposition* of Christology" (JGM, 404). He notes the element of truth in his critics' call for a supplementation by a christology "from above," which points to the need for a systematic treatment beyond the task of his monograph. This would be possible

> only within the context of the doctrine of God and thus within the overall framework of a comprehensive dogmatics. This poses the task of thinking about christology in connection with God's relation to the world in general and especially in connection with his relationship to humanity in the course of its history.[4]

Notice, however, that the idea that christology "from below" already presupposes (or "pre-requires" as a condition) some idea of the reality of God — and so is concerned with the relation of Jesus to God — was already present in the text of the first edition. The procedure of christology requires that "the idea of God must be presupposed historically and in substance" (JGM, 20), although precisely this idea is treated as problematic and clarified in the study of Jesus. In this sense, he already notes a "relative justification" (35) for the "from above" moment because

> . . . while Christology must begin with the man Jesus, its first question has to be that about his unity with God. Every statement about Jesus taken independently from his relationship to God could only result in a crass distortion of his historical real-

---

4. JGM, 406. Notice here Pannenberg's emphasis on *sub ratione Dei* as the driving force of theological inquiry, and his allusions to what would become ATP and ST. Christoph Schwöbel notes ("Wolfhart Pannenberg," 182) that while Pannenberg starts "from below," even in JGM he does not "stay" below. In an earlier review essay, "Rational Theology in Trinitarian Perspective: Wolfhart Pannenberg's *Systematic Theology*," *Journal of Theological Studies* 47, no. 2 (October 1996): 508, Schwöbel suggests that the entire ST "must be read in two ways: as an application of the doctrine of the immanent Trinity to the divine economy, and as an application of the divine economy to the trinitarian doctrine of God." This suggestion confirms not only our contention here that "from above" and "from below" are inherently related, but also our arguments in the last chapter about his Grundprinzip.

ity . . . the specific element in the Christological question about Jesus is that it does not begin with some preliminary aspect of his deeds and words or of his effect on men, but with his relation to God as it is expressed in the whole of his activity on earth. (JGM, 36)

This statement is not unique; Pannenberg says the same thing in other words in various places. These methodological decisions are shaped by his belief that "the question about God and that about man *can only be answered together*. . . ."[5]

One year before the "Afterword" to the christology book, Pannenberg went into more detail about this central problem in christological method in his article "Christologie und Theologie." Here he explicitly calls for overcoming the alternative between "from above" and "from below." This will require a "deepening and widening of the place from which concentrated theological reflection on the man Jesus of Nazareth begins." This new approach finds both "the world and humanity already within the Circle of divine life," which Pannenberg articulates in terms of the relation between the trinitarian persons and the infinity of God, which is not "simply set over against" the finite world, but "at the same time contains it."[6] In other words, the method of christology is to be couched within the dynamic relations of the "true infinite" and the Trinity, as they disclose the relation of all things to God.

In spite of this clear statement of the need for two movements in theological method, early reactions missed this reciprocal relation, and Pannenberg was misinterpreted as suggesting that christology and indeed all theology is exhausted by the "from below" movement. In 1973 Frank Tupper expressed concern that Pannenberg's writings had not discussed the divine intention in the cross. In a

5. "Analogy and Doxology," in BQT, I, 232. Emphasis added. In 1959, he tried to show "how closely the elements of the metaphysical concept of God are related to ideas about the structure of inner-worldly being and of human cognition," BQT, II, 173.

6. In *Grundfragen, II*, 135, 140. My translations. In BQT, II, 103, Pannenberg makes it clear that the finitude of human existence stands already in association with the infinite.

"postscript" to Tupper's book, Pannenberg responded that his method in JGM was "anthropological-historical," and promised to expand on the "self-explication of God in the history of Jesus"[7] at a later time. He spelled this out three years later in the "Afterword" to the 1976 German edition.

Unfortunately, this misreading continued to prevail. We will take Colin Gunton as representative. Gunton calls Pannenberg's distinction between these "two ways of doing Christology" a "gross oversimplification."[8] Gunton wants to differentiate between two types of theology "from above." Type A allows theological concepts to be "determined or heavily conditioned by philosophical considerations that operate independently of the particular elements of Christology," while Type B moves methodologically "*from* rather than *towards* explicitly theological judgments about Jesus."[9] We might ask here who would ever accept the label of "Type A" (even before modernity), as well as whether it is *possible* for particular elements of christology to *be* independent of philosophical considerations.

My point here, however, is that Gunton missed the fact that Pannenberg's method incorporates the concerns of "Type B," for he *does* accept a theological movement (namely a "dogmatic" or "systematic" moment) that moves *from* explicitly theological judgments. Gunton's misreading is further disclosed by his comment that "Pannenberg's process of thought is continuous, a movement from the finite to the infinite."[10] As we saw in Chapter Three, in several works published prior to Gunton's book, Pannenberg made it clear that he is interested in the mutual relation of infinite and finite and not in working from only one direction. Gunton's misreading is unfortunate, for Pannenberg could have been used as a resource for the former's own call for a "harnessing together" (52) of christology from above and from below.

7. Frank Tupper, *The Theology of Wolfhart Pannenberg* (Philadelphia: Westminster, 1973), p. 305.

8. Colin Gunton, *Yesterday and Today: A Study in Continuities in Christology* (Grand Rapids: Eerdmans, 1983), p. 51.

9. Gunton, *Yesterday and Today*, pp. 34, 44.

10. Gunton, *Yesterday and Today*, p. 20.

Several scholars *have* recognized the two movements in Pannenberg's theological method and offered widely varying descriptions of their relationship.[11] We will look briefly at three reconstructions: Elizabeth Johnson, Nancey Murphy, and George Sumner. In her 1981 dissertation, Johnson thematized the close relationship between Pannenberg's christology and his view of reality. This relationality does not result in a "narrow christologism" that invalidates non-Christian views of reality, nor in a "generalized reality theory" that compromises the uniqueness of Christ. Johnson notes that in expositing the two concepts in Pannenberg's thought she could start by describing either side, for the profound relationship between his view of reality and the Christ event is "a rigorous unity which coheres by the force of its own logic."[12] She argues that

Pannenberg's interpretation of the Christ event and his understanding of reality are ingredient to one another. Even the remotest trace of dualism is prevented from arising between the two by the proleptic structure which he sees in each and by the interrelationships which he posits between them. The truth of

11. E.g., Ted Peters sees Pannenberg as constructing a "single framework for theology which encompasses both" the task of methodology and that of apologetics; see his "Truth in History: Gadamer's Hermeneutics and Pannenberg's Apologetic Method," *Journal of Religion* 55 (1975): 56. William Placher has argued that Pannenberg has never claimed, pace critics, that arguments about the particular history of Jesus' resurrection can "be separated from Christian's understanding of their experience and of the whole of reality"; rather, these arguments move with an "element of circularity." See Placher, "History and Faith in the Theology of Wolfhart Pannenberg" (Ph.D. diss., Yale, 1975), p. 501.

12. Elizabeth Johnson, "Analogy/Doxology and Their Connection with Christology in the Thought of Wolfhart Pannenberg" (Ph.D. diss., Catholic University of America, 1981), p. 114. The basic theses of her dissertation are summarized in her article "The Right Way to Speak about God? Pannenberg on Analogy" (*Theological Studies* 43 [1982]). Johnson also shows how this structurally constitutive relation between the two is a "pattern of thought" that solves (for Pannenberg) the problems of the relation between appearance and being, time and eternity, theological and historical hermeneutic, anthropocentric and theocentric views of history, faith and reason, sacred and profane, "and the whole panoply of problems arising from the encounter of Greek with biblical insights finds a satisfying solution" (*Analogy/Doxology,* pp. 115-16).

reality is that it is oriented toward the future, the end of which has already arrived in the history and destiny of Jesus Christ. The truth of Jesus Christ is that he is one with that future and is therefore the point of unity and meaning for all reality. Christology and theory about reality do not coincide in Pannenberg, but neither are they separated spheres: they are inextricably interrelated in the overall gestalt of his thought.[13]

Although Johnson does not offer an explicit model for conceptualizing the relation, she clearly sees the two movements as intertwined in a relational unity. She is writing before the ATP book, and so can only anticipate the direction Pannenberg will go. However, both in her dissertation and in another article the following year, she has recognized the crucial move programmatically outlined in his "Christologie und Theologie" article, calling for (as Johnson summarizes it) "a broader and deeper christology from below more strongly linked with anthropology and presented as a true christology from above, i.e., a christology of the self-realization of God."[14]

Johnson notes the "circularity" in his thought,[15] but she is not concerned with methodology per se and so does not spend considerable time in describing the structure and nature of this relationality. Nevertheless, she does recognize that Pannenberg sees both movements as occurring within the same structure of human knowing, which he views as already inside the circle of the divine life,[16] because of the mediation of the Son and Spirit in the creation of the world and humanity. However, the problem with the picture of "circularity" is that, while it emphasizes the real unity, it does not capture either the asymmetry or the bipolarity of the two movements.

Nancey Murphy goes into more detail in her attempt to describe

13. Elizabeth Johnson, "The Right Way to Speak about God?" pp. 117-18.

14. Elizabeth Johnson, "The Ongoing Christology of Wolfhart Pannenberg," *Horizons* 9, no. 2 (1982): 247. In this context, she also recognizes the centrality of the themes of the true infinite and the Trinity.

15. Johnson, "Analogy/Doxology," p. 109. She is not making the charge of vicious circularity in the logical sense, but simply pointing to the mutual influence of ideas.

16. Johnson, "Analogy/Doxology," p. 274.

the two movements in Pannenberg's theology. Her *Theology in the Age of Scientific Reasoning* begins and ends with Pannenberg. Second only to her Lakatosian proposal, she finds his methodology to be the most promising available option for responding to Hume's challenge to theology, viz., showing that it qualifies as "rational" in an age of probabilistic reasoning. Murphy concludes that Pannenberg's method ultimately fails to overcome Hume, but that if one reconstructs Pannenberg into a nonfoundationalist along Lakatosian lines, Hume is defeated and theology becomes methodologically indistinguishable from science. I have criticized this approach above in discussing the relation of "individual and community" in Chapters Two and Three.

My purpose here is to illuminate the way in which Murphy recognizes but misconstrues Pannenberg's view of theology as taking place "between two tendencies," i.e., between the faithful understanding of what the Christian tradition says about God and the testing of the tradition's concept of God as the best explanation of the whole of experience. She describes Pannenberg's method in this way:

> Theology begins with two sets of concentric circles. One set involves the texts of the Christian Scriptures. In Pannenberg's theology the texts concerning Jesus' resurrection are at the very center, surrounded by circles representing the increasingly broad contexts required for their full understanding — most immediately, the rest of the New Testament. The apocalyptic worldview of the first century would in turn form an important context for understanding the New Testament. Besides this first series of concentric circles is another representing our own experience and the ever-broadening contexts within which we attempt to interpret it. At some point moving outward we reach a circle that encompasses both the texts and our own experience. . . . The Christian view of God, based upon Jesus' resurrection, is finally represented by the outermost circle, intended to encompass and give meaning to all experience and to all other contexts of meaning.[17]

17. Nancey Murphy, *Theology in the Age of Scientific Reasoning* (Ithaca, N.Y.: Cornell University Press, 1990), p. 33.

173

In her contribution to a symposium held in Pannenberg's honor in 1988, Murphy offered a graphic representation of this interpretation of the "two tendencies" in his methodology.[18] Her representation there showed two concentric circles overlapping at the outermost circles, which looked something like a cell in the process of dividing. Murphy then went on to reconstruct Pannenberg in Lakatosian terms, having a "hard core" with "auxiliary hypotheses" that mutually shape each other. In his response to the symposium, Pannenberg notes that

> the account she [Murphy] gives is actually closer to my view of the task of theology than the image of concentric circles which she attributes to me. In terms of *systematic structure* the framework of theological explanation as I envision it may be adequately described in Lakatosian terms. The question of *method* is somewhat different.[19]

We might suggest here that *any* complex explanation could be reconstructed by a Lakatosian in Lakatosian terms, for the latter is simply a description of the structural way in which a person has explained something. The question of method, as Pannenberg notes, is different; at the methodological level the "concentric circles" picture does not capture the asymmetric control or the real relational unity of the two tendencies in Pannenberg's thought.

George Sumner also sees two related dynamics in Pannenberg's thought, which he calls an "anthropological" and a "doxological" movement. The picture he uses to describe them is of two tunnels being simultaneously dug toward one another, meeting in the middle.

> When thought twice, theology following this same pattern, in the wake of that resurrection, must employ the concept of *Vorlauefigkeit* in two ways. In brief, theology *"von unter"* will be

18. Nancey Murphy, "A Lakatosian Reconstruction of Pannenberg's Program," in *Beginning with the End: God, Science, and Wolfhart Pannenberg*, ed. C. R. Albright and J. Haugen (Chicago: Open Court, 1997), p. 413.

19. W. Pannenberg, "Theological Appropriation of Scientific Understandings," in *Beginning with the End*, p. 431.

dominated by the concept of contestation *(Strittigkeit)* or struggle in accordance with the "root metaphor" of testing or verification according to the natural sciences. Theology *"von oben"* will be dominated by the concept of encompassing or sublation with heavy reliance (as well as important emendations) on dialectical thinking. It is important to see that two logics are at work. The critical rationalist is digging one side of the tunnel, the universal historical dialectician the other.[20]

As another visual aid, Sumner refers to the drawings of Escher, which often make sense from one of two perspectives (39). For Sumner, Pannenberg's approach fails because on the issue of the unique salvific importance of Jesus Christ, the anthropological and doxological movements diverge. He sees this as the key problem that emerges "in that tricky ravine which runs down the middle of the *spannungsvolle Einheit* of Pannenberg's apologetic-systematic project" (42). In other words, the issue of salvation in Jesus alone causes the tunnels not to meet, or destroys the unity of the Escherian optical illusion, allegedly leading to the need for a nonfoundationalist theological method, which Sumner attempts to outline at the end of his dissertation.

Sumner has properly seen that Pannenberg's method is a "tension-filled unity," and he notices that "each side of the theological endeavor is field-encompassing. From each side all the subjects theology must confront can be addressed" (38). He has correctly grasped the dynamic of "sublation" between the movements, but wrongly assumes that they try to sublate *each other;* he thinks Pannenberg's goal is "equipoise" between the movements (176-77). Sumner's use of the "two tunnels" picture does not capture the real dynamic unity of Pannenberg's approach, but suggests instead two *opposite* movements that must be made to meet in the middle. Here he has not seen as well as Elizabeth Johnson did in 1981 that Pannenberg views both movements as occurring within their al-

20. George Sumner, "Pannenberg and the Religions: Conflictuality and the Demonstration of Power in a Christian Theology of the Religions" (Ph.D. diss., Yale, 1994), p. 38. Page numbers in the next two paragraphs refer to this text.

ready-embeddedness of the circle of the divine life. Sumner's model of Pannenberg's method also does not capture the mutual conditioning of these movements, nor the asymmetric control (only the "systematic" sublates the "fundamental") that we have seen at work in Pannenberg's corpus.

What then *is* the relationship between the two movements? For Pannenberg, the way that an anthropological thematization of religion brings us to theological (dogmatic) issues and the way that the theological revelatory truth claims of the Christian faith illuminate anthropological experience suggest that there is a reason the two moves keep appearing to meet each other. They are movements in the mind (moments in a single process of knowing) that reflect our condition of existing *sub ratione Dei*. All theological statements (in either movement) are provisional, but point to our relation to a (contested) all-determining reality as a condition for explaining our experience of reality.

In the final section of Chapter Three we noted that this relationality may be provisionally described as involving "Aufhebung." Our historical survey below will show that Pannenberg clearly sees the "systematic" movement as sublating the "fundamental" movement. But what does he mean by this? His use of the word "aufheben" does not make him a Hegelian. The term itself simply implies a taking up of one level into another, whereby the first level is negated in some sense but is preserved as it is elevated into the new level. While Hegel saw this dynamic as a metaphysical self-actualization of the Absolute Spirit, Pannenberg is using the term here in a methodological sense simply to describe an explanatory procedure. The levels are conceptual, although the relation between the levels has both epistemic and hermeneutic ramifications.

"Aufhebung" alone, however, is not sufficient to capture the reciprocity we see in Pannenberg's view of the two movements. The result of the conceptual relation is not merely a synthesis. Rather, both movements are still clearly differentiated, maintaining their own integrity. Yet, they exist in a relational unity that constitutes the two "poles." For Pannenberg, the conceptual level that does the sublating ("systematic" moment) does not exist in a separate sphere "before" it comes into the relation with the sublated conceptual level ("fundamental" moment). Rather, the two are "mutually conditioning," which means a more radical unity already constitutes the differentiated reciprocity. The systematic level only *is* what it is in its relation to the fundamental level, which it sublates. For Pannenberg, the goal is not to start with two supposedly separate levels and then engage in sublation; rather, our idea of God and our human self-understanding are already inextricably linked. The goal is to *recognize* the sublation, and argue critically about the coherence, illuminative power, and experiential adequacy of the explanation.[21]

Further, the "from above" (systematic) move has material primacy, and thus asymmetric control over the "from below" (fundamental) move. Therefore an accurate model of this reciprocity must account for the differentiated *bipolarity,* the *asymmetry,* and the relational *unity* evident in Pannenberg's theological argumentation. An accurate description will need to encompass the concept of "Aufhebung" itself as it seeks to develop a way of modeling this reciprocity. After illustrating his use of anthropology in the following section, we will propose a new heuristic model for clarifying the nature of this reciprocal relationality. The model will then be applied to his theological anthropology in order to test its explanatory value. It is this relationality, then, that may be critically appropriated for the postfoundationalist task of theology. Those readers who are more interested in this dialogue may want to treat the following historical review as an "excursus," and move directly to the final major section of this chapter, which synchronically presents his theological anthropology.

---

21. This relation is also illuminated by Pannenberg's occasional references to the Roman Catholic distinction between "fundamental" and "systematic" theology. He criticizes their strong division of labor between these two aspects of theology, arguing that systematic theology inevitably incorporates within itself the concern of fundamental theology to confirm the truth of Christian faith (ST, I, 48). For Pannenberg there is "no opposition in principle between philosophical theology and Christian theology" (ST, I, 339). Opposition occurs only when the former does not take religious tradition and experience into account or when the arguments of the latter assume in advance the truth of biblical teaching; in other words, when these two inherently related aspects of the task of theology attempt to operate separately.

Diachronic Survey of Pannenberg's
Use of Anthropology

As we move through this selective chronological presentation of Pannenberg's use of anthropology,[22] we will pay special attention to the emergence of his emphasis on the true infinite and to themes related to his trinitarian doctrine of God. With this background we will be able to make a synchronous presentation of his theological anthropology proper, focusing on the reciprocal relation between the two movements described above. Already in earlier works, however, we will see the emergence of an asymmetrical relational unity.

Pannenberg's first major treatment of explicitly anthropological questions was his 1962[23] *What Is Man?* (WIM), which was based on his 1959/60 lectures at Wuppertal. Here we find in at least kernel form most of the issues that emerged in much greater detail in ATP (1983). Like the latter book, WIM begins with openness to the world (and openness to God) and ends with "history" as the most concrete dimension of humanity. The former theme was already evident in *Revelation as History,* which had appeared the previous year. In his fifth "dogmatic thesis" he noted there that "the thought about the immortality of the soul was in fact an expression of the unending openness of man to go beyond any given situation, so that even death is not to be taken as a limit. The modern expression of this would be man's openness to the world by the very nature of his constitution."[24]

22. Because we have examined TPS and ST carefully above (especially in Chapter Three), these major books will not be included in the following survey except for the purpose of pointing out important anticipations of or allusions to them.

23. In order to maintain a sense of the actual chronological development of Pannenberg's thought, the dates mentioned in the main text of the following survey represent the publication of the original German, although the titles may be discussed in English translation. The details of publication will be provided in the footnotes and the bibliography. *Was ist der Mensch? Die Anthropologie der Gegenwart im Lichte der Theologie* (Göttingen: Vandenhoeck & Ruprecht, 1962). *What Is Man?* trans. Duane A. Priebe (Philadelphia: Fortress Press, 1970).

24. Edited by Pannenberg in association with Rolf Rendtorff, Trutz Rendtorff, and Ulrich Wilkens, *Revelation as History,* trans. David Granskou (New York: Macmillan, 1968), p. 148. German: *Offenbarung als Geschichte* (Göttingen: Vandenhoeck & Ruprecht, 1961).

Even at this early stage, Pannenberg recognized the contextual conditioning of human reason. "Whenever a man makes creative decisions, these decisions always remain related to the biological and sociohistorical conditions of his situation, that is, to his own life history as well as to the spirit of his time" (WIM, 3). Nevertheless, this openness presupposes (or requires, *voraussetzen*) dependence on an unknown infinite; "man's openness to the world presupposes a relation to God" (12).

All of the issues in WIM are argued in a much more scholarly way in ATP, which we will discuss in detail below, so a simple summary should suffice. The main point here is that each of the chapters of WIM aims to describe the data of human existence, from biology to history, *sub ratione Dei*. Although Pannenberg does not use the term here, the idea permeates his argument. He shows that various anthropological phenomena presuppose an openness beyond the world, which in turn requires the thematization of the infinite. This holds true for human imagination which emerges through language (chapter 2), for the need to trust our environment in order to survive (3), for the constitutive human hope that looks beyond death (4), for the broken egocentricity of the human self (5), for the experience of time which presupposes eternity (6), for the social mediation of human identity (7), for the need for love as the basis for justice in institutions and culture (8), for the reductionism of pseudoreligious descriptions of the social process like Marxism (9), for the transmission of traditions which presupposes an openness to a future totality (10), and finally for the historical particularity of human existence which presupposes a divine guarantor for its unity (11). At this early stage Pannenberg tended to speak of the requirement of an infinite or God as obvious or almost a given, a tendency he tried to correct in later writings.

In "Analogy and Doxology," an article also published in 1962, Pannenberg treats the issue of the religious basis of the concept of "person" as involving non-manipulability. He notes that our idea of what it means to be a (human) person emerged in response to the experience of a divine ground to the "whole" or totality of reality. In a footnote, he points out that "the question about God and that about man *can only be answered together,* although the one may not be used to dissolve the other."[25] In 1963, Pannenberg treated similar anthropological issues in "Hermeneutic and Universal History."

> Is it not the case that man cannot expect an answer to the question about himself without knowledge of the world, of society, of history, and of God? If this is the case, however, then self-understanding cannot become thematic irrespective of previous understanding of the world and also, in a certain sense, of God. The understanding of the world and of God are not merely the *expression* of man's question concerning himself [Bultmann], but, on the contrary, the relationship to the world, to society, and to God is what first *mediates* man to himself. Only by means of the mediation of these relationships does he gain self-understanding. (BQT, I, 110-11)

Clearly, even at this early stage, Pannenberg is working out of a basic methodological commitment that human nature can only be understood *sub ratione Dei*. The structure of human being has an essentially religious element.

The term "God," however, remains problematic in the "from below" or "philosophy of religion" movement, as we saw above. So he is not assuming that it is obvious to the non-Christian that human nature is incomprehensible without the biblical God; rather, he is arguing that *some* concept of God, in the sense of an all-determining reality, is a necessary condition for explaining the fact of our experience of openness beyond the world. The "from above" or "history of religion" aspect of a theology of religions argues (in the case of Christian theology) that the biblical triune God, self-revealed in Jesus Christ, is the best explanation for this openness of human existence. Seeds of this approach were already present in a 1964 article, "On Historical and Theological Hermeneutic." Here, too, he emphasizes that a human self-understanding presupposes an anticipation of a totality, and "presumably it is not even possible to speak of the whole of reality without in some way thinking of God" (BQT, I, 156). But the focus of the end of this article is showing that human

---

25. BQT, I, 232. Emphasis added.

experience, the data with which anthropology deals, is explained in the history and message of Jesus Christ.

> It is possible to find in the history of Jesus an answer to the question of how "the whole" of reality and its meaning can be conceived without compromising the provisionality and historical relativity of all thought, as well as openness to the future on the part of the thinker who knows himself to be only on the way and not yet at the goal. (BQT, I, 181)

In "What Is Truth" (1962), Pannenberg treated the specific issue of the role of the idea of God in human knowledge. Tracing the development of the idea of truth in the history of philosophy, he argues that since Nicholas of Cusa "God is the presupposition from which alone the agreement of human thought with extrahuman reality can be explained and guaranteed" (BQT, II, 17). This approach was particularly evident in Descartes's *Meditations*, which linked the concepts of the finite self and the infinite.

In his "Toward a Theology of the History of Religions" (also 1962), Pannenberg expressly treated the role of a phenomenology of religion as contributing to an anthropology of religious experience. Its function (as a preliminary movement) must be to engage the whole of anthropological research, recognizing that the ultimate goal is to describe humanity in its concreteness, not simply to find abstract and identical structures of human behavior. In an allusion to the last part of WIM, he develops an emphasis on the concrete historicality of human existence that will become even more explicit in ATP. Pannenberg suggests that

> it is only through historical portrayal that one comes as close as possible to the actual course of the concrete life of man. In contrast to this, all general forms of anthropology, be they biologically, psychologically, or sociologically oriented, remain preliminary abstractions, which are indeed indispensable for a first approximation to an understanding of human behavior but can nevertheless have only a preparatory character, and must pass over to the phase of a historical representation if the science of

man wishes to reach the concrete actualization of human experience. (BQT, II, 78)

In this same article, Pannenberg deals with a theme we will find recurrent and dominant in his thought, i.e., the need for an appropriate response to Feuerbach's anthropological reduction of theology. He notes that arguments about the rationality of talk about God must be made on anthropological terrain. He wants to take on Feuerbach, Marx, and Freud on their own turf, arguing that their accounts of human nature are reductionistic. For Pannenberg, abstract anthropological statements about "exocentricity" imply that human existence "naturally" or inherently moves beyond itself, and everything finite, toward a transcendent mystery. But this leaves open the question whether God actually exists.

> For this reason, the decisive step first occurs with consideration of the fact that the abstractness of statements about the anthropological structures can be overcome. If it belongs to the structure of human existence to presuppose a mystery of reality transcending its finitude and to relate oneself to this as the fulfillment of one's own being, then in actuality man always exists in association with this reality. . . . The reality of the mystery of being, to which the structure of man's existence points, must be demonstrated in such actual association with this mystery. (BQT, 103-4)

Two years earlier (1960), Pannenberg had dealt with the Feuerbachian challenge in much more detail in "Types of Atheism and Their Theological Significance." He rejects the Barthian response as "an act of spiritual capitulation," and suggests that

> Theology has to learn that after Feuerbach it can no longer mouth the word "God" without offering any explanation; that it can no longer speak as if the meaning of this word were self-evident; that it cannot pursue theology "from above," as Barth says, if it does not want to fall into the hopeless and, what is more, self-inflicted isolation of a higher glossolalia, and lead the whole church into this blind alley. . . . The struggle over the con-

cept of God has to be conducted indeed in the fields of philosophy, the sciences of religion, and anthropology. If Feuerbach should prove right in these fields then the proof of atheism for which he strove would in fact be accomplished. (BQT, II, 189-90)

Pannenberg argues that Feuerbach's analysis was wrong; he falsely assumed the infinity of the human race (BQT, II, 236). Even the more recent anthropological use of the terms "openness to the world" and "exocentricity" are misleading, for they require the "infinite," a ground beyond the world. Pannenberg asks: What is the *relation* of human self-transcendent questioning to this ground? Feuerbach conceded that human existence presupposes an openness to infinity beyond itself, but argued that this could be explained by the infinity of human nature. Pannenberg alludes to the need for a "philosophical anthropology worked out within the framework of a general ontology" as a part of the theological response.

In 1965, he critiqued the various ways of treating "The Question of God" in theologians like Bultmann and Ebeling, suggesting instead that it be treated in light of the idea of "exocentricity."

Whether this characteristic openness of human behavior presupposes such a supporting ground, different from the entire realm of existing beings (that is to say, from the world) precisely because what is being inquired into is man's openness to inquire beyond everything in existence; or whether this openness is only an expression of the self-creative power of man as an "acting being" is probably the central problem inherent in the modern idea of man's "openness to the world" or self-transcendence — an idea about which there is such remarkable agreement among the most diverse trends of modern thought. (BQT, II, 221)

Here he emphasizes the emergence of the idea of "person" as deriving from the religious experience of the non-manipulability of the infinite or transcendent. He points to "the priority of the relation to God for the phenomenon of the personal."[26]

26. BQT, II, 230. Here he was building on an earlier article, "Person," *Die Religion in Geschichte und Gegenwart,* vol. 5 (Tübingen: J. C. B. Mohr, 1961), pp. 230-35.

In "On the Theology of Law" (1963), Pannenberg again critiqued Barth's methodology, arguing that trying to use only the revelation of Christ obscures historical data. Pannenberg saw the source material of both theological and philosophical anthropology to be the same, namely the phenomena of human existence. The difference is that theology places the phenomena in a broader framework, offers better explanations, and so aims to be "true philosophy."

> ... if theology is to be able to assert such a comprehensive claim to truth, it must establish criteria for its propositions by means of which they can be tested and distinguished from mere assertions. Such a criterion for the questions we are examining must be that theological statements deal more adequately with anthropological phenomena than do other explanations.[27]

In light of the postmodern critique of reason, the issue of determining which explanations are "more adequate" is more problematic than Pannenberg implies. Nevertheless, the difficulty of the task does not mean we should stop searching for intersubjectively criticizable criteria.

Although Pannenberg's well-known 1964 monograph JGM was focused on christology, already here we see the contours of his intuition of the way christology and anthropology ought to be related. For example, the openness of Jesus to God is "not alien to the humanity of man as such" (JGM, 344). Jesus' sonship is the fulfillment of human destiny, of the openness to the world and to God that constitutes human nature. The most obvious treatment of anthropology in the book is in the second section, which examined the activity and fate of Jesus in his humanity, especially chapter 5, "The True Man." We see here not only a restatement of old themes, like openness to God as "the real meaning of the fundamental structure of being human which is designated as openness

---

27. "On the Theology of Law," in *Ethics,* trans. Keith Crim (Philadelphia: Westminster, 1981), p. 36. German: *Ethik und Ekklesiologie: Gesammelte Aufsätze* (Göttingen: Vandenhoeck & Ruprecht, 1977).

to the world in contemporary anthropology" (193), but also a more explicit treatment of the fulfillment of that destiny as participating in the self-distinction that characterized Jesus' life and work.

> ... Theology must take into consideration the complex totality of Jesus' historical individuality and seek to formulate his universal significance, even though it is probably only able to perceive that totality as relevant for humanity under one aspect or another that is related to the anthropological problematic of the time. ... The saving character of the universal relevance that belongs to Jesus' figure is determined by whether Jesus is to be understood as the *fulfillment* of the hopes and deep longing of humanity. (JGM, 204-5)

In *Theology and the Kingdom of God,* Pannenberg included anthropological themes of the relation to God in his discussions of the power of the future. The first essay (1967) explains that "in relation to the God of the power of the future, man is free: free for a truly personal life, free to accept the provisionality of everything, free with regard to nature and society, free for that creative love that changes the world without destroying it" (TKG, 69). He also treats the effect of this openness to the future Kingdom on issues such as ethics, politics, and the relation of the church to society.

In his "Response to the Discussion" at the end of *Theology as History* (1967), Pannenberg emphasized again the role of anthropological argument. At that time it was popular for theologians to speak of human existence as a "questioning" toward God. Pannenberg notes that one cannot deduce from this fact either what God is like or even that God exists. Responding to a critic, Pannenberg insists that he does not see human openness beyond the finite as "self-evident"; rather, he attempted to establish this claim through argumentation with anthropologists in his WIM, with special reference to their concept of *Weltoffenheit.* In that argumentation itself, he was not starting with the premise of a Christian view of God nor attempting to "prove" the existence of God theoretically, for "a *recognition* of the reality presupposed in man's self-transcending personal dependency comes to pass only through the *experience* of this reality itself as concrete meeting."[28] Here he was pointing to the need for the "history of religion" movement.

In the important collection of essays under the title *The Idea of God and Human Freedom*, Pannenberg treated a variety of issues related to anthropology. In "Speaking about God in the Face of Atheist Criticism" (1969), he explained:

> The basic question posed by modern atheism is this: Does man, in the exercise of his existence, assume a reality beyond himself and everything finite, sustaining him in the very act of his freedom, and alone making him free, a reality to which everything that is said about God refers? Or does the freedom of man exclude the existence of God, so that with Nietzsche, Nicolai, Hartmann and Sartre we must postulate the non-existence of God, not his existence, for the sake of human freedom? This must be the central question by which modern atheism stands and falls. And a decision on this question is an indispensable basic condition, though not a completely sufficient condition in itself, for any justification of our speaking about God. This statement means that the first and fundamental choice between theology and atheism in fact lies in the understanding of man, in anthropology.[29]

Because of the atheist anthropologizing of the idea of God, the field in which theology must battle atheism is not the terrain of atheist theories, but that of anthropology, wherein lie their basic assumptions. In 1971, Pannenberg insisted that this means "theological anthropology nowadays has the status of a form of fundamental

---

28. W. Pannenberg, "Response to the Discussion," in *Theology as History*, ed. Robinson and Cobb (New York: Harper and Row, 1967), p. 225.

29. W. Pannenberg, *The Idea of God and Human Freedom*, trans. R. A. Wilson (Philadelphia: Westminster Press, 1973), p. 106. German: *Gottesgedanke und menschliche Freiheit* (Göttingen: Vandenhoeck & Ruprecht, 1971). In this same article, Pannenberg makes it clear that his early treatment of the doctrine of predestination in the Middle Ages led to his realization that it resulted in an antinomy between traditional theistic conceptions of God and the possibility of real human freedom.

theology."[30] Here we can see more clearly the emergence of themes that will explicitly shape ATP. We see especially the growing sense of urgency the task has for Pannenberg. For the atheist to succeed, he or she must show that the essence of human being can be completely described without the use of religious categories. Conversely, the movement of a fundamental-theological anthropology "cannot be expected to do more than demonstrate the religious dimension" of human existence, but it can and must do that.[31]

In his 1972 *The Apostles' Creed*, Pannenberg recapitulated his conviction about the importance of anthropological argumentation for the debate with atheism, and his call for a demonstration that human existence is essentially dependent on a "sustaining infinite reality." In the context of that book, however, he was interested in making sense of Christian faith "in light of today's questions." This means moving beyond the "from below" task of fundamental-theological anthropology:

> The decision about the reality of God is made in the wider context of experience of reality in general. Here we must go beyond the limitations of mere anthropological argumentation. For the assertion of a divine reality is an assertion of its power over the world and over men. Even if, as we have seen, the idea of God itself is, in the context of modern thought, no longer deducible from knowledge of the world — if, that is to say, it has another origin as an idea — its truth still depends on the power which emanates from it to illumine and elucidate the whole of man's experience of reality. At the same time, we cannot decide once

---

30. Pannenberg, "Anthropology and the Question of God," in *The Idea of God and Human Freedom,* p. 90.

31. Pannenberg, "Anthropology and the Question of God," p. 94. "Thus a theological anthropology which is to serve as a fundamental theology must, if it is seriously to face the challenge of atheism, deal at appropriate length with the different fields of anthropological study, with their methods, results, and problems, and with the history of the problems resulting from philosophical reflection upon human subjectivity; and it must also discuss them with regard to their implications for the religious dimension of human existence" (93). This was precisely what ATP would aim to do.

and for all whether an idea of God can prove itself against experience of reality. For our experience of the world and of ourselves continually alters.[32]

Notice here that as Pannenberg engages in the "from above" movement, the systematic presentation of Christian faith as explaining reality, he holds onto the postfoundationalist valuation of both intelligibility and fallibility.

In *Spirit, Faith, and Church* (1970), Pannenberg had treated an issue that would be of continued interest in later writings. In his first contribution, he argued against the idea of the "human spirit" as fundamentally distinct from the "divine spirit." In the final section of this chapter, we will return to this theme as articulated in ST, II, but it is important to note that already here he was concerned to link the work of the Holy Spirit in the life of the Christian and the Church to the work of the Spirit of God in creation.[33] The human creature does not "have" spirit, but participates in the divine spirit, "by being elevated beyond itself in the ecstatic experience that illustrates the working of the spirit." Rather than accepting a natural/supernatural dualism, Pannenberg believes that the idea of spirit "allows us to do justice to the transcendence of God and at the same time to explain his immanence in his creation."[34] This shows clearly his interest in the explanatory power of what he would later call the "true infinite."

Another theme in his anthropological thought is the common

32. W. Pannenberg, *The Apostles' Creed: In Light of Today's Questions,* trans. Margaret Kohl (Philadelphia: Westminster Press, 1972), p. 25. German: *Das Glaubensbekenntnis* (Hamburg, 1972).

33. We can see an emphasis on this topic in some of Pannenberg's early sermons; e.g., "Gott ist Geist," in *Gegenwart Gottes: Predigten* (München: Claudius, 1973): 100-108. The importance of the concept of "spirit" for the dialogue with natural science is clear in Pannenberg's 1972 essay "The Doctrine of the Spirit and the Task of a Theology of Nature" and his 1971 "Spirit and Energy," both reprinted in W. Pannenberg, *Toward a Theology of Nature: Essays on Science and Faith* (Louisville: Westminster/John Knox, 1993). The dialogue with natural science for Pannenberg is always connected to anthropological issues as well.

34. W. Pannenberg, *Spirit, Faith and Church* (Philadelphia: Westminster Press, 1970), p. 21.

destiny of all humankind as inseparable from the destiny of the individual. In "The Future and the Unity of Mankind" (1972), he argued that "a final resolution of the antagonism between the individual and society clearly remains an eschatological ideal . . . it finds expression in the uniting of the kingdom of God and the resurrection of the dead."[35] This is also related to ecumenical concerns and the unity of the church, as Pannenberg argues in "The Unity of the Church and the Unity of Mankind,"[36] concerns that drive ST, III, as we saw above in relation to the third postfoundationalist couplet.

In a 1973 article, Pannenberg argued against the traditional tendency that allows for soteriological interests to determine christology, calling instead for "The Christological Foundation of Christian Anthropology." He believes that the specific history of the one man Jesus of Nazareth ought to illuminate and critique general anthropological views. That is, christology itself "ought to have a constitutive value for general anthropology." But the history of Jesus contributes not by offering a radically new starting point, but "by *including within itself and thus transforming* the already existing reality of man and his historical question about himself."[37] Here again we see Pannenberg describing the dynamic of the "from above" movement sublating a "from below" movement.

This article outlines several material issues that will become central ten years later in ATP, including Herder's assertion that the image of God refers to a destiny and not an original state. The issue of human "freedom," which goes back at least to his dissertation on the doctrine of predestination in Duns Scotus,[38] is also raised in a new way here, and indicates the outline of future essays that would focus more on this theme. However, this article also in-

35. Pannenberg, *Ethics*, p. 187.

36. Reprinted in *The Church*, trans. Keith Crim (Philadelphia: Westminster, 1983). Original German essay, 1973, reprinted in *Ethik und Ekklesiologie* (Göttingen: Vandenhoeck & Ruprecht, 1977).

37. W. Pannenberg, "The Christological Foundation of Christian Anthropology," in *Humanism and Christianity* (Concilium, vol. 86), ed. Claude Geffré (New York: Herder and Herder, 1973), p. 87. Emphasis added.

38. W. Pannenberg, *Die Prädestinationslehre des Duns Scotus in Zusammenhang der scholastischen Lehrentwicklung* (Göttingen: Vandenhoeck & Ruprecht, 1954).

troduces several "from above" themes; e.g., Christians see Jesus as the "new man" (life-giving spirit) but in such a way that he is related to the "first man" (living being). The Christian answer to the inherent longing of the "exocentric" person is defined by Jesus' existence in relation to the Father. In both movements, we see the *sub ratione Dei* theme.

> Christians are, however, bound to ask why man's being constituted in relation to God and why he is characterized by being religious are so neglected by modern non-Christian anthropology. They are, however, also bound to recognize that even this form of anthropology still deals *de facto* with man whose being is constituted in relation to God.[39]

Also in 1973, in a dialogue with Kosseleck and others on whether the unity of history requires a "subject," Pannenberg sets out some of the same claims that will figure so prominently in ATP. He argued that human "action" (Handeln) cannot be the basis for the unity of history, because the actions of finite subjects cannot be explained by some timeless abstract structure of human nature. Christian anthropology recognizes that human nature includes a determination to overcome its limitations by actions, but takes this partial truth up into *(aufgehoben)* the claim that humans achieve their destiny not by action, but by being elevated beyond themselves. Thus the subjectivity of God not only explains the unity of history, but also serves as the "ground of possibility for human freedom *(Ermöglichungsgrund menschlicher Freiheit)*."[40]

The same year, Pannenberg published his *Theology and the Philosophy of Science;* this book showed the way philosophy of religion and history of religion are linked by anthropology in a "theology of religion." We explored the structure of this link in Chapter Three, and are now tracing the development of his use of anthropology in order

---

39. Pannenberg, "The Christological Foundation," p. 93.

40. W. Pannenberg, "Erfordert die Einheit der Geschichte ein Subjekt?" in *Geschichte — Ereignis und Erzählung* (Poetik und Hermeneutik, V), ed. R. Koselleck and W. D. Stempel (Munich: Wilhelm Fink Verlag, 1973), p. 489.

to gain a better understanding of the reciprocity that constitutes this link.

In 1974, Pannenberg coedited a book on the "fundamentals" *(Grundlagen)* of theology, which included a transcript of a dialogue between the contributors. Pannenberg's main concern is to argue for the fact that statements about God (theological assertions) are claims to truth, and must be susceptible to some form of (provisional) confirmation. The important thing for our present survey is Pannenberg's emphasis here on the "Religionsthematik" as central to the task of fundamental theology.[41] Later, the arguments of ATP will aim to show that a religious theme is essential to a description of human nature.

In 1975, Pannenberg published a series of essays under the title *Faith and Reality*. The fourth essay, "Man — The Image of God?", continued his emphasis on the essentially future-oriented religious nature of human beings.

> The destiny of man is to be truly himself in openness to the divine mystery of his life by freely giving himself to the world and to his fellow men; his destiny is his still-unachieved future which is only from God. . . . In history, God and man are always manifested together, but man is so in the light of his experience of God. . . . Consequently the religious theme cannot simply be brushed aside when man is in question.[42]

In 1976, Pannenberg published "Person und Subjekt," an article that set out several of the key theses that would play a central role in ATP. He traced the concept of "person" beginning with Greek thought, showing the Christian roots of the modern concept of subject and their relation to the trinitarian concept of persons. Explaining the difference between "subject" and "hypostasis" is an issue of continuing importance for theology, with serious anthropo-

---

41. W. Pannenberg, G. Sauter, S. M. Daecke, and H. N. Janowski, *Grundlagen der Theologie — Ein Diskurs* (Stuttgart: Kohlhammer, 1974), pp. 68-69.

42. W. Pannenberg, *Faith and Reality*, trans. John Maxwell (Philadelphia: Westminster, 1977), p. 49. German: *Glaube und Wirklichkeit: Kleine Beiträge zum christlichen Denken* (Munich: Chr. Kaiser, 1975).

logical implications. Pannenberg believes that the Christian idea of Trinity, if it overcomes the traditional view of person and subject as synonymous, can help solve some of the problems in anthropological theory.

In this context, he introduces a thesis that will become the linchpin for his argument in chapter 5 of ATP: "Person is the presence of the self in the moment of the ego, in the claim laid upon the ego by our true self and in the anticipatory consciousness of our identity."[43] He sees this reversal in the conventional relation of I and Self as the basis for a new determination of the concept of person. While Hegel's solution involved "die *Aufhebung* der Substanz in das Subjekt," which became a foundational thought in his system, Pannenberg on the other hand argues: "so ist Subjectivität aufgehoben in das Personsein, als ein Moment der Personalität."[44]

This new conception of "person" has at least four implications, Pannenberg explains. (1) It explains the value or dignity of human personhood as grounded in the mystery of their unfinished history, because they are on the way to their destiny. (2) It resolves some of the problems of "dialogical personalism" in terms of the determination of the individual in relation to the Thou. (3) It clarifies the trinitarian personhood of God, so that the personhood of each is mediated through the others, without the separation of I and self. (4) It also clarifies christological conceptual problems, so that the identity of the man Jesus Christ is mediated through his relation to the Father.

The issues of "foundationalism" and rationality come to mind again when we hear him arguing that christology and the doctrine of Trinity should become the "starting point" *(Ausgangspunkt)* for a clear consideration of human personality. We have seen that while Pannenberg can "start" either with the fundamental or with the systematic movement, they are always already mutually conditioned. Throughout this discussion is the underlying theme that

43. "Person ist die Gegenwart des Selbst im Augenblick des Ich, in der Beanspruchung unseres Ich durch unser wahrhaftes Selbst und im vorwegnehmen den Bewußtsein unserer Identität" (*Grundfragen, II*, 92). This sentence is repeated in *Anthropologie in theologischer Perspektive*, p. 233. English: ATP, 240.

44. *Grundfragen, II*, p. 94.

human essence cannot be fully explained without reference to the relation to God. His Grundprinzip is clearly operative in the final sentence of his 1977 article "Die Subjectivität Gottes und die Trinitätslehre," where he argues that only if we understand the subjectivity of God in terms of the relations of the three persons in their glorifying of one another will it be possible to conceptualize God as "the true infinite, at the same time immanent and transcendent to the world."[45]

In the 1977 article "Gottebenbildlichkeit und Bildung des Menschen," Pannenberg revisits several earlier issues, but pays special attention to the relation between the German mystical tradition (Eckhart) and the "formation" of persons as it is related to the mediating role of the church as persons are conformed to the image of Christ.[46] In the 1978 article "Die Auferstehung Jesu und die Zukunft des Menschen,"[47] Pannenberg exposits many of the biblical texts relevant to these issues, especially the image of God, the "new man" in Christ. He discusses the failure of secular treatments of "freedom," or the hope for a new "man-type" produced by society, to fulfill the longings of humans for the future. His insistence that the destiny of human beings is not *external* to the creatureliness of human nature is also emphasized here. These themes are filled out, as we will see below, in ATP and ST.

In *Human Nature, Election and History* (1977), we see the development of familiar issues. The first two essays focus on the Christian emphasis on the "eternal value" of the individual, and the social responsibility that follows from this: "The responsibility of the Christian is, in short, to assist other persons (as opportunity permits) in their realization of their human destiny, in their becoming human beings in the full sense of existing in the image of God."[48] The sec-

---

45. ". . . nur so ist Gott der wahrhaft Unendliche, der Welt zugleich immanent und ihr transzendent." Reprinted in *Grundfragen, II,* p. 111.

46. *Grundfragen, II,* pp. 207ff.

47. *Grundfragen, II,* 104-87. This article is translated by M. B. Jackson as "The Resurrection of Jesus and the Future of Mankind," in *The Cumberland Seminarian* 19 (1981): 41-51.

48. W. Pannenberg, *Human Nature, Election, and History* (Philadelphia: Westminster, 1977), p. 35. These essays were lectures originally presented in English univer-

ond part of the book introduces his interpretation of the doctrine of election as related to the eschatological fulfillment of all humanity in the consummation of history, anticipating the presentation of ST, III.

In 1983 Pannenberg published *Christian Spirituality*, which had been lectures from 1977. The most important essay for our purposes is the final one, "A Search for the Authentic Self,"[49] which is an argument that the Christian idea of salvation is a better answer to human longing than the Buddhist idea. He mentions Luther's idea of *extra se in Christo*, which will become important in later writings.

> ... the identity of the human person, the authentic self, is realized outside ourselves in Christ, as Luther said, and this perspective allows Christian teaching to include also the human experience of nonidentity and inauthenticity in its interpretation of the human predicament. Thus it can do justice to the history of the individual in search of the true self, which nevertheless is already present in some way in this same process. (109)

Luther's concept of Christian existence "outside the self in Christ" is explicated in ATP in connection with "exocentricity" and in ST as giving new meaning to the doctrine of *imago Dei*.

In the same year (1983), Pannenberg published the massive *Anthropologie in theologischer Perspektive*. Because this book will be the subject of careful summary and analysis below, we will limit ourselves here to a review of its general structure and basic arguments. In the Introduction to ATP, Pannenberg mentions four general anthropological disciplines, viz., biology, psychology, sociology, and history. This list moves from the most abstract to the most concrete description of human nature. It seems plausible to see the three

---

sities and then published in German the following year as *Die Bestimmung des Menschen* (Göttingen: Vandenhoeck & Ruprecht, 1978).

49. W. Pannenberg, *Christian Spirituality* (Philadelphia: Westminster Press, 1983). Cf. his Buddhist dialogue in "Auf der Suche nach dem wahren Selbst. Anthropologie als Ort der Begenung zwischen christlichem und buddhistischem Denken," in A. Bsteh, ed., *Erlösung in Christentum und Buddhismus* (Mödling, 1982), pp. 128-46.

main parts of the book as representing three movements "between" these disciplines: Part I, "The Person in Nature,"[50] moves from biology to psychology; Part II, "The Human Person as a Social Being," connects psychology to sociology; and Part III, "The Shared World," goes from sociology to history.

The movement from abstract to concrete is important. Pannenberg notes that even the most concrete presentation of humans and history in chapter 9 will still involve abstraction (ATP, 22; cf. 486), and reminds us along the way (e.g., 158) that the method of ATP involves an "abstract" form of reflection on human existence. This is important because it reminds us that in ATP, Pannenberg is doing what he proposed in TPS that a "philosophy of religion" movement ought to do; viz., treat the phenomenon abstractly and conceptually, moving toward more concrete description. The latter then "must be subsumed *(aufgeheben)* in the complexity of the historical reality of religions" (TPS, 419). The ST will represent Pannenberg's attempt to accomplish the "history of religions" movement (as a concrete history of the transmission of the tradition of the Christian religion and a provisional confirmation of its truth), but only within the context of his broader "theology of religion."

The themes treated in ATP are similar to his earlier WIM, although the analysis is much more exhaustive. We find, too, the development of themes introduced in several of his earlier essays. The concept of "identity formation" plays a central role. Not only is "the problem of identity" the title of the central chapter (5), but the entire book can be seen as a demonstration of the thesis that human identity or personhood cannot be explained by the concept of action (which is dominant in non-theological anthropology), but requires the presence of the totality of meaning in each moment of human life as constitutive of the person's destiny. This means that humans only anticipate their true identity, and are constituted by their openness to and beyond the world, which implies that human existence contains within itself the religious thematic of the relation

---

50. The German title for this first part is "Der Mensch in der Natur und die Natur des Menschen." The English translation does not capture the emphasis of this latter phrase, which raises the important question of human nature.

to the infinite. This may be unthematically experienced in biological life, illustrated in the phenomenon of basic trust, the sharing of meaning in social institutions, etc. However, further reflection on these leads us to the thought of the "true infinite."

Throughout the book Pannenberg is concerned to thematize the religious dimension of all human phenomena, demonstrating "the fact that the question of God goes together with the question of human beings about themselves" (ATP, 73). We will see this expressed in his ST as a "mutual conditioning" of the idea of God and human self-understanding. The point here is that ATP represents a crucial step in Pannenberg's use of anthropology in his overall theological method. It is the "from below" move, which always has the "from above" move in sight, but limits itself to demonstrating the way in which anthropological data point to religious themes and call for theological explanation. For Pannenberg, the latter will require a trinitarian understanding of God, which illuminates human nature as the destiny of persons for participation in the fellowship of the Son with the Father by the Spirit.[51]

In a 1984 article, "Constructive and Critical Functions of Christian Eschatology," Pannenberg outlined the relation between eschatology and anthropology. Here he followed Rahner, according to whom "eschatology repeats the statements of theological anthropology on human nature, though in a modified way, in the mode of consummation."[52] Pannenberg suggests, however, that setting up an opposition between an anthropological approach and the "strictly theological" argument is too rigid and misleading. Instead he insists that the two approaches "complement" each other because

---

51. In the years immediately following ATP, Pannenberg contributed articles to journals in order to develop more thoroughly particular aspects of his analysis. E.g., on the relation between "personality" and "subjectivity," see "Die Theologie und die neue Frage nach der Subjektivität," *Stimmen der Zeit* 202 (1984): 805-16. On the importance of anthropology in the early discussion between Platonic thought and Christian theology, see "Christentum und Platonismus," *Zeitschrift für Kirchengeschichte* 96, no. 2 (1985): 147-61.

52. W. Pannenberg, "Constructive and Critical Functions of Christian Eschatology," *Harvard Theological Review* 77, no. 2 (1984): 121.

... the argument focusing on the concept of divine promises as basis of eschatological hope requires a positive relation of their content to human nature, while the arguments from the implications of human existence remain in need of an agency that could provide what they postulate. ... The *interaction of the divine and the anthropological element* in the foundation of eschatological hope will prove its relevance when we now turn to the functions of eschatological thought in human self-understanding.[53]

This quote supports our thesis that Pannenberg sees the two movements "from above" and "from below" as mutually conditioned. Unlike the foundationalist, neither side is self-justifying; unlike the nonfoundationalist, beliefs in the web are susceptible to transcommunal criteria for judging explanations of reality.

In the wake of the debate caused by ATP, Pannenberg edited *Sind wir von Natur aus religiös?* (the title itself summarizing the concern of ATP). This book offers many insights into Pannenberg's attitude toward the methodological use of anthropology in "fundamental" theology and its relation to "systematic" theology, which we will examine synchronically in the next section. He begins his first contribution by asserting that one of the defining characteristics of humans that sets them apart from animals is that they "have religion."[54] This fact does not "prove" that God exists, but it can show that humans are by nature religious. Religion is a necessary and essential dimension of human life (23).

Pannenberg argues that the situation for theology since the nineteenth century has been one in which anthropology has fundamental significance. This means that if theologians want their theological assertions to claim general validity, rather than express the thoughts of subjective faith, they must argue for this validity on the

---

53. Pannenberg, "Constructive and Critical Functions of Christian Eschatology," 123. Emphasis added. The inherent connection between religion and the general human longing for meaning is spelled out in Pannenberg, "Meaning, Religion, and the Question of God," in *Knowing Religiously,* ed. Leroy S. Rouner (Notre Dame: University of Notre Dame Press, 1985), pp. 157f.

54. W. Pannenberg, *Sind Wir von Natur aus Religiös?* (Düsseldorf: Patmos, 1986), p. 9.

basis of anthropology (88). He describes the *working hypothesis* of the ATP book; in the investigation of the anthropological sciences into human reality, the religious dimension has been pushed away or allowed to fade away from the analysis. The task of ATP was to ask: "in how far can this dimension be restored?"[55] He does not think the discussion is now over; it is just beginning. However, he will feel successful if his book has awakened the public consciousness of the problem.

He admits that the question whether humans are by nature religious is contestable; he does not take it to be obvious or self-evident (93). However, the Christian theologian may argue *for* this claim. He admits, too, that he begins with a subjective interest in the religious thematic, but insists that he does not begin his *argument* with unquestioned premises that derive from this interest. The argument must tackle the anthropological data, including the question and contestability of what presents itself in the phenomenon. In response to a common criticism, Pannenberg points out that his argument is not carried out as though the concerns of dogmatic anthropology did not exist. On the contrary, it shows how these data can be placed into explicit relation with the assertions of dogmatic anthropology; Pannenberg did this especially with the doctrines of image of God and sin. *Imago Dei* is brought into dialogue with the anthropological concept of exocentricity, and sin with the concept of centrality. Thus, anthropological themes are not unimportant to theology, although the descriptions of the human sciences are taken only as approximations, taken up in theological perspective into a discussion of the relation of humans to God (103).

In response to O. Pesch's question why he did not treat the doctrines of justification and salvation in the ATP book, Pannenberg explains that these themes break out of the limits of simple anthropology; this is why he limited himself primarily to image of God and sin, which are easily connected. To discuss salvation requires a christological foundation, and should be treated in relation to the doctrines of Trinity, reconciliation, church, and eschatology; that is

---

55. *Sind Wir,* 92, my translation.

"within a total presentation of Christian dogmatics *sub ratione Dei.*"[56]

Pannenberg states that he wrote ATP with Hegel's "Phenomenology of Spirit" incessantly before his eyes.[57] It is interesting to note the organization of the book, which has three parts with three chapters each, reminiscent of Hegel. Like Hegel, Pannenberg thinks that anthropology has fundamental philosophical significance. However, the whole argument of ATP involves an implicit critique of the course of Hegel's thought, for the latter fails to solve the problem of human "identity." Hegel saw "spirit" as the actualization of self-consciousness, but Pannenberg sees it as the elevation of a human being above his or her ego.[58]

Pesch had accused Pannenberg of surrendering theology to anthropology with his "fundamental theological" method. Pannenberg insists that the theologian can appropriate the findings of the human sciences without surrendering to their reductionistic method, which allows the religious thematic to fade from view; theology reinterprets the findings of anthropology (146). Pannenberg gladly admits that the "theological perspective" he brings to ATP includes a sensitivity to the issue of salvation and justification by grace. He recognizes the danger of projecting his theological assumptions into his reading of the phenomena. It is precisely because of this danger that he tried to argue in ATP, so far as possible, on the soil of anthropological *(humanwissenschaftlichen)* analysis, making reference to dogmatic themes only at the margins (164).

He concludes the book with a concise statement of his under-

56. ". . . im Zusammenhang einer Gesamtdarstellung der Dogmatik *sub ratione Dei* ausgefuhrt werden" (*Sind Wir,* p. 135).

57. "Dazu muß ich sage, daß mir tatsächlich bei der Abfassung meines Buches unablässing Hegels' Phänomenologie des Geistes' vor Augen gestanden hat" (*Sind Wir,* p. 141).

58. ". . . sondern eine Erhebung des Menschen über sein Ich" (*Sind Wir,* p. 142). Pannenberg addresses similar issues in dialogue with theories of the evolution of the brain in "Bewußtsein und Geist," *Zeitschrift für Theologie und Kirche* 80 (1983): 332-51. Following up on the issues of ATP, in 1984 Pannenberg severely criticized Hegel's view of "Geist" in "Der Geist und sein Anderes," in *Hegels Logik der Philosophie: Religion und Philosophie in der Theorie des absoluten Geistes,* ed. D. Henrich and R.-P. Horstmann (Stuttgart: Klett-Cotta, 1984), pp. 151-59.

standing of "fundamental-theological" method, which confirms our overall interpretation of his use of anthropology. He insists that he does not see the whole of Christian doctrine as anthropology. Rather he points to the "ironic element" *(ironische Moment)* in the designation of anthropology as fundamental-theology, for it certainly does *not* form the "Fundament" of theology; only *methodologically* is anthropology fundamental. The "Fundament" is God and God's revelation in Jesus Christ (165). Pannenberg insists that his occupation with anthropology has always had the intention of taking up *(aufzuhoben)* its fundamental function into the development of a systematic theology.[59]

Here we have one of the clearest statements of Pannenberg's view of the inherent relation between the two moves. It does involve "Aufhebung," but note the quality of the relationship: in line with his metaphysical views, Pannenberg is materially starting with the "from above" movement, which affirms the ontological priority of the future. This move is the "Fundament," but in such a way that it must be tested and confirmed against the "from below" movement. We will introduce a heuristic picture of this relational unity below, and analyze his theological anthropology in light of it.

In 1988, Pannenberg published *Metaphysics and the Idea of God,* which contains a chapter treating some of the issues from ATP in relation to "Self-consciousness and Subjectivity." Here he brings these concepts into explicit dialogue with metaphysical questions, with special attention on the problematic implications of trying to ground the idea of God in the concept of the "absolute subject."

> Feuerbach was right: if we begin with the thesis that self-consciousness is the "ground" and "truth" of all consciousness of objects, then every thought of an absolute ground of subjectivity must be the product of subjectivity. . . . Over against the assumption of transcendental philosophy — that there is an ego

---

59. "Meine lezte Absich bei der Beschaftigung mit der Anthropologie geht dahin, sie hinsichtlich ihrer Fundamentfunktion aufzuheben, namlich aufzuheben in das Konzept einer systematischen Theologie" *(Sind Wir,* p. 166). Pannenberg notes that he had already begun this sublation in WIM in 1962.

which as the condition of the unity of experience, precedes all experience and is conscious of itself — stands the thesis that the genesis of the ego lies within the process of experience itself. (MIG, 46-49)

The basic question is whether the subjectivity of individuals is sufficiently explained by positing their being conditioned by social interactions, or whether it requires a higher context that ascends "above the context of society" (MIG, 61). Pannenberg wants to focus on the *conditions* for the origin both of the world and the ego and their relation to the Absolute.

> The metaphysics of the Absolute that I am proposing would not merely attempt, on the grounds of subjectivity, to reconstrue the constitution of the subject through some source in the Absolute that precedes it. Instead, it would carry out the "rising above" toward the idea of the Absolute from a starting point that encompasses worldly experience, self-consciousness, and their *reciprocal mediation.* (MIG, 61-62, emphasis added)

We saw in Chapter Three how this approach is linked to the post-foundationalist idea of interpreted experience. For Pannenberg, it is still possible to do metaphysics, but "every conception of the absolute One must today prove its worth by showing itself to be not only the source and completion of the world but also the constitutive ground and highest good of subjectivity" (MIG, 62). The Christian solution, of course, is that human destiny is fellowship with the infinite trinitarian God.

Systematische Theologie was published during 1989-93 and understandably took up most of Pannenberg's attention.[60] The role of an-

---

60. In 1990, in response to some criticisms of his ATP, Pannenberg defended his use of the term "sin" *(Sünde)* in a non-dogmatic context. See Pannenberg, "Sünde, Freiheit, Identität: Eine Antwort an Thomas Pröpper," *Theologische Quartalschrift* 170 (1990): 289-98. He argued there that it is part of human nature to act always *sub ratione boni* (297), which leads to the need to clarify the relation of religious speech about God to the philosophical concept of infinity (298). For a discussion of the "anthropic principle" and the importance of the future for under-

thropology here will be discussed in conjunction with ATP in the next section. All three volumes, but especially the second, represent the "taking up" of the fundamental-theological anthropological move into the dogmatic move that aims to present the truth of Christian doctrine.

In 1996, Pannenberg published *Theologie und Philosophie*. The longest chapter is "The Turn *(Wendung)* to Anthropology," which traces the history of this turn that he has always found so important, and which shapes the basis for his belief that theology must account for anthropology in its fundamental-theological task. He focuses especially on the post-Hegelians (Feuerbach, Marx, Stirner, Kierkegaard, and Dilthey) and the new understanding of human existence after the "death of God" in Nietzsche's nihilism and Heidegger's existentialism. Of decisive importance was the emergence of "philosophical anthropology" with its emphasis on the Exzentrizität of human being, human openness to and beyond the world. He then shows how this anthropological turn was extended to the philosophy of nature in, e.g., Bergson and Whitehead. Theology today must do its work in this intellectual milieu. Philosophy and theology have a common theme in the whole of reality, although they approach the theme differently. Both, however, must deal with the pertinent anthropological criteria as they critically examine the relation between the concepts of the world as a whole and the idea of God.[61]

1997 saw the publication of *Problemgeschichte der neueren evangelischen Theologie in Deutschland*, which not surprisingly revisits the role of anthropology at several critical points in this history. His analysis involves primarily the identification of factors shaping trends in German theology. He concludes by stressing that an understanding of the recent history of theology helps us see the importance of an intimate knowledge of anthropology *(Vertrautheit mit den Wissenschaften vom Menschen)*, as well as of natural science and philosophy, in discussing the starting point and leading ideas that should guide the

standing the universe, see Pannenberg, "Breaking a Taboo: Frank Tipler's *The Physics of Immortality*," *Zygon* 30, no. 3 (June 1995): 309-14.

61. W. Pannenberg, *Theologie und Philosophie: Ihr Verhältnis im Licht ihrer gemeinsamen Geschichte* (Göttingen: Vandenhoeck & Ruprecht, 1996), p. 366.

outline of systematic theology.[62] The next section will now demonstrate how Pannenberg's own ST attempts to do this.

Synchronic Presentation of Pannenberg's Theological Anthropology

My goal here is to show how the theses, arguments, and structure of ATP anticipate and point toward the presentation of ST, which in turn takes up these arguments into a doctrinal presentation aimed at explaining the religious dimension of the anthropological phenomena. After a brief overview of some structural and material similarities, I will set out a heuristic model for picturing the reciprocity of these moves, which will then be explicitly applied to his treatment of human nature, image of God, and sin.

Pannenberg describes what a "full" theological anthropology would look like in chapter 8 of ST, II, "The Dignity and Misery of Humanity." There are two basic anthropological statements in Christian theology, viz., *imago Dei* and sin, which Pannenberg correlates to human dignity and human misery. He emphasizes that these doctrines are the presupposition of the redeeming activity of God in Jesus Christ. "Redemption" implies freedom for the redeemed, which in turn implies becoming what we are naturally intended to be. If the fellowship with God mediated by Christ is to help us achieve self-identity, then our identity must be naturally connected to a destiny for fellowship with God.

This destiny is the theme of the doctrine of the creation of humanity. "But presentation of this doctrine needs a more general anthropological basis that will ensure the connection between theological anthropology and the doctrine of creation on the one side, and christology on the other" (ST, II, 180). This quote shows how all the chapters of volume II (7-11) represent a coherent single phase of his overall argument. In this context, "general anthropological ba-

---

62. W. Pannenberg, *Problemgeschichte der neueren evangelischen Theologie in Deutschland: von Schleiermacher bis zu Barth und Tillich* (Göttingen: Vandenhoeck & Ruprecht, 1997), p. 356.

sis" refers to a third dogmatic theme, the constitution of human nature, which traditionally has dealt with the unity of body and soul, as well as the concepts of person and spirit.

These three are the traditional loci of theological anthropology, which Pannenberg treats in chapter 8 under the titles (§1) Personal Unity of Body and Soul, (§2) Human Destiny, and (§3) Sin and Original Sin. However, Pannenberg explains that these three alone do not comprise a complete theological anthropology.

> That would require more than a description of our destiny and the situation of alienation from it. A full theological anthropology would have to include as well the actualizing of this destiny, which is the theme of God's redeeming work, its appropriation to and by us, and its goal in the eschatological consummation. A full anthropology would also include not only the biological foundations of the human form of life, its nature, and its position in the world but also the social relations in which human life is lived and which help to condition individual identity in the process of socialization. (ST, II, 180-81)

Here he is referring both to the explicit arguments of ATP and to the dialogue with anthropology throughout ST. Pannenberg's development of the doctrine of creation (chapter 7), especially in his understanding of the emergence of creatures toward independence from the Creator, points to the issues of anthropology (chapter 8), as well as christology (chapters 9-11).[63] In a footnote, he adds: "Christology and eschatology then of course must be brought into anthropology, the former as a basis for being in grace, the latter as its consummation. Nor must ecclesiology be left out, for it describes the community life within which our being in grace is actually lived" (ST, II, 180). This means that in all of the remaining doctrines to be treated in ST (including volume III) anthropological themes will be present (as sublated). This reinforces his concern that redemption not be seen as something external and foreign to our creatureliness:

---

63. In ST, II, 278, he says that chapters 9-11 as well are "still in the general context of anthropology and the doctrine of creation."

It is not as if, before meeting Jesus, we had no general concepts of our nature and destiny, of God, of the Logos as the epitome of the world's order, or of our relation to God. Only through Jesus, however, do these general concepts acquire their true content. It is herein that the specific person and history of Jesus have universal relevance. (ST, II, 295)

This does not mean that everything is reduced to anthropology, but that a full presentation of Christian doctrine must include the anthropological dimension as a constitutive moment.

In our summary of ST in Chapter Three, we saw how Pannenberg explicitly sees the "fundamental" movement, which engages anthropology and religion, as being taken up into *(Aufhebung)* a theological treatment that starts with the primacy of the trinitarian God (ST, I, 128). This "taking up" continues throughout ST, and is particularly obvious in chapter 8, which is in constant dialogue with the theses and argumentation of ATP. It is interesting to note that ATP presented the themes in virtually the same order; the first three chapters of ATP are (1) "The Uniqueness of Humanity," which introduced the issue of human nature and spirit, (2) "Openness to the World and Image of God," and (3) "Centrality and Sin."

As we saw in our summary of ATP above, the issue of human "nature" goes far beyond chapter 1, and the concept of "spirit" is not finally resolved until the final chapter. In chapter 8 of ST, we find the material similarly structured. He notes that the general issue of human "nature" is not only the starting point (i.e., part 1 of the chapter), but also will form a kind of climax: "the concrete relation of human life to the life-giving Spirit of God will then be dealt with at the end of the chapter and will form a transition to christology" (180). Here he is referring to the fourth subpart of ST, II, chapter 8, (§4) "Sin, Life and Death." In precisely the fashion of ATP, we see him moving from the abstract to the concrete, although here he is arguing "systematically" for the truth of the Christian trinitarian explanation of the anthropological religious phenomena.

In the synchronic presentation that follows, the goal is to set the two movements side by side in order to illustrate how they "mutually condition" one another. This process will clarify the purpose of ATP, which has so often been misinterpreted. Some early responses to ATP criticized it for not being a specifically "Christian" anthropology. Yet a full Christian anthropology was not Pannenberg's goal; he was offering a "fundamental-theological" anthropology (ATP, 21). This has become even more clear in ST. In ATP he is making the "from below" move, while showing its relevance for the "from above" move. Pannenberg explained this in *Sind Wir von Natur aus Religios?* (1986), which unfortunately has not been translated for the English-speaking academy.

Pannenberg emphasized even then that he *rejects* the view that anthropology stands "over against theology as something different from the latter, and theology, which in turn stands over against the anthropology as something different from it, is supposed to establish contact with this very different thing" (ATP, 19). Rather, the anthropological data implicitly "contain" a theologically relevant dimension. He explicitly rejects the idea of searching for a "point of contact," insofar as such an approach assumes we are dealing with two wholly separate spheres that must somehow be connected. A model of Pannenberg's reciprocity must therefore capture the real *unity* of the movements.

Our analysis so far has shown that while Pannenberg does refer to the reciprocity as involving "Aufhebung," this term does not capture all of the nuances of the relationality, which includes a differentiated *bipolarity*, a clear *asymmetry*, and an actual relational *unity*. The picture of this relation that I find most helpful in capturing these aspects of Pannenberg's method is provided by James Loder and W. Jim Neidhardt, in their appropriation of the Möbius band as a model of what they call "asymmetric bipolar relational unity."[64] This band is the subject of a well-known drawing by M. C. Escher,

64. James E. Loder and W. Jim Neidhardt, *The Knight's Move: The Relational Logic of Spirit in Theology and Science* (Colorado Springs: Helmers and Howard, 1992). The Möbius band has been used in several other contexts by scholars concerned with interdisciplinary convergence; e.g., Douglas R. Hofstadter, *Gödel, Escher, Bach* (New York: Vintage, 1980). See also Ruth Nanda Anshen, "The Möbius Strip," in her preface to the books in the *Convergence Series,* which she edits (e.g., Noam Chomsky, *Knowledge and Language* [London: Praeger, 1986], pp. xxiiff.).

but it differs from many of his other works in that it is not an optical illusion,[65] but an actual topological space.[66]

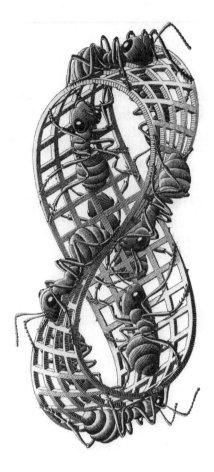

Figure 2: Escher's *Möbius Strip II (Red Ants)*, Woodcut, 1963.
© 1992 M. C. Escher/Cordon Art. Baarn, Holland

65. G. Sumner (see the first section of Chapter Four above) seems to have the Escherian "optical illusion" images in mind in his attempts to picture Pannenberg's method. In the optical illusions drawn by Escher, "two perspectives" are required, as Sumner notes. For the Möbius band, on the contrary, the unity can only be seen by grasping the whole.

66. For a history of August Möbius's discovery and its impact, see J. Fauvel et

If one traces the path of the ants, one discovers that what appears to be two sides of the band is really a single side. Yet, the differentiation of two sides within the unity is still clear. The sides and the unity are mutually constitutive. This topological space is made possible by the 180° "twist" in the band.

Loder and Neidhardt develop a complex model based on the Möbius band and highlight several aspects of the relationality. They apply the model to diverse fields and phenomena, with special attention to the works of Kierkegaard, Piaget, Einstein, and T. F. Torrance. One key dynamic they add in their appropriation of the band is the concept of "asymmetry," wherein one side of the band is conceptualized as having "marginal control" over the other side. Pointing to Escher's rendering, they refer to the "top" and the "bottom" of the band. For the sake of simplicity, I will use the following graphic to capture the essential aspects of their model that are relevant to our analysis:

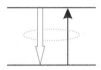

Simplified model of asymmetric bipolar relational unity

The two lines on the top and the bottom of the figure represent the bipolarity, the real differentiation involved in the relation. In the following description of the model, it is important to remember that it is intended to capture the dynamics of the image of the Möbius band, so that these two "lines" in the simplified model should not be thought of as *separate* spheres, although the moves can be distinguished. The "block" arrow (pointing downward) represents the systematic movement "from above," which implies the sublation as well as the illumination of the "lower" level. However, it also has material primacy and so provides a dominant guiding force. This captures the asymmetry of the reciprocity. The "line" ar-

al., eds., *Möbius and His Band: Mathematics and Astronomy in Nineteenth-Century Germany* (Oxford: Oxford University Press, 1993).

row (pointing upward) represents the fundamental movement "from below," which can be described as "calling for" explanation at a higher level, "pointing to" religious themes or, in Pannenberg's words, "leading to" (ATP, 21) theological concepts.[67]

The broken circle represents the twist that unifies the movements, and so aims at capturing the real relational unity of the entire theological task.[68] One can only see this unity when the whole is taken in its totality. I argue that this model is a more accurate expression of Pannenberg's methodology "between two tendencies" than the proposed images we reviewed in the first section of this chapter. Only by taking in both movements (ATP and ST) at once can we grasp the relational unity of Pannenberg's approach.[69]

If, for heuristic purposes, we think of Pannenberg's use of "from above" (systematic theology) at the top of Escher's rendering of the

---

67. Loder and Neidhardt use terms like "molds, sustains, motivates . . ." to describe the dynamics of the block arrow, and terms like "is responsive to, dependent upon, points to . . ." to describe the line arrow. They use Polanyi's distinction between tacit and focal awareness in the unity of human knowledge as a key illustration (*The Knight's Move*, 57). They also point to Gödel's Incompleteness Theorems in mathematics, which show that a complex conceptual system cannot completely explain itself but is open to and requires higher levels of explanation.

68. To illustrate this kind of relational unity, Loder and Neidhardt refer to the corpuscular and undulatory characteristics of light. Their goal is to show that this kind of relational unity is ultimately disclosed in the unity between the divine and human natures of Jesus Christ as expressed at Chalcedon; the relational nature of creaturely phenomena are only proximate manifestations which reflect the nature of the One through whom they were created.

69. Loder and Neidhardt interpret Pannenberg as emphasizing totality over relationality and therefore as failing to illustrate the kind of epistemological model they propose. Perhaps their interpretation of Pannenberg was a result of viewing only his ATP (from below) move, rather than seeing the whole. In light of ST (but already in ATP and other works), we can see that his inherently relational trinitarian hermeneutic is the answer to, and has marginal control over, the concept of universality. For Pannenberg, "spirit" is not the tension between exocentricity and centrality (as Loder and Neidhardt suggest, *The Knight's Move*, 53), but the presence of meaning in human life that transcends and makes this tension possible (ATP, 519-20). I believe that my analysis above and in previous chapters suggests that Pannenberg offers a prime example of the kind of interdisciplinary thinking Loder and Neidhardt favor.

Möbius band, and "from below" (fundamental theology) as starting from the bottom, we can imagine how the two mutually condition one another. Using Loder and Neidhardt's terminology, this would imply that the "from above" move has "asymmetric control" in the relational unity. In Pannenberg's terms, this means that "systematic theology" has material primacy, although anthropological-religious thematization of openness to the infinite in "fundamental theology" has methodological primacy, in the sense that we start there. However, this "starting there" is not *remoto deo*, for the whole thrust of all of Pannenberg's anthropological treatments over the last few decades is focused precisely on thematizing human nature under the aspect of its relation to God, *sub ratione Dei*.

In the next three subsections we will test the model by applying it to his treatment of the traditional loci of theological anthropology, where we would expect the reciprocity to be particularly clear. Note that the columns in the chart below represent the material treated in chapter 8, §§1-3 of ST, II, as well as chapters 1-3 of ATP.[70]

Trinitarian God "from above" movement	Spirit	Image of God	Sin
True Infinite "from below" movement	Personal Identity	Exocentricity	Centrality

Let me emphasize again: ST is not merely on the "top," nor is ATP only on the "bottom." The value of this model is that it insists on the real coinherence of the movements; they are inextricably intertwined and overlapping. Yet, within the unity we clearly differentiate two movements. Notice that this analysis offers the added benefit of further confirming our interpretation of his basic principle as understanding and explaining all things *sub ratione Dei*, materially played out in the trinitarian fulfillment of the "true infinite" con-

70. We will not limit ourselves to these sections, but they will be the primary focus. §4 of ST, II, chapter 8, will be examined briefly in the context of the discussion of §3.

cept. As the notes to the left of the chart suggest, each of the "from above" moves offers a trinitarian explanation of a "from below" phenomenon that illustrates the implicitly religious dimension of human existence, which expresses a relation to the true infinite.

Pannenberg has been interpreted as attempting a synthesis of Karl Barth and Ernst Troeltsch.[71] We see something like this also in his methodology. In the relation between from above and from below, we may think of Barth as privileging the former, so emphasizing "christology" that the "anthropological" side was sometimes eclipsed, while Troeltsch so elevated the anthropological dimension that his doctrine was in danger of becoming reduced to social teaching.[72] Pannenberg, on the other hand, tries to hold theology and anthropology together in a relational unity without denying the valid roles and integrity of either disciplinary endeavor.

The background question during the following synchronic exposition of these two treatments of theological anthropology will be whether Pannenberg collapses into foundationalism (on either side) or into nonfoundationalism. I believe that he does not, and that his performance in holding the two together is a good example of the aim of postfoundationalism, even if finally we may disagree with him on some material issues, and even though we may want to refigure some of his language (which carries over from his early critical rationalism). I will be focusing on the salient methodological moves (rather than aiming for exhaustive material exposition) vis-à-vis my goal of critically appropriating his method through a postfoundationalist reconfiguration.[73]

---

71. This is Buller's thesis in *The Unity of Nature and History in Pannenberg's Theology*.

72. See, for example, Barth in *Church Dogmatics*, III/2, § 43.2, especially pp. 25f., and Ernst Troeltsch in *The Social Teaching of the Christian Churches*, trans. O. Wyon (London: George Allen & Unwin, 1931). Much of the debate between conservatism and liberalism in the last two centuries might be traced to this issue.

73. In Paul Sponheim's response to ATP, "To Expand and Deepen the Provisional," in *Beginning with the End*, he hopes that theology can work on the distinction that Pannenberg has opened up: "theological argument in the ambiguous middle distance [that] can be distinguished from axiomatic proof on the one hand and from sheer authoritarian appeal on the other" (385). This sounds very much in line with "postfoundationalism," and I am arguing that this is precisely what Pannenberg is doing in ST.

Human Nature: Personal Identity and Spirit

In a pattern we will see repeated in the next subsections, Pannenberg begins his presentation in ST, II, chapter 8, §1, "Personal Unity of Body and Soul," with a survey of the historical development and exegetical background of the doctrine. Any anthropology today must account for the fact of consciousness and its link to bodily life. Modern anthropology with its emphasis on the unity of human life has rendered untenable the substance dualism of Platonic as well as Cartesian metaphysics. The Aristotelian assumptions were closer to the biblical view of the unity of human life, and Thomas Aquinas followed out these implications. However, here, too, the concept of soul as "substance" led theology astray, for the OT clearly uses the term "soul" *(nephesh)* to refer to the whole person (e.g., Gen. 2:7). Pannenberg also points to the difference between much patristic thought and the OT view of the "spirit." For the OT, spirit refers not to the intellect but to a "vital creative force."

Further, the OT does not see humans as unique in their relation to spirit; animals, too, are *nephesh hayya* (Gen. 2:19) and have the spirit of life in them (Gen. 1:20; 6:17). The OT clearly differentiates between reason and spirit. Reason, like all other functions of life, depends on the actualizing power of the Creator Spirit of God. What sets humans apart in the OT is not spirit or reason, but "the destiny of fellowship with God and the position of rule associated with closeness to God" (ST, II, 190). Although we can follow the patristics in adopting the Johannine idea of the Logos and the participation of the human *nous* as sharing in it, we must not identify *nous* and *pneuma*. We may still hold for reason a dominant role in human life, and even see in it a natural disposition for being actualized by the Spirit, but this must be understood in the relation of the *whole person* to the Spirit.

With this background Pannenberg launches into a review of material originally treated in ATP. The key themes here include imagination, feeling for life, and the constitution of personal identity. Let us summarize these briefly, referring primarily to the ATP treatments, in order to show how these phenomena of human life point to an inherently religious thematic, namely, openness to the infinite. This will illustrate the function of the fundamental "from below" movement in pointing to and calling for theological explanation. Then we will demonstrate how in ST the systematic "from above" movement takes up these concepts and explains them in light of the trinitarian God.

In his treatment of "imagination" in ATP, Pannenberg emphasizes its relation to reason and attention. He traces the philosophical use of the idea from Aristotle to Sartre, showing that the tension between particular and universal is key. This tension in the life of the imagination, "which shows itself in perceptual consciousness as the relation of objects to space . . . forms the framework for the activity of reason" (ATP, 382). Rational reflection always "already operates at every point within the tension of gestalt and field, part and whole, particular and universal" (383). Even when it is not thematized, this means that humans always have at each moment of knowledge a relation to an "ultimate comprehensive unity," the presence of an anticipated "totality." For Pannenberg, this is the presence of the infinite.

In human "feeling" (Gefühl), too, we have the presence of the whole in experience. ATP traces this concept in the philosophical and psychological literature, with special attention on thinkers who have identified the dynamic of receptivity and dependence on the "totality" within the affective life. Pannenberg notes that in "moods," whether good or bad, the whole of one's life is involved. He focuses on Schleiermacher's analysis of feeling, which he believes still best explains the immediate self-consciousness. The latter "embraces the difference between subject and object . . . so that in the consciousness of its own 'dependence' the feeling in question also gives expression to the dependence of nature in its entirety" (ATP, 247). Pannenberg critiques Schleiermacher, however, for using the transcendental idealist's concept of "self-consciousness" to describe this phenomenon, for it obscures the original symbiotic solidarity of self and world that obtains prior to the differentiation of self from world (250).

In ATP the concept of personal identity is central. Literally, it is the center of the book. The chapter on "The Problem of Identity" (5) is precisely in the middle, halfway between the treatments of biology (1) and history (9). This problem is crucial for Pannenberg: it incorporates the concerns of everything between chapters 1 and 9, holding together all the dimensions of his analysis. As we saw in our earlier summary, the overall thesis of ATP is that human identity (or personhood) cannot be explained by the concept of "action" (as most nontheological anthropologies attempt), for action presupposes the identity of the subject who acts. Thus he argues for the *historical* formation of persons, who have their identity through anticipation of their selfhood; this in turn implies the presence of meaning in human life, which Pannenberg sees as the creative activity of the Spirit. In this way, he connects the concepts of person, identity, and spirit.

> In the person the whole of the individual's life "appears" in the present. . . . The word "person" establishes a relation between the mystery — which transcends the present of the ego — of the still incomplete individual life history that is on the way to its special destiny and the present moment of the ego. Person is the presence of the self in the moment of the ego, in the claim laid upon the ego by your true self, and in the anticipatory consciousness of our identity. . . . The transcendence of selfness in relation to its social situation corresponds to the reference to God proper to basic trust, which already transcends its initial link to the mother. . . . Because selfness is ultimately grounded in the *relation to God* [emphasis added], persons can be free in the face of their social situation. . . . The person is the ego as a "face" through which the mystery of the still unfinished history of individuals on the way to themselves manifests itself. (ATP, 240-41)

In the ninth and final chapter of ATP, "Human Beings and History," the centrality of the concepts of person and identity in their relation to the "Spirit" becomes even more clear. All of the previous chapters are seen as pointing to the presence of the totality of meaning in human experience. In the last section, he explicitly says that the phenomenon of "person," in which we experience the unity of our identity, is a creation of the Spirit. "In the medium of the human soul and in the place that is the ensouled body, the presence of the spirit constitutes the identity of the person as a presence of the self in the instant of the ego" (ATP, 528). The identity of each person is constituted by the relation to the Spirit of God. This may take one of two forms, openness to fellowship with God or a closed resistance to this destiny. These of course lead to the Christian doctrines of *imago Dei* and sin, which also ramify into social relations. ATP closes with a brief allusion to the explanatory power of the biblical trinitarian God in light of these phenomena:

> The correspondence between the image of God in human beings and the Trinitarian life of God is in fact fulfilled in the human community and specifically in the community of God's kingdom, whose King-Messiah is Christ the Servant (Luke 22:28) and in which all dominion of human beings over one another will be eliminated. (ATP, 531-32)

Let us now turn to his *Systematic Theology* and examine the way in which Pannenberg's presentation of the trinitarian God takes up his fundamental-theological anthropological arguments. Here Pannenberg couches his considerations of "imagination" in the context of the influence of fifteenth-century theologian Nicholas of Cusa, who explicitly linked the imagination to a higher form of receptivity than sense impressions; viz., to "an openness that relates the infinite ground of subjectivity to finite data of the consciousness" (ST, II, 192). As the development of these ideas through Fichte and Hegel showed, the presence of the unity-in-distinction operative in imagination leads us to a further step in reflection in which we distinguish the infinite from the finite. But another step leads us beyond that distinction, for if the infinite were defined merely as a something opposed to (and therefore limited by) something else, then the infinite would be finite; instead, the infinite must also "comprehend" everything finite (195).

His treatment of "feeling for life" in the systematic movement similarly focuses on the way it points toward the true infinite, which in turn is explained by the trinitarian God.

> The feeling for life as an expression of the presence of Spirit with that of the indefinite totality of life that precedes and overarches the subject-object distinction underlies, then, the formation of

the field of consciousness within which a survey of different contents is possible . . . the presence of the infinite ground of being, the Spirit, which declares itself in the feeling for life, transcends, however, the difference of subjects. . . . (ST, II, 193-94)

In other words, only such a view of the Spirit can explain the phenomenon. However, not just the Spirit but also the Logos is involved, and together they work to actualize the destiny of persons who were created for fellowship with God.

Here the concept of "personal identity" comes to the fore. Pannenberg argues that even historically we can see the connection, for reflection on the human existence of Jesus led to the concept of "person" as referring to a special relation to God. We, too, are now seen to be "persons" in our relation to God, by whose creative Spirit we experience our identity in anticipation. We can see the divine Logos also at work in human intelligence, which is viewed as participating "in the self-distinction of the eternal Son from the Father by which he is not merely united to the Father but is also the principle of all creaturely existence in its individuality" (196). In a crucial passage, he claims that

. . . As the Son, in his self-distinction from the Father, is united with him by the Spirit in the unity of the divine life, and as, in his creative activity, he unites what is distinct by the power of the Spirit, so the differentiating activity of human reason needs the Spirit who enables it, by mediating the imagination, to name each thing in its particularity, and in all the distinction to be aware of the unity that holds together what is different. In the process human reason is not of itself filled with the Spirit. In its creatureliness it needs, like every other vital function, to be quickened by the living power of the Spirit if it is to be active, and it also needs the inspiration that lifts it above its own finitude and that in all its limitation makes it aware of the presence of truth and totality in the individual.[74]

74. ST, II, 196. See his more detailed description of the participation of human reason in the Logos in Pannenberg's discussion of methodology in Christology (ST,

In ST Pannenberg takes up his critique in ATP of the primacy of action in much non-theological anthropology (summarily presented at ATP, 520), arguing now, in the systematic movement, that "the unity and integrity of human life are constituted in another sphere that precedes all action" (ST, II, 202). This personal identity, which is rendered thematic in ATP, finds it full explanation in ST in the context of the constitutive relation of human creatures to the trinitarian God. This relation, which is mediated by the Spirit and the Logos, may take one of two structural forms; these point us to the Christian doctrines of *imago Dei* as human destiny (§2) and of sin (§3).

This subsection demonstrated that in the arguments of both ATP and ST Pannenberg moves back and forth between "from below" and "from above," illustrating the way in which he sees them as "mutually conditioning." Clearly, he wants his arguments to be adequate to our human experience, and he "starts" there; but this starting with the (interpreted) data of experience calls for and leads to theological concepts. The phenomena discussed in ATP are illuminated by the revelation of God in Jesus Christ; the latter has material primacy. I have also tried to show the underlying presence of his *sub ratione Dei* basic principle, which is at work in both ATP and ST. ATP is indeed "fundamental" but not *remoto Deo;* rather, that fundamental move emerges out of the *relation* of reciprocity between anthropological self-understandings and the Christian idea of the trinitarian God, *both* of which are held together in both ATP and ST. The same dynamic will now be explored in his presentation of the image of God.

Human Dignity: Exocentricity and Imago Dei

In Pannenberg's treatment of human dignity in ATP and ST we find another example of the reciprocity at work in his theological

II, 292f.). Pannenberg's interpretation of "Spirit" is operative in other places in ST, especially chapter 7 on creation, but also in ST, III, in connection to Christian life and the community of God (e.g., 19, 132). The emphasis on the way in which the Spirit elevates the human above his or her finitude was already present in ATP (e.g., 519, 527, 532).

method. "Human Destiny," §2 of ST, II, chapter 8, focuses on the anthropological concepts of "basic trust" and "openness to the world." Because he is examining one of the two forms that the relation to God takes in human existence, it is not surprising that the issue of personal identity also continues to play an important role. Before summarizing the findings of ATP, which attempt to show that these phenomena inherently point to the human relation to the infinite, and taking them up into an explanation of the destiny of human beings for fellowship with the trinitarian God, Pannenberg first provides a detailed exposition of the historical development of the doctrine of the image of God, and the role of the exegesis of relevant biblical passages.

The subsections in §2 are: (a) "The Image of God in Adam and Christ," (b) "The Image of God and Our First Estate," and (c) "Divine Likeness as Human Destiny." The first two subsections and part of (c) are primarily a critical review of the traditional interpretations of the relevant biblical texts and a history of the development of the doctrinal idea of the image of God. In order to understand Pannenberg's constructive proposal in (c) as well as the importance of the anthropological findings of ATP, it will be helpful to review his treatment of this history.

The main task for biblical theology here is finding a coherent link between the OT concept of the image of God as inherent in the creatureliness of Adam and the NT emphasis on Jesus Christ as the definitive image of God. Pannenberg begins with the OT material, illustrating the general agreement among exegetes that the intention of Genesis 1:26ff. is to connect the image of God to the function of dominion in the world. This does not mean exploitation, for we are representatives of God's own dominion, which will be eschatologically fulfilled. The divine likeness, however, is not the function of ruling over creation itself, but that which makes this ruling possible. What exactly *is* this likeness? Pannenberg suggests that none of the attempts in the tradition has led to a satisfactory result (ST, II, 205). He critiques the Barthian idea of the image as "co-humanity" (in its basic form of male-female relations) as exegetically untenable, and rejects the patristic identification of reason as the image of God because it fails to account for the OT references to the whole person.

Christian theology, argues Pannenberg, must start with the NT sayings about Jesus Christ as the image of God and interpret the OT passages in their light. Irenaeus attempted this, but his strong distinction between image and likeness, as well as his emphasis on the "restoration" of what Adam lost, was unable to resolve the tension between the OT likeness concept and the NT christological concept. This was due primarily to Irenaeus's insistence on the idea of a "first estate" wherein Adam and Eve were perfectly righteous and immortal. This leads to section (b) and Pannenberg's critique of the concept of the "Fall." The rejection of this traditional idea is a crucial and distinctive move in Pannenberg's theology.[75]

He insists that our general destiny as creatures is brought to fulfillment in Jesus Christ (ST, II, 210). This must be maintained without conflating the ideas of our general divine likeness and the elucidation of this likeness in Jesus Christ. Pannenberg believes that the Reformation treatment of this doctrine succumbed to this dangerous conflation. Their tendency was to "equate the statement of the first creation story in Genesis 1:26 with what Colossians says about the renewing of believers in the knowledge of God according to the image of their Creator (3:10) and with what Ephesians says about the new man as God created him in true righteousness and holiness (4:24; cf. 5:9)" (ST, II, 211). This meant that the "image" in the first parents had to include an original righteousness, and that with their fall both the image and the likeness (which the early Reformers identified) were lost.

The problems here led the Protestant Scholastics back to a distinction between the image and likeness, often using the terms "substance and accident." However, this was exegetically problematic because both the OT and the NT passages refer simply to the *nature* of those in whom the image is actualized. Pannenberg argues that there

---

75. Scholars who miss this move in Pannenberg will have difficulty understanding his anthropology. Brian Walsh, e.g., in "A Critical Review of Pannenberg's *Anthropology in Theological Perspective," Christian Scholar's Review* 15, no. 3 (1986): 258, worries that Pannenberg has made "fallenness constitutive to creatureliness." Since for Pannenberg humans are not "fallen," because there was no "fall," how could fallenness be constitutive? Pannenberg makes this point central in ST, II, but it was already clear in ATP (e.g., 137).

is no biblical basis for the older dogmatic idea of a paradisaic perfection, whether in the form of perfect knowledge or perfect holiness (ST, II, 212-13). In fact, even the idea of a loss of the divine image through a "fall" is not rooted in the biblical account. Genesis 5:1ff. repeats Genesis 1:26, implying that Adam's descendants still have the image, and the prohibition against murdering other humans (Gen. 9:6) is based on the fact that each individual has a divine likeness.

This leads Pannenberg to his own attempt to reconcile "the ongoing reality of creation in the divine image to our interpretation of the Pauline thesis that not we as such but only Jesus Christ is the image of God, and that all others need to be renewed after this image in their relation to God" (215). First he points to the fact that Genesis says not simply that we *are* the image of God but that we are created *according to* the image of God. This suggests that we are the copy of an original, which implies likeness. The copy can only represent the original if it is "like" it; yet, this likeness may be one of degrees. Humans are according to God's image, in varying degrees, but only in Jesus "did the image of God appear with full clarity" (216). This allows Pannenberg to see our original creatureliness as implicitly related to our destiny of full actualization of the image of God. He critically appropriates J. G. Herder's conception of the image as a direction, a disposition or goal, i.e., as a "destiny."

At this point in the chapter he is almost ready to "take up" his fundamental argument from ATP (and elsewhere) into a presentation of the explanatory power of the trinitarian conception of God. His thesis is that our "destiny of fellowship with God" forms an indestructible basis for an understanding of morality (ST, II, 224) that avoids the disintegrating trends toward ethical autonomy in the Enlightenment. For this thesis to hold, two things are required:

> First, that religion is not dispensable in the search for a proper understanding of human reality, that it is not a relic of a past age, but that it is constitutive of our being as humans. Second . . . that there are sufficient reasons for regarding the God of the Bible as the definitive revelation of the reality of God that is otherwise hidden in the unsearchable depths of the world and of human life. (ST, II, 225)

Fulfilling the first requirement was the task of ATP, and the second requirement can be seen as the task of the whole of ST, I-III. His specific objective in this context is to show the inherent connection between our natural openness to the world and the fulfillment of that openness in our destiny of fellowship with the trinitarian God. To illustrate this mutual conditioning, let us first review his presentation of the concepts of "basic trust" and "openness to the world" in ATP.

In ATP, Herder plays a more central role, because there the anthropological phenomena are the focus. Chapter 2 of ATP contains the major treatment of *imago Dei*, although the concept runs like a thread throughout the other chapters, especially in the emphasis on "identity" in chapters 5 and 9. Pannenberg sees Herder as the eighteenth-century predecessor of the concept of "exocentricity," which has dominated twentieth-century philosophical anthropology. Here again we find a case in which doctrinal concerns historically led to the development of explanatory constructs for understanding anthropological reality. As we saw above in the diachronic survey, the idea of "openness to the world" was prevalent in Pannenberg's earlier writings, especially his 1962 WIM.[76]

Pannenberg describes "exocentricity" as a tensional relation grounded in our biological nature, whose effects can be seen to point ultimately to the "religious thematic" of human life.

> . . . The opposition between the striving for pleasure and the objectivity of the human relation to the world . . . may now be described as a conflict between basic factors in the structure of human existence, as an expression of a tension between the centralized organization of human beings and their exocentricity. . . . In its exocentric self-transcendence the ego is originally present to what is other than its body, but it is in knowing the otherness of the other, which is identical with its body, as distinct from all else, that it knows itself to be distinct from it-

---

76. In *The Idea of God and Human Freedom*, he described this idea of openness as "the outer aspect of the freedom, the inner aspect of which is the theme of the problems of subjectivity" (93).

self. . . . This exocentric self-transcendence, this being present to what is other than the self . . . constitutes the ego or person. At the same time, however, the ego, in its identity with "itself," also places itself over against the other. (ATP, 84-85)

What is peculiar to human beings is the fact that their identity may be clarified "in terms of the twofold reference of human self-consciousness that corresponds to the tension between centrality and exocentricity."[77] Humans are present to what is other than themselves *as other;* they find their center "outside" themselves but at the same time their awareness of all that is other is oriented (through the functioning of the ego) toward the center of the self. Humans are constituted by a drivenness to anchor their being in something beyond themselves, ultimately in something beyond the grasp of finite perishability. This means that humans are not "finished"; rather, they are on their way to becoming themselves. Pannenberg shows that this emphasis in Herder was argued more rigorously in the twentieth century by thinkers like Scheler, Gehlen, and Plessner.

Pannenberg argues that this openness to the world "reaches beyond the totality of all given and possible objects of perception, that is, beyond the world" (ATP, 68). This becomes clear only upon reflection, but at this level of reflection it also becomes clear that this reaching out implies a relating exocentrically to a *reality* prior to the individual perception (69). This relation to the infinite is never direct or unmediated; rather, it is always mediated through the experience of finite reality, and especially through the social relations that shape their identity (70).

A psychological phenomenon that points to this constitutive aspect of human being is "basic trust," which Pannenberg deals with briefly in chapter 2 of ATP, but at length in chapter 5 on the problem of identity. The appropriation of Erik Erikson's use of this

---

77. ATP, 105. For a helpful discussion of Pannenberg's concept of "openness to the future" in comparison to the concepts of "openness" in Heidegger, Whitehead, and Rahner, see J. Ipe, "The Hermeneutics of Human Openness" (Ph.D. diss., Lutheran Theological School at Chicago, 1988), pp. 59ff.

phrase "basic trust" is in fact crucial to the concluding pages of chapter 5 (ATP, 226ff.), which leads up to his radically new definition of "person" that we reviewed above. Erikson showed the importance of the formation of basic trust in the child as a necessary prerequisite for differentiation between the self and the world, and the importance of a continued basic trust for the development of a healthy personality. This is not referring to a naïve trust, but to an original response to the symbiotic whole of the infant's experience. For Pannenberg, "trust is directed to a reality that transcends the self and in which the self has its ground" (229). This trust typically manifests itself in relation to the mother or primary caregiver, but it is directed toward an agency that transcends the limitations of the mother. In other words, basic trust is "antecedently a religious phenomenon . . . God is the true object of basic trust even in its beginnings" (231), although this does not become thematic until later life, if at all.

In an important critique of Hans Küng, we find a distinction offered by Pannenberg that bears on our appropriation of his method for the postfoundationalist task of theology. Like Küng, Pannenberg sees an objective link between the idea of God and basic trust. However, his view of the link, unlike that of Küng, "does not involve a 'foundation,' whether for basic trust itself or for the reality to which the basic trust is first of all directed" (ATP, 233). Rather, Pannenberg sees the link as an orientation of the trust to its object. In a footnote, he explicitly rejects the search for an "absolute justification," which would provide a foundation for the reality of God, as Küng seems to do. For Pannenberg, "basic trust" does not prove the reality of God, but it does show that the "theme" of God is inseparable from the living of human life because of "the *implications* of this fundamental phenomenon in human behavior" (233).

For Pannenberg, the constitutive exocentricity of human life that is manifested in "basic trust" *points to* the religious theme of human life, i.e., an inherent openness to the infinite. The analysis in ATP thematizes these phenomena *sub ratione Dei*, showing how they imply that human existence is essentially oriented toward that which is beyond itself, and beyond the world. "The transcendence of selfness in relation to its social situation corresponds to the reference to God proper to basic trust . . . because selfness is ultimately grounded in the relation to God, persons can be free in the face of their social situation" (241).

Let us now turn again to his *Systematic Theology* and examine the way in which Pannenberg takes up these anthropological arguments into a (provisional) presentation of the truth of the Christian doctrine of the trinitarian God. The key move here is an "eschatological turn" to the interpretation of the image as fellowship with God that was developed in the Jewish wisdom literature. The latter insisted that the idea of "image" must have its basis in a similarity to God's eternal being. This literature found the link in the glory of Adam. In the NT, however, Paul links our sharing in God's wisdom and righteousness to the revelation of the image of God in Jesus Christ (2 Cor. 4:4). This means that the image "is reinterpreted as our final destiny which is manifested already in Jesus Christ and in which believers share already through the power of the Spirit, who is already effecting the eschatological reality of the new man in them" (ST, II, 220).

For Pannenberg, the Christian doctrine of *imago Dei* claims that the exocentric destiny of human beings is fellowship with God, a destiny revealed in Jesus Christ but already unthematically present in our natural creaturely openness beyond the world. In this context he explicitly critiques Barth, whom he characterizes as describing fellowship with God "as a purpose for us creatures that is external to our essential nature" (ST, II, 226). Already in ATP, he had identified this concern, showing the contrast between Barth and Herder. For Herder, humans are involved in the question of their destination, so

> it is not possible that this destination, though grounded in the divine creative intention, should remain purely external to them; rather, their being must be understood as constituted by the divine creative intention. Otherwise the intention would remain ineffectual and would therefore not be understood as a true intention of God in his creative activity. . . . In Barth's theology the externality of God's creative intention in relation to "the phenomenon of the human" prevents the divine creative intention from showing itself, to the same extent as in Herder, as determining the

entire range of natural human dispositions and existential conditions and thus as an *effective* creative action. (ATP, 59-60)

Pannenberg believes that Barth's emphasis on the concealment of this human determination implies that our creaturely reality is not of itself oriented to God and to being with God. He argues that Barth's use of co-humanity as the parable of the *imago Dei* renders the original act of Creation impotent in "setting this work in motion toward the appointed goal."[78] Pannenberg attempts to avoid this problem of externality by systematically linking his description of constitutive anthropological relationality as our *exocentric nature* to the corresponding doctrine of the image of God as *exocentric destiny*. This is consistent with his earlier emphasis on the "correspondence between the image of God in human beings and the Trinitarian life of God" (ATP, 531).

Pannenberg reminds us of his treatment (in ATP) of an "indefinite trust that opens up the horizon of world experience and intersubjectivity" (ST, II, 228). Here he connects basic trust to our "restless thrust toward overcoming the infinite." We are unable to accept our finitude; we find ourselves limited but we are constitutionally open to that which is beyond the finite, even if this only becomes thematic in explicitly religious forms of life. Yet this life is always ambivalent because we are tempted to take this destiny of ours into our own hands, to achieve it through human action, perhaps by participation in the cultus.

At this point in ST, Pannenberg tries to show how the trinitarian

---

78. ST, II, 227. Cf. Barth's *Church Dogmatics*, III/2, 321. Pannenberg's critique of Barth seems right on this point, and may be buttressed by the following observations. In CD, III/1, Barth argued that the *humanum*, "and therefore the true creaturely image of God," is the principle of differentiation and relationship (186). But at the end of §45.2 (III/2, 276), he says that "there are two determinations of man which do not belong at all to his creatureliness and therefore to his nature." These are humanity's determination by the inconceivable acts of sin and mercy. For Barth, the basic form of humanity, the image of God, the *humanum*, is not lost after the fall (III/2, 324); it is "unbroken by sin" (III/2, 43). These statements certainly imply an "image of God" that is somehow ontologically quarantined from current human existence. That is, "sin and mercy" are things that happen externally to who we *really* are.

understanding of God can explain this phenomenon. We can only glorify God by accepting ourselves as creatures, i.e., by differentiating ourselves and everything finite from God, thus honoring his deity. However, we cannot do this by our own choice or on the basis of our own action, because our ability to distinguish ourselves from God (or other finite things) is only possible "where we are already lifted above ourselves by the Spirit of God" (230). The Spirit elevates us above our finitude (without annihilating or absorbing it) so that we can participate in the fellowship of the Son with the Father.

> Only by accepting our finitude as God-given do we attain to the fellowship with God that is implied in our destiny of divine likeness. In other words, we must be fashioned into the image of the Son, of his self-distinction from the Father. . . . In the Son the image is achieved in the sense of full likeness, not because God made himself the same or similar, but because the Son distinguished himself from the Father and the Father from himself in order to reveal the Father as the one God. In this way the Son is so in accord with the being of God as Father that only in relation to him is the Father eternally Father and God. Only to the degree that the self-distinction of the Son from the Father takes human form in the human distinction from God do we find a person who corresponds to God, who as the image of God is destined for fellowship with him. (ST, II, 230-31)

In ST we find the same human phenomenon explored *sub ratione Dei,* but in this case "from above," attempting to show the explanatory power of the trinitarian conception of God. Our goal in this subsection was to illustrate the mutual conditioning of the ideas of exocentricity and *imago Dei* in Pannenberg's treatment in both ATP and ST. The actual performance of his argumentation suggests that he is not a *foundationalist,* for he does not accept either side as immediately self-justified. Rather, together they offer an explanation of human experience that he finds experientially and epistemologically adequate. On the other hand, he is clearly not a *non-*foundationalist because he allows experience (and anthropological data) to shape theological understandings, and aims for broader intersubjective and transcommunal criteria for the rationality of theological explanations. Before attempting to summarize our comparison and contrast of Pannenberg and the emerging *post-foundationalist* model of rationality, we will demonstrate the reciprocity of movements in one final area: the doctrine of sin.

Human Misery: Centrality and Sin

In §3 ("Sin and Original Sin") Pannenberg begins with a thorough review of the historical development of the issue, again with special attention to the exegesis of relevant biblical passages. This subpart of ST, II, chapter 8, has three subsections. (a) "The Difficulty of the Topic," is wholly devoted to explaining the problems in the doctrine due to the historical factors that have shaped it. The second two subsections also begin with a review of historical and exegetical concerns, but focus on concerns related to the specific issues of (b) "Forms of Sin and Their Root," and (c) "The Universality of Sin and the Problem of Guilt." In ATP the entire third chapter is devoted to "Centrality and Sin," although these issues permeate his discussions throughout the book.

Our synchronic presentation will show that Pannenberg was already concerned in ATP with the same two basic questions that he treats in ST (correlated to the last two subsections) under the doctrine of sin: (b) What is the essence or *root* of sin that is the source of its manifestations? and (c) How can humans be responsible or *guilty* for something about which they personally had no choice? After a presentation of some of the relevant historical background, we will examine Pannenberg's treatment of the issues in ATP, and then show how in each case he takes those treatments up into his presentation in ST, which explains the relation of the phenomenon of "centrality" to the resistance of humans to their destiny of fellowship with the trinitarian God.[79]

79. In a footnote that refers to his interpretation of Kant in ATP, Pannenberg makes a comment that reveals the difference in methodology between ATP and ST: "I was not there [ATP] offering a theological evaluation but was dealing with the structural parallels in philosophy and the humanities" (ST, II, 246n.).

Pannenberg suggests that the doctrine of sin presents more difficulty for Christian anthropology today than any other theme. At least two factors have contributed to this situation. First, the classical formulation of the doctrine of "original sin" finally dissolved in eighteenth-century Protestant theology after centuries of failed attempts to uphold it. Second, because Protestant piety attached extreme importance to the recognition of sin as a condition for salvation, when the doctrine of original sin collapsed, this opened revivalist piety up to the criticism that it merely produces inauthentic guilt feelings (ST, II, 232ff.). It seemed morally objectionable that God would impute to his descendants the sin of Adam before they had committed any sins themselves. Some Protestant scholastics and nineteenth-century theologians tried to anchor the doctrine in "acts" of sin, but this failed to retain the universality of sin. As a result, most Christian talk about sin became linked to moralism and legalism. Against some christocentric approaches that argued that only the eyes of faith can know sin, Pannenberg insists that "Christian faith does not create the fact of sin but presupposes it, even though awareness of its depth comes only in the light of the knowledge of God mediated through Jesus Christ" (236). This means we should find the core content of sin in something that "characterizes the whole phenomenon of human life," and not merely in anonymous social structures, but primarily in the human individual, as the classical prophets of Israel insisted.

This leads Pannenberg to his first question: What is the root of sin, the source of all of its formal manifestations? The majority of material in ST, II, chapter 8, §3 (b) was treated in ATP in the context of his "fundamental" theological movement. For this reason, we can move immediately into a summary of his treatment in ATP and then show how it is taken up into the "systematic" movement in ST. In Chapter 3 of ATP, "Centrality and Sin," Pannenberg paid special attention to the contributions of Augustine to the doctrine of sin. Although we must move beyond his emphasis on sexuality and his metaphysical conception of the natural order, the central aspect of Augustine's analysis retains its explanatory power today.

This aspect is Augustine's insistence that sin has to do with a structural relation of the self, a "failure of human beings in relation to themselves" (ATP, 95). Although Augustine often equates sin with desire or concupiscence, Pannenberg points to passages (which he interprets as more central) that emphasize the formal structure that underlies the concept of concupiscence, a structure that has to do with the relation of the self to itself, manifested in a failure to attain selfhood. Pannenberg finds this to be consonant with the findings of modern philosophical anthropology, which emphasize the brokenness of the ego and the self as a result of the tension between exocentricity and centrality. In our self-consciousness, we are aware "not only of identity but also of nonidentity with ourselves" (81). That is, we are aware of a struggle within us between our ego and our desires, whether instinctual or "spiritual."

The main development beyond Augustine has been the modern framing of the question in terms of the constitutive "subjectivity" of human persons. Pannenberg traces this through Kant and Hegel, and finds Kierkegaard's contribution to be particularly helpful. In his investigation of all these thinkers, Pannenberg emphasizes the extent to which their treatments properly deal with the relation to God, confirming my interpretation of his Grundprinzip. However, Pannenberg wants to move beyond merely framing the problem in terms of self-consciousness, as Plessner does.

> The fact of self-consciousness yields only a difference between the self-knowing ego and its own body, and this difference is immediately canceled by the consciousness of identity as well. The fact that in self-consciousness human beings experience an opposition of the ego in itself is not yet made intelligible. Light is shed on this phenomenon only by the fact that exocentricity by its nature means a being present to the other; it is then from the vantage point of the other that the ego approaches its own body and, in its body, the embodiment of its impulses and its striving for pleasure. In its exocentric self-transcendence the ego is originally present to what is other than its body, but it is in knowing the otherness of the other, which is identical with its body, as distinct from all else, that it knows itself to be distinct from itself . . . this exocentric self-transcendence, this being present to what is other than the self (i.e., originally what is other than the

body) constitutes the ego or person. At the same time, however, the ego, in its identity with "itself," also places itself over against the other. This is the root of the break in the ego, the root of its conflict with its own exocentric destiny. (ATP, 84-85)

So we see Pannenberg aiming to find the root of sin in a structural relation that constitutes human existence per se, not simply self-consciousness. This attempt to ground the doctrine of sin in broader anthropological concerns is in keeping with his desire to move beyond the limitations of the reflection logic of German idealism. However, Pannenberg recognizes that this "subjectivist" *(subjektivitätstheoretische)* analysis, especially in Kierkegaard, made an important leap beyond Augustine. In both *The Concept of Anxiety* and *The Sickness unto Death,* Kierkegaard defines sin in terms of the relation of the self to itself. Pannenberg believes Kierkegaard has demonstrated in these books that the human self cannot achieve its identity on its own. This achievement depends on the "Power that posits the self." However, Pannenberg argues that Kierkegaard still has not shown the *root* of sin, for both anxiety and despair are already manifestations of the structural relation that constitutes the self. Here Kierkegaard, too, was held back by a desire to maintain the concept of a state of original innocence. Yet, Kierkegaard correctly saw that the opposite of sin was faith.

This leads us to Pannenberg's comment in ST that, with certain qualifications, we can accept the conclusion of Reformation theology that "unbelief" is the root of sin (ST, II, 251). Pannenberg had mentioned this in ATP (93), but in the context of his systematic movement it becomes the focal point. Anxiety is a natural condition of human existence. The other option is confidence in the future, but "trust in this sense, of course, is not yet faith in the sense of turning to the God of the Bible" (ST, II, 251). Here we see Pannenberg bringing his ATP analysis of "basic trust" into the discussion. In the sense that all humans naturally have a disposition to trust that which can provide a basis for confidence (though that basis remains unthematic), and insofar as we find humans unable to have this confidence, we may say that "unbelief" is a general anthropological phenomenon. But this is not yet the "unbelief" the Bible calls sin, in the sense of rejecting the biblical God; this occurs only in historical encounter with this God. "We indeed suffer the consequence of a life in anxiety, unbridled desire, and aggressiveness, but only in encounter with the God of historical revelation may we say that this unnatural manner of life is sin against God and in so doing identify unbelief as its root" (ST, II, 252).

In ATP, Pannenberg argues that we must find the root of sin in the *natural conditions* of human existence, i.e., in the very structural tension that constitutes human selfhood.[80] Aware of the danger of Flacianism here, Pannenberg is quick to explain:

> But even if human beings are in this sense sinners *by nature,* this does not mean that their nature as human beings is sinful. In this seemingly paradoxical statement the word "nature" has two different senses. In the first half it means the *natural conditions* of our existence; in other words, those limitations which human beings transcend in virtue of their exocentricity as they transform the natural conditions of their lives by dint of the behavior that creates culture. In the second half of the statement, on the other hand, the word "nature" means the essence, the essential nature of the human being as the kind of exocentric being just described. (ATP, 107)

The implications of this move for systematic theology can hardly be underestimated. Let us examine how this treatment in ATP is taken up into ST. In the latter Pannenberg argues that the attempt

80. Pannenberg has been criticized for viewing "exocentricity" as always and essentially good. This complaint was already voiced in 1973 by Galloway (*Pannenberg,* 24). The concern is that he fails to see that this dynamic of being centered outside the self may itself take a neurotic form (or worse). That is, it is also sin to lose the self in the other, destroying the balance of the tension between the ego and the world. Pannenberg admits, in ST, II, 229, that his statements in WIM often focused only on the one side (centeredness) of sin. However, already in ATP Pannenberg saw that exocentricity can also take a "demonic" form (ATP, 530). Further, Pannenberg explicitly notes that Kierkegaard's concept of the "despair of the infinite" (which is a distorted form of the exocentric dynamic of human existence) is sin (ST, II, 248). All living things are exocentric, but they do not all reflect the image of God. *Imago Dei* is a certain kind of exocentricity, viz., finding one's identity *extra se in Christo.*

to find the origin of sin in creaturely freedom had the purpose of absolving the Creator from responsibility for evil (ST, II, 264). However, this attempt has repeatedly failed, so Pannenberg argues instead that

> Christian theology ought to find in the permission of sin the cost of the creaturely independence at which God's creative action aims. As creatures that have attained to full independence, we humans must develop and become what we are and ought to be. In the process we can all too easily give our independence the form of an autonomy in which we put ourselves in the place of God and his dominion over creation. But without creaturely independence the relation of the Son to the Father cannot manifest itself in the medium of creaturely existence. (ST, II, 264-65)

Here we see the importance of the trinitarian conception of God as an explanation for the natural conditions of human existence, which include the structural relation to the self that is the root of sin.

This emphasis on sin in the natural conditions of human existence has a further implication for systematic theology; for Pannenberg it helps to solve the aporia of human responsibility and guilt for the sin in which individuals (universally) find themselves. This leads us to the second major question (c) that Pannenberg treats in subsection §3. Here he takes up the earlier analysis of the concepts of responsibility and guilt in ATP (113ff., 293ff.) and sets them in the context of systematic presentation. His argument is that we can only speak about responsibility and guilt when we imply choice and decision on the part of the agent. These arise only on the conditions that a norm has been transgressed, and that the agent has subjectively accepted this norm. "Thus the sense of guilt, the conscience, and responsibility in some sense concern the linking of awareness of our own identity as an obligation to certain norms and to the demands that they make on our conduct" (ST, II, 262). For Pannenberg, our identity cannot be achieved on our own, but only as the Spirit elevates us beyond our finitude and we are fashioned in the image of the Son by accepting our distinction from the Father. Our failure to accept our finitude, which is the only way to achieve our destiny, is sin. Sin deceives us, promising life. "Our voluntary committing of it is enough to make us guilty" (ST, II, 263). Already in ATP, we see Pannenberg pointing to the need for this kind of understanding:

> Only a concept of guilt that, insofar as it involves the "acceptance" of responsibility by individuals for their own lives, is based on a consciousness of the demands connected with their destiny can be true to the perspective, justified by Christian revelation, that is operative in the Pauline thesis of the universality of sin. (ATP, 136)

So ATP is pointing to religious themes, calling for theological explanation, while ST takes up the call and sublates the anthropological material in a presentation of the fulfillment of human life in relation to the infinite trinitarian God.

We may briefly point to the same dynamics in §4 (of chapter 8 in ST, II) "Sin, Death, and Life." In a historical review, Pannenberg shows that most of the tradition for centuries held that sin was the cause of physical death. In the eighteenth century, however, the idea that death is simply part of the finitude of human nature (as for all finite creatures) became dominant. In the NT Paul does see an inner logic between sin and death, but its presupposition is that all life comes from God. "Since sin is turning from God, sinners separate themselves not only from the commanding will of God but also from the source of their own lives. Death, then, is not just a penalty that an external authority imposes on them but lies in the nature of sin as its consequence" (266). In a footnote, Pannenberg refers to his treatment of these issues in ATP. There he examined them in a five-page excursus in chapter 3. He pointed to the problem that biology understands life as a function of the living cell (ATP, 140), and not as dependent on the operation of the Spirit of God. He found Tillich's concepts of self-integration and self-destruction (which involve participation in the dimension of "spirit") as helpful in moving toward a relating of the biological and theological ideas.

In his ST treatment of sin Pannenberg makes an important

movement beyond the analysis of ATP; he emphasizes that in view of the resurrection of Jesus, Paul sees death in a wholly new light. It no longer has its sting; it is not seen as separation from God. For those linked to Christ, physical death no longer means the end of the human person. He faces the objection that death seems to follow from our finitude, rather than from sin. Here he points to an important theological argument. Christians hope for a life without death (1 Cor. 15:52ff.), but this life with God does not involve an absorption into God. "The finitude that is part of creaturely life will not be set aside by participation in the divine life"; from this it follows that "finitude does not always have to include mortality."[81]

> Fear of death pierces deep into life. On the one hand it motivates us to unrestricted self-affirmation, regardless of our own finitude; on the other hand, it robs us of the power to accept life. Either way we see a close link between sin and death. The link is rooted in sin to the extent that only the nonacceptance of our own finitude makes the inescapable end of finite existence a manifestation of the power of death that threatens us with nothingness. (ST, II, 273)

In Pannenberg's treatment of sin we have seen the interplay of both movements in ST and ATP. The anthropological phenomenon of anxiety in relation to the self and the failure to have confidence in the (unthematic) object of basic trust are clarified and illuminated in the systematic move by arguing that the God of the Bible is that object. Only by participation in the self-distinction of the Logos by

---

81. ST, II, 270-71. Brian Walsh misinterprets Pannenberg on this point. In "Pannenberg's Eschatological Ontology," *Christian Scholar's Review* 11, no. 3 (1982): 246, Walsh asserts that Pannenberg's metaphysics is a "contradictory monism," which results in a view of salvation "whereby the finite loses its finitude" (249). Although ATP had not been published at the time of Walsh's article, Pannenberg had already made it clear that even in the eschatological consummation of human salvation, individuals will not lose their finitude. See, e.g., "Tod und Auferstehung in der Sicht christlicher Dogmatik" (1974), reprinted in *Grundfragen, II,* 152ff. Pannenberg also treats the relation of sin, death, and finitude to Jesus Christ in "A Theology of the Cross," *Word and World* 8, no. 2 (Spring 1988): 169f.

the power of the Spirit can the human self achieve its true identity and destiny, viz., fellowship with the trinitarian God. Similarly, the human experience of feelings of guilt, "which accompanies the consciousness of a concrete fault [and] is an unthematic knowledge of the person's own nonidentity" (ATP, 293) is made thematic in Christian systematic theology, and answered by the doctrine of sin and its remedy, which is the reception of one's identity in relation to God. Finally, the human longing for unlimited life is explained in light of the Trinity: "We achieve liberation from sin and death only where the image of the Son takes shape in human life through the operation of the Spirit of God" (ST, II, 275). From start to finish, Pannenberg's theological anthropology is characterized by the asymmetric bipolar relational unity of "from below" and "from above." Not only does this rebut the charge of foundationalism; it also provides a relational thought-form that may help in the development and articulation of the emerging postfoundationalist model of rationality.

CHAPTER FIVE

Pannenberg and the
Postfoundationalist Task of Theology

The thesis of this book is that the structural dynamics of the relational unity between Pannenberg's "fundamental" and "systematic" theological movements may be critically appropriated for the postfoundationalist task of theology, which is

> to engage in interdisciplinary dialogue within our postmodern culture while *both* maintaining a commitment to intersubjective, transcommunal theological argumentation for the truth of Christian faith, *and* recognizing the provisionality of our historically embedded understandings and culturally conditioned explanations of the Christian tradition and religious experience.

I have not argued that Pannenberg was a proto-postfoundationalist, nor that he now fits exactly into the postfoundationalist camp. Clearly, the postfoundationalist will want to go beyond him, responding to the concerns voiced in Chapter One. In this concluding chapter, I will first summarize the major contributions of Pannenberg to the emerging postfoundationalist model, then examine the areas in which he stands in most need of critique from the postfoundationalist point of view. Finally, I will explore some of the implications of the analysis in the preceding chapters for the constructive and interdisciplinary task of theology in our postmodern culture.

First, let us offer a summary of the argument in reverse. The overall goal of the last part of Chapter Four was to offer a synchronic exposition of the traditional loci of theological anthropology in Pannenberg's ATP and ST in order to demonstrate the reciprocity between the two movements they represent, viz., the "fundamental" (from below) move and the "systematic" (from above) move. The *reciprocity* itself was emphasized because these are not two *separate* movements, but are mutually conditioned, unthinkable apart from each other. This exposition showed how the relationality model of Loder and Neidhardt offers a heuristic picture that captures the dynamics of this reciprocity, including its characteristic asymmetry, bipolarity, and real relational unity. We saw in each of the doctrines examined (human nature, image of God, and sin) that Pannenberg's analysis in ATP pointed to the religious thematic of openness to the infinite and called for further theological explanation. In ST he took up (sublated) the ATP analysis into a presentation of the truth of Christian faith in the trinitarian God. ST attempts to provide sufficient reasons for considering the biblical God to be the definitive revelation of the all-determining reality, the object of our unthematized basic trust and openness to the infinite, i.e., the anthropological phenomena discussed in ATP.

Pannenberg's (full) theological anthropology can only be understood by grasping the reciprocal relational unity of his "fundamental" and "systematic" theological moves. With the appearance of ST, it has become clear that many early responses to his ATP did not fully comprehend the overall goal of his project. G. R. Lewis, e.g., argued that Pannenberg's ATP was inconsistent in "not acknowledging the special revelatory sources of the theological propositions that he so well confirms from general revelation."[1] Our review of ST,

---

1. G. R. Lewis, review of *Anthropology in Theological Perspective*, by W. Pannenberg, in *Journal of Psychology and Theology* 14, no. 1 (Spring 1986): 65. In a review article, "Pannenberg's Theological Anthropology," *Perspectives in Religious Studies* 13, no. 2 (Summer 1986): 169, Roger Olson raises the general criticism that ATP "is more a 'religious' or 'theistic' anthropology than a specifically *Christian* one. . . . The revelation of true humanity in Jesus Christ plays a very minor role in this volume. . . ." I

II, has shown that Pannenberg did not intend ATP as a "full" Christian anthropology, nor even as a limited "dogmatic" anthropology. This should have been clear to readers of ATP, for already there he emphasized that it was an exercise in "fundamental-theological" anthropology (ATP, 21). Understanding the reciprocal relation between ATP and ST (which was already proposed in TPS) is the key to interpreting Pannenberg. Those scholars who expected dogmatic statements in the pages of ATP missed the overall reciprocity of Pannenberg's "theology," a reciprocity that has become even more manifest with the publication of ST.

The earlier sections of my Chapter Four (above) had prepared the background for this analysis, first by expositing the "mutual conditioning" of from below and from above in Pannenberg's works. This involved a critique of previously proposed models that aimed to account for Pannenberg's claim that theology takes place in the tension "between two tendencies." The second section of that chapter provided a historical survey, tracing the development of Pannenberg's use of anthropology in his theological method over four decades. There we focused on his own terminology, where we often found the concept of "Aufhebung."

This emphasis was not a surprise, for already in Chapter Three where we analyzed Pannenberg's attempt to link "philosophy of religion" and "history of religion" *via* a general anthropology as the "basis" for a "theology of religion," we found several uses of "aufheben" (in TPS) to describe the relation. It was suggested that this "linking" might be structurally analogous to the postfoundationalist goal of "linking" epistemology and hermeneutics. Earlier in that chapter, I made an initial case that Pannenberg is consonant with the postfoundationalist model by bringing him into dialogue with the four "couplets" that summarize that view of theological rationality. The first part of Chapter Three set the stage for this dialogue by proposing a new interpretation of the basic principle that drives his the-

---

would argue that we cannot call ATP a "theological anthropology" (see Olson's title) without the careful qualification that it is the "from below" move that anticipates the (christological and trinitarian) "from above" move in ST. Of course, this became more clear with the publication of ST.

ology: understanding and explaining all things *sub ratione Dei,* materially filled out by the trinitarian resolution of the true infinite concept. This interpretation was more fully confirmed in Chapter Four, where we also had to move beyond "aufheben" in order to provide a model that captured all the dynamics of his theological argumentation.

Chapter Two was a presentation of the emerging postfoundationalist model of theological rationality. It was suggested that this more nuanced model can help overcome the dichotomy between absolutist foundationalism and relativist nonfoundationalism, and enable us to appropriate Pannenberg for the contemporary task of theology in postmodern culture. The major middle section of this chapter exposed this model in terms of couplets that described the relation between four pairs: experience and belief, truth and knowledge, individual and community, explanation and understanding. Finally, it set out the most distinctive characteristic of postfoundationalism, the attempt to link epistemology and hermeneutics in a broader concept of rationality.

The postfoundationalist model was selected because it provides the ability to respond to Pannenberg's systematic theology in a way that captures his actual practice. Chapter One reviewed many of the reactions to his method that labeled him a "foundationalist." I attempted to demonstrate there that the assumption that Pannenberg accepts either anthropological or theological foundations as immediately self-justifying is unwarranted; his writings (materially and formally) contradict this reading. The exposition of his thought in light of the postfoundationalist model of rationality has supported this initial conclusion. I am now ready to summarize the findings and make the stronger claim that in spite of a need for serious critique vis-à-vis his failure to deal with postmodernity, Pannenberg may contribute to the most distinctive goal of postfoundationalist thought: the linking of epistemology and hermeneutics.

Pannenberg's Contributions to Postfoundationalism

Whether or not one agrees with Pannenberg on specific material issues, the reciprocity operative in his methodology offers resources for developing and clarifying the postfoundationalist model of rationality. His contributions seem to lie in three basic areas: (1) supporting the four postfoundationalist couplets, (2) providing a relational model for linking epistemology and hermeneutics, and (3) demonstrating how to bring the uniquely Christian concept of God into the interdisciplinary dialogue on the nature of rationality.

First, as we argued in Chapter Three, Pannenberg's treatment of epistemology and hermeneutics, understood within the context of his broader anthropological concerns, helps to buttress the four postfoundationalist couplets. Pannenberg's view of the relation between experience and belief fits the postfoundationalist emphasis on the "already interpreted" nature of human experience, while at the same time affirming that beliefs are engendered and nourished by human experience of reality. He affirms the search for intelligibility in human knowledge, but recognizes the fallibility and provisionality of truth claims. Pannenberg is aware of the social conditioning of individual rational judgments, but believes that this does not affect the nature of rationality itself, which still searches for the best explanations of experience. Finally, Pannenberg's whole interdisciplinary approach emerged out of his concern to see theology as involving both explanation and understanding. Overall, Pannenberg's treatment of the issues within the context of broader anthropological concerns can only help the postfoundationalist cause. In fact, this kind of effort converges with van Huyssteen's call for the development of a broader theory of experience to accommodate all the cognitive, pragmatic, and evaluative dimensions that shape rationality.

A second major contribution was examined in the last section of Chapter Three. There we argued that Pannenberg's attempt to link the history of religion and the philosophy of religion *via* anthropology may be structurally similar to the postfoundationalist goal of linking epistemology and hermeneutics *via* a broader concept of rationality. With the analysis offered in Chapter Four in mind, we can now make a stronger claim. The reciprocity that constitutes Pannenberg's movement "between two tendencies" suggests a heuristic model of relational unity that can help in the conceptual development of this distinctive aspect of the postfoundationalist model.

Using the apparatus developed above, we can illustrate the comparison as follows:

Hermeneutics
History of Religion   (postmodern emphasis)

Philosophy of Religion   Epistemology
(modern emphasis)

On the left, we see the bipolar asymmetric relational unity of Pannenberg's "theology of religion," which we outlined in Chapter Three and illustrated with a synchronic presentation of his theological anthropology in Chapter Four. The figure on the right suggests a similar reciprocity for postfoundationalism. The postmodern concern with hermeneutics drives us to a constant interrogation of our epistemological assumptions. However, the modernist concerns about issues of human knowledge *(episteme)* are not simply negated or left behind; rather, they are taken up into a new critique and reconstruction. This is in accord with the reading of postmodernity outlined in Chapter Two; rather than the end of modernity, postmodernity is a to-and-from movement. Even materially, Pannenberg may be helpful here. In TPS he accepted to a large extent Dilthey's "turn to hermeneutics." Yet as he made that turn, he did not simply leave "dialectic" and questions about truth behind; they were brought into the discussion.[2] Of course, Pannenberg has not engaged explicitly postmodernist concerns, but his treatment of hermeneutic and dialectic suggests that his overall approach would not preclude a move in this direction.

Note the way in which this new heuristic figuration of relationality captures more of the postfoundationalist intention than the simple picture of horizontal arrows presented at the end of Chapter

---

2. E.g., see TPS, 160, and ATP, 491, 512.

Two. The model borrowed from Loder and Neidhardt can help the postfoundationalist emphasize the *bipolarity* of epistemology and hermeneutics, the real differentiation of their respective tasks. It also illustrates the *asymmetry* of the link between them; concrete hermeneutical interrogation has marginal control over (elevating without annihilating) the more abstract concerns of epistemology. Finally, the model captures the actual relational *unity* (or "fusion," to use van Huyssteen's term) of the tensions inherent in the postfoundationalist view of rationality; hermeneutics and epistemology are mutually conditioning, unthinkable apart from each other. Even here, we have no reason to be frightened of the term "Aufhebung," which has proved useful in describing the phenomenon of postmodernity.[3]

Pannenberg's third contribution is in the area of the interdisciplinary dialogue with non-theological discussions of rationality. He illustrates a willingness to bring the Christian commitment to a unique conception of God into these discussions. He believes that Christian theology can still aim to provide the best explanation for the conditions underlying the fact of the contestability of truth claims (pluralism), the best understanding of this experienced reality. Pannenberg can argue that his conception of the "true infinite," which supports a view of truth that finds its unifying unity in God, is a *better explanation* than other philosophical options (such as the non-theological approaches of Haack and Schrag).

The appeal to the divine as a way of securing human knowledge goes back at least to Plato. However, the fact that this appeal has often been made in a foundationalist fashion does not rule out all appeals whatsoever. It is still possible that the idea of God (in some sense) may be brought into a postfoundationalist refiguring of the nature and function of rationality. Such a move, however, would still be intended as an explanation, not only *from* experience but also (as van Huyssteen suggests) *for* experience.

Pannenberg's whole theology has an apologetic force — it shows the illuminative power of the Christian idea of God as the reality

---

3. E.g., see Paul Lakeland's use of the term in a context where he suggests that "the postmodern is the simultaneous cancellation and preservation of the past . . ." *Postmodernity* (Minneapolis: Fortress, 1997), p. 3.

that transcends and upholds the distinction between God and the finite world. Such an interdisciplinary argument must be carried out in all fields, including epistemology, anthropology, philosophy, and history. In this process, the Christian idea of God cannot be held onto as a self-justifying foundation. Nor can it be abandoned to float on a nonfoundationalist raft, abrogating the critical-realist ideal of intersubjective and transcommunal criticizability. The *post*foundationalist Christian, standing critically within the tradition, may reflect on experience and rationally reconstruct (explain) the conditions of knowledge, being, and doing, in light of the Christian idea of the Holy One (true Infinite), testing the illuminative power of the revelation of the trinitarian God in Jesus Christ.

As we saw in Chapter Two, Susan Haack's foundherentist model is concerned with the truth-indicativeness of claims to knowledge. However, because of her *a priori* dismissal of the possibility of using religious experience as justificatory, ultimately all she can say is that "*if* any truth-indication is available to us, satisfaction of the foundherentist criteria of justification is as good an indication of truth as we could have."[4] She seems to be aware of the philosophical intuition that without some concept of God there is no way to explain the conditions of knowledge in any more conclusive way. She traces Descartes's use of the concept of the infinite to secure the knowledge of the finite doubter,[5] and she rejects him precisely for this reason, settling for a more tentative claim about truth-indicativeness.

However, the Christian idea that there must be a unifying unity as the condition for knowledge may offer a better explanation of the human experience of the intelligibility of the world and its susceptibility to intelligent inquiry. The only reason for keeping theological concepts like the "true infinite" out of the conversation would be a foundationalist philosophical adherence to a metaphysical naturalism that antecedently rules out the possibility of a reality that transcends finitude. But leaving huge dimensions of experience out of

---

4. Susan Haack, *Evidence and Inquiry: Towards Reconstruction in Epistemology* (Oxford: Basil Blackwell, 1993), p. 220. Emphasis added.

5. This common unilateral interpretation of Descartes's intentions in the *Third Meditation* has been challenged by Pannenberg; e.g., ST, I, 350ff.

one's attempt at explanatory integration does not seem to be an adequate way of intersubjectively justifying one's beliefs.

In a footnote Haack anticipates and implicitly disparages the complaint of some proponents of "Reformed epistemology" that her model of rationality fails to account for the widespread rational abnormalities caused by "sin."[6] I want to emphasize that the postfoundationalist apologetic being unfolded here explicitly rejects such an appeal to the Christian view of sin as a *premise* in the argument. Proponents of other religions could simply respond that it is Christians who are "sinful" and that this prevents them from seeing the truth. We have here another foundationalist immunization of intrasystemic beliefs that can never produce truly intersubjective and transcommunal dialogue. The doctrine of sin does have a rightful place in apologetic argument, but it must be brought into dialogue with the anthropological sciences that explore human experience and placed into an overall systematic presentation of the explanatory power of Christian faith. Unless it is carefully qualified in this way, it seems to me that *appealing to the noetic effects of sin is among the most appalling of noetic sins.*

Haack finds Descartes's attempt to prove God in the third of his *Meditations* to be viciously circular as well as inappropriately aimed at providing certainty. The postfoundationalist can affirm both of these concerns. Haack accepts the pre-analytic intuition that the human mind operates in such a way that it reaches out for greater breadth of understanding, continually searching for the conditions of its own actual processes of knowing; that is, it aims to know what is true. It is precisely here that the Christian theologian may point out the reductionism. How do we explain the conditions underlying the ever-broadening human search for truth? What is the unifying unity beyond the complex systems we are struggling to understand? Haack is unable to appeal to any such unity, because she has antecedently blocked any reference to religious experience. While Descartes's solution was *too* satisfying, Haack's answer is not satisfying enough. Just because some foundationalists inappropriately appeal to the concept of God as

---

6. Haack, *Evidence and Inquiry*, p. 234n.16.

the ground of certainty does not mean that *any* appeal to the concept of God is inappropriate.

A similar dialogue might take place between the Christian postfoundationalist and Calvin Schrag. We have seen how Schrag's interest converges with the "middle way" of postfoundationalism. He recognizes (following Lyotard) the to-and-fro movement between the modern and the postmodern. Schrag's contribution to those who find themselves thus situated in this "between" is his articulation of the concept of "transversal" reason, which passes "between the Scylla of a hegemonic and ahistorical universalism and the Charybdis of a lawless, self-effacing particularism and enervated historicism . . . [and] charts the course of comprehending the configurative practices and forms of life that comprise our socio-historical inherence."[7]

The question is whether Schrag's appeal to a "transversal" logos that is operative in human rationality requires something "beyond" it, i.e., a Logos that is universal in some sense. His refigured (transversal) logos is intended to replace the Greek idea of the universal ordering principle of the cosmos. For Christians, the "Logos" is ultimately understood as the second person of the Trinity and is not exhaustively defined by the function of ordering the creation, but transcends that order as its free source, existing fully in the eternal trinitarian divine life.

The postulation of the existence of such a Logos (a belief engendered and nourished by interpreted experience of God's self-revelation) might better *explain* why transversal arguments lead to such convergence between intelligence and intelligibility. In his more recent book, Schrag criticized traditional theistic dualisms, such as finite/infinite, arguing instead for a view of the self that is tempered by a *transcendence* understood as "robust alterity," as a "condition for a transversal unification that effects a convergence without coincidence."[8] Can this vision of transcendence accomplish the task that Schrag has set for himself: setting out the *conditions* for understanding

---

7. Calvin Schrag, *The Resources of Rationality: A Response to the Postmodern Challenge* (Bloomington: Indiana University Press, 1992), p. 9.

8. Calvin Schrag, *The Self after Postmodernity* (New Haven: Yale University Press, 1997), p. 148.

and explaining the "self" after postmodernity? The postfoundationalist Christian philosophical theologian may engage Schrag (and others) precisely at this point, debating the explanatory power of various understandings of the conditions behind or underlying the transversal play of critique, articulation, and disclosure.

In fact, we have seen Pannenberg's attempt to overcome "theistic dualisms" as well, which suggests that his model might accommodate Schrag's desire to "disassemble the metaphysical construal of the transcendent-immanent relation."[9] After the disassembly, which reconstruction offers the best explanation? The Christian may argue that the trinitarian conception of God better explains the existence and order of the world, as well as the human experience of transcendence. The postfoundationalist should not expect the atheist to instantly become a Christian upon hearing these explanations; Pannenberg clearly does not. However, there is no longer any reason to claim that religious beliefs *eo ipso* are not rational.

Whether or not one agrees with Pannenberg's specific interpretation of infinity or of the Trinity, surely he has correctly identified one of the desiderata of theological presentation: to solve (insofar as possible) philosophical issues in a way that explains human experience of reality better than other approaches, thereby supporting the Christian claim that the reality of the world is the creation of the God of the Bible. Of course, Christian endeavors to speak of this God and attempts to justify the rationality of theological statements are susceptible to the same limits that constrain all human language and knowledge. Pannenberg recognizes that reason has limitations, but he does not seem to have taken seriously the claims of (reconstructive) postmodernity about the extent of these limits.

A Postfoundationalist Critique of Pannenberg

My goal in this book has been to suggest ways in which Pannenberg's methodology may be *critically* appropriated for the postfoundationalist task of theology. Any adoption of Pannenberg's

---

9. Schrag, *The Self after Postmodernity*, p. 135.

theological method will need to be qualified in at least three ways: (1) a call for more serious engagement with the challenges of postmodern hermeneutics, (2) a recognition of the way in which the postmodern debates about rationality have altered the anthropological terrain on which theology carries out its interdisciplinary task, and (3) a refiguring of Pannenberg's terminology, which still carries the marks of a critical rationalist separation between the "contexts" of discovery and justification.

First, we need to take the postmodern challenge more seriously than Pannenberg does. Perhaps the clarification of the difference between positive and negative modes of postmodernity can help here. "Deconstructive" approaches tend to collapse into self-exempting fallacies, and offer no resources for accounting for the creativity, productivity, and progress of human thought. "Reconstructive" approaches, however, recognize the limits of human knowledge, but accept the challenge to search more rigorously for intelligible explanations. This search does not hope for finality or closure (this side of the eschaton), but for progressively more adequate explanations. Perhaps Pannenberg's failure to engage postmodern hermeneutics is due to his having seen only the "negative" side of postmodernity, a side which postfoundationalism also critiques.

While we may follow Pannenberg in thematizing the truth of Christian doctrine in systematic theology, we must recognize that our postmodern situation requires another step: the very idea of the unity of truth (as guaranteed by and requiring some concept of God) must itself become a theme. The radical nature of the postmodern challenge is precisely at the level of the very need to define truth conditions. It is dangerous to privilege the concept of a unity of truth the way Pannenberg does; this is what has led to his being simply dismissed by so many postmodern thinkers, particularly in North America. The concepts of truth, rationality, knowledge, and objectivity have come under rigorous attack, and the postfoundationalist will insist on taking this attack seriously.

Yet it can be taken seriously without being facilely embraced. The postfoundationalist can still argue that deconstructive readings of postmodernity do not adequately explain human experience. Although we must be careful not to immunize the idea of the true infinite, we can bring our commitment to it into the dialogue, arguing that the Christian intuition of the true infinite, disclosed in the revelation of the trinitarian God in Jesus Christ, illumines all things. However, if we enter the discussion assuming that consensus on the necessity of the "unity of truth" (as a condition for knowledge) may be reached somewhat readily, our arguments may find little hearing.

This leads to a second concern, which is based on the observation that the interdisciplinary dialogue has not been standing still during the last four decades. While Pannenberg makes a good case in his writings that anthropology has been the appropriate terrain for discussing and defending the credibility of theological claims, in our current intellectual milieu the terrain has changed and continues to change. Today the question of the possibility of *having* an intersubjective, transcommunal terrain has become the new terrain. Here the work of postfoundationalist thinkers can move beyond Pannenberg to address the contemporary debate as it has been shaped by postmodernity. For postmodern hermeneutics, the metaphysical question "What Is Man?" (Pannenberg) has been exchanged for the historically relative existential question "Who Am I?"[10] Notice, however, that both questions are still broadly speaking "anthropological." The postfoundationalist Christian can take up Pannenberg's metaphysical concerns about human *nature* into the postmodern hermeneutical discussions, which are increasingly open to the need for this reconstructive move.[11]

10. See Gary B. Madison, *The Hermeneutics of Postmodernity* (Bloomington: Indiana University Press, 1988), p. 155.

11. In "The New Creationism: Biology under Attack," *The Nation* (June 9, 1997), Barbara Ehrenreich and Janet McIntosh decry the deconstructivist rejection of any talk about "natures," which has led some to reject the existence of DNA as common to humans: "But the notion that humans have no shared, biologically based 'nature' constitutes a theory of human nature itself" (12). Here again we see the self-referential problem. These authors argue that "this climate of intolerance, often imposed by scholars associated with the left, ill suits an academic tradition rhetorically committed to human freedom. What's worse, it provides intellectual backup for a political outlook that sees no real basis for common ground among humans of different sexes, races and cultures" (16). Another point of contact is in the postmodern emphasis on the "imagination" (Madison, *Hermeneutics*, 178ff.), an emphasis shared by Pannenberg, as we saw above in our exposition of his anthropology.

These two concerns lead naturally to (or perhaps arise out of) a third problem. The postfoundationalist who wants to appropriate Pannenberg's reciprocity for the task of linking epistemology and hermeneutics in a new model of rationality will need to avoid the terminology in Pannenberg that led so many to consider him a foundationalist. Clearly, his language, which strongly distinguishes two levels or contexts (invention and argumentation), is a carryover from his early interaction with Popper's critical rationalism. Although Pannenberg criticized Popper's vision of "neutrality," his adoption of the "two contexts" framework sounds foundationalist to Anglo-American ears. We have noted that the language of ST is much less foundationalist sounding than ATP, which in turn used less Popperian parlance than TPS. We have also emphasized that the German usage of terms like "foundation" is quite different from English usage. Nevertheless, in our postmodern culture, merely using such terms inevitably raises the specter of foundational*ism*. The new language of postfoundationalist thought, with its concepts of interpreted experience, traditioned understanding, and transversal thinking will better serve theology in its interdisciplinary dialogue within postmodern culture. We may hope that postfoundationalism, with its more robust theory of experience and broader definition of rationality (as being shaped by evaluative, pragmatic, and cognitive factors), may help us transplant Pannenberg's anthropological arguments into the postmodern dialogue.

Implications for the Constructive Task of Theology

If we accept the postfoundationalist critical appropriation of Pannenberg's contributions as described above, what are the implications for the constructive task of theology? First of all, we must see that the constructive task is also inherently an interdisciplinary task. For theology to avoid the insularity of nonfoundationalism, without regressing into foundationalism, it must seriously engage other contemporary attempts to understand and explain the various aspects of reality, which Christian faith asserts is the creation of the biblical God. Further, this *inter*disciplinary task can only be fulfilled by *intra*disciplinary cooperation. By transgressing the strict boundaries between philosophical theology, systematic theology, biblical studies, and historical and practical theology, without effacing the differentiation of their functions, Christian theology as a whole can more effectively engage in coherent and constructive discussion with the worldviews of postmodern culture.

Another important ramification of our analysis impacts the issue of "prolegomena" in systematic theology. Rather than restricting methodological discussions to the beginning of a theological presentation, the postfoundationalist model suggests the need for what we might call "*para*legomena." By this neologism, I mean the ongoing articulation and engagement of methodological issues "alongside" and intertwined with material doctrinal presentation. We can see this idea in van Huyssteen: ". . . the project of theological methodology and 'prolegomena' now becomes part of theological reflection as such, that is, as part of an ongoing interdisciplinary inquiry within the practice of theology itself."[12] In our synchronic presentation of Pannenberg's anthropology, we saw that he integrates methodological issues throughout his dogmatics. He states explicitly that methodological reflections "need to be based on interaction with the subject matter and presentation. They should not be offered abstractly in advance, especially in a situation in which there is so little general agreement on what the subject matter of theology really is, and therefore on what method is appropriate to it" (ST, I, xii).

Nonfoundationalist theologians are fond of quoting Jeffrey Stout's comment that if you clear your throat too long, you will lose your audience.[13] The complaint is that methodological discussions can go on indefinitely and no real theological work be accomplished. This naïve assumption that we can stop talking about method and simply start doing theology only makes sense if one ei-

---

12. J. Wentzel van Huyssteen, *Essays in Postfoundationalist Theology* (Grand Rapids: Eerdmans, 1997), p. 228. Cf. Philip Clayton, *Explanation from Physics to Theology* (New Haven: Yale University Press, 1989), p. 152.

13. E.g., Timothy R. Phillips and Dennis L. Ockholm, eds., *The Nature of Confession: Evangelicals & Postliberals in Conversation* (Downers Grove, Ill.: InterVarsity Press, 1996), p. 19.

ther accepts foundationalism, and claims to have secured the necessary foundations, or if one accepts nonfoundationalism, and claims that methodology is only subject to criteria internal to the community. While Stout may be correct, it is also true that if you do not clear your throat sufficiently, the audience will not be able to understand you. *Can we not clear our throats as we go along?* The postfoundationalist will attempt to intercalate methodological and material reflections, incorporating epistemological and hermeneutical concerns as he or she does constructive theology.

Further, I would suggest that the postfoundationalist model of rationality offers resources to reconfigure Pannenberg's basic principle itself. The phrase *sub ratione Dei* might suggest a neutral observer, for whom "all things" and "God" are two objects of analysis. This image could imply that the theologian is outside the relation, faced with the mental task of describing the relation. To account for the personal commitment of the theologian, and the postmodern concern for existential situatedness, we might suggest instead that the task of theology is understanding and explaining all things *ab intra ratione Dei* (from within the relation to God).[14] This would emphasize more clearly the personal dimension of the theological task as well as the range of the theologian's contextuality, without sacrificing the commitment to a real objective relation. Such a basic theological principle could still accommodate Pannenberg's concern that theology be intimately linked with anthropology (in both a "fundamental" and "systematic" sense). At the same time, it could incorporate the postfoundationalist passion to link hermeneutics and epistemology in a broader conception of rationality. This model would recognize that the human endeavor of theological thinking is always already dynamically embedded in the historically mediated relation of the communally conditioned individual and his or her interpreted experience of God.

Finally, a postfoundationalist method can foster the construc-

14. The intention of this phrase is to point to a dynamic reality that is difficult to express in any language, viz., the constitutive being-in-relatedness out of which all knowing emerges. While it is not a properly formed Latin grammatical phrase, *ab intra ratione Dei* aims to convey this sense of existential already-embeddedness within the religious relation.

tive task of theology in its presentation of specific material issues. The rigorous thematization of relationality that characterizes this view of rationality lends itself to attempts to conceptualize some of the central aspects of Christian doctrine. First, we have already noted the revival of trinitarian doctrine in the last half-century, emerging concurrently with the radical changes in philosophy of science traced above. The doctrine of the Trinity is perhaps the most relational thought possible for the human mind, and the "relational turn" in philosophy may indeed help theologians articulate the uniquely Christian concepts of God and the God/world relation, which in turn will offer opportunities for clarifying the constitutive relational dynamics in ecclesiology and eschatology. The doctrine of the Incarnation obviously requires careful analysis of relationality, in this case between God and humanity in the person of Jesus Christ. Ways of thinking about types of relational unity that involve neither fusion nor mere conjunction are particularly helpful here; the concept of the "true infinite" may be especially parturient in this doctrine. The actual living out of the Christian faith is constituted by a relational unity — the relation between the Holy Spirit and the human spirit, whereby the person linked to Christ is "one Spirit with the Lord" (1 Cor. 6:17). This kind of theological valorizing of reflection on "relationality" per se may also open up conceptual space for eclucidating the destiny of the self. In all of these doctrines, Pannenberg has served us by his tireless efforts to present their truth to contemporary culture. My hope is that developments in the postfoundationalist model of rationality may provide theologians with conceptual tools that will prove their fecundity in radical interdisciplinary dialogue with postmodernity.

Bibliography

Works by Wolfhart Pannenberg

Pannenberg, Wolfhart. "Analogie." In *Die Religion in Geschichte und Gegenwart,* vol. 1, pp. 350-53. Tübingen: J. C. B. Mohr, 1957.

————. *Analogie und Offenbarung: Eine kritische Untersuchung der Geschichte des Analogiebegriffs in der Gotteserkenntnis.* Heidelberg Habilitationschrift, 1955.

————. *Anthropology in Theological Perspective.* Translated by Matthew J. O'Connell. Philadelphia: Westminster Press, 1985. German: *Anthropologie in theologischer Perspektive.* Göttingen: Vandenhoeck & Ruprecht, 1983.

————. *The Apostles' Creed: In Light of Today's Questions.* Translated by Margaret Kohl. Philadelphia: Westminster Press, 1972.

————. "Die Aufgabe christlicher Eschatologie." *Zeitschrift für Theologie und Kirche* 92, no. 1 (1995): 71-82.

————. "Auf der Suche nach dem wahren Selbst. Anthropologie als Ort der Begegnung zwischen christlichem und buddhistischem Denken." In *Erlösung in Christentum und Buddhismus,* edited by A. Bsteh, pp. 128-46. Mödling, 1982.

————. *Basic Questions in Theology,* vols. 1 and 2. Translated by George Kehm. Philadelphia: Fortress Press, 1970 and 1971. Originally published as one volume in German: *Grundfragen systematischer Theologie.* Göttingen: Vandenhoeck & Ruprecht, 1967.

————. "Die Bedeutung der Kategorein 'Teil' und 'Ganzes' für die

Wissenschaftstheorie der Theologie." *Theologie und Philosophie* 53 (1978): 481-97.

————. "Bewußtsein und Geist." *Zeitschrift für Theologie und Kirche* 80 (1983): 332-51.

————. "Breaking a Taboo: Frank Tipler's *The Physics of Immortality*." *Zygon* 30, no. 3 (June 1995): 309-14.

————. "Christentum und Platonismus." *Zeitschrift für Kirchengeschichte* 96, no. 2 (1985): 147-61.

————. *Christian Spirituality*. Philadelphia: Westminster Press, 1983.

————. "The Christian Vision of God: The New Discussion on the Trinitarian Doctrine." *The Asbury Theological Journal* 46, no. 2 (Fall 1991): 27-36.

————. "Christliche Glaube und menschliche Freiheit." *Kerygma und Dogma* 4 (1958): 251-80.

————. "The Christological Foundation of Christian Anthropology." In *Humanism and Christianity* (Concilium, vol. 86), edited by Claude Geffré, pp. 86-100. New York: Herder and Herder, 1973.

————. *The Church*. Translated by Keith Crim. Philadelphia: Westminster, 1983. From Part II of *Ethik und Ekklesiologie*. Göttingen: Vandenhoeck & Ruprecht, 1977.

————. "Constructive and Critical Functions of Christian Eschatology." *Harvard Theological Review* 77, no. 2 (1984): 119-39.

————. "The Emergence of Creatures and Their Succession in a Developing Universe." *The Asbury Theological Journal* 50, no. 1 (1995): 17-25.

————. "Erfordert die Einheit der Geschichte ein Subjekt?" In *Geschichte — Ereignis und Erzählung* (Poetik und Hermeneutik, vol. 5), edited by R. Koselleck and W. D. Stempel, pp. 478-90. München: Wilhelm Fink, 1973.

————. *Ethics*. Translated by Keith Crim. Philadelphia: Westminster, 1981. From Part I of *Ethik und Ekklesiologie*. Göttingen: Vandenhoeck & Ruprecht, 1977.

————. "The Experience of Meaning, Religion, and the Question of God." In *Knowing Religiously*, edited by Leroy S. Rouner, pp. 153-65. Notre Dame: University of Notre Dame Press, 1985.

————. *Faith and Reality*. Translated by John Maxwell. Philadelphia: Westminster, 1975. German: *Glaube und Wirklichkeit*. Munich: Chr. Kaiser, 1975.

————. "Der Geist und sein Anderes." In *Hegels Logik der Philosophie: Religion und Philosophie in der Theorie des absoluten Geistes*, edited by D. Henrich and R. Phorstmann, pp. 151-59. Stuttgart: Klett-Cotta, 1984.

————. "God's Presence in History." *The Christian Century* (March 11, 1981): 260-63.

————. "Gott ist Geist." In *Gegenwart Gottes: Predigten,* by W. Pannenberg, pp. 100-108. Munich: Claudius, 1973.

————. *Grundfragen systematischer Theologie: Gesammelte Aufsätze, Band II.* Göttingen: Vandenhoeck & Ruprecht, 1980.

————. "History and Meaning in Lonergan's Approach to Theological Meaning." *Irish Theological Quarterly* 40, no. 2 (1973): 103-14.

————. *Human Nature, Election and History.* Philadelphia: Westminster, 1977. These essays were lectures originally presented in English universities and then published in German the following year as *Die Bestimmung des Menschen.* Göttingen: Vandenhoeck & Ruprecht, 1978.

————. *The Idea of God and Human Freedom.* Translated by R. A. Wilson. Philadelphia: Westminster Press, 1973. German: *Gottesgedanke und menschliche Freiheit.* Göttingen: Vandenhoeck & Ruprecht, 1971.

————. *An Introduction to Systematic Theology.* Edinburgh: T. & T. Clark, 1991.

————. *Jesus — God and Man.* Translated by Lewis L. Wilkins and Duane A. Priebe. Philadelphia: Westminster, 1968. (2nd ed. 1977). German: *Grundzüge der Christologie.* Gütersloh: Gerd Mohn, 1964. (7th ed. 1990).

————. *Metaphysics and the Idea of God.* Translated by P. Clayton. Edinburgh: T. & T. Clark, 1990. German: *Metaphysik und Gottesgedanke.* Göttingen: Vandenhoeck & Ruprecht, 1988.

————. "Möglichkeiten und Grenzen der Anwendung des Analogieprinzips in der evangelischen Theologie." *Theologische Literaturzeitung* 85 (1960): 225-28.

————. "The Nature of a Theological Statement." *Zygon* 7 (1972): 6-19.

————. "Offenbarung und 'Offenbarungen' im Zeugnis der Geschichte." In *Handbuch der fundamentaltheologie: vol. 2 — Traktat Offenbarung,* edited by W. Kern et al., pp. 84-107. Freiburg: Herder, 1985.

————. "Person." In *Die Religion in Geschichte und Gegenwart,* vol. 5, pp. 230-35. Tübingen: J. C. B. Mohr, 1961.

————. "Eine philosophisch-historische Hermeneutik des Christentums." In *Verantwortung für den Glauben: Beiträge zür fundamentaltheologie und Ökumenik,* edited by P. Neuner and H. Wagner, pp. 35-46. Freiburg: Herder, 1992.

————. *Die Prädestinationslehre des Duns Scotus in Zussammenhang der scholastichen Lehrentwicklung.* Göttingen: Vandenhoeck & Ruprecht, 1954.

————. *Problemgeschichte der neueren evangelischen Theologie in Deutschland:*

von Schleiermacher bis zu Barth und Tillich. Göttingen: Vandenhoeck & Ruprecht, 1997.

————. "Problems of a Trinitarian Doctrine of God." *Dialog* 26, no. 4 (1987): 250-57.

————. "Providence, God and Eschatology." In *The Whirlwind of Culture,* edited by D. Musser and J. Price, pp. 171-82. Bloomington, Ind.: Meyer-Stone, 1988.

————. "Die Rationalität der Theologie." In *Fides quaerens Intellectum: Beiträge zur Fundamentaltheologie,* edited by M. Kessler, W. Pannenberg, and H. J. Pottmeyer, pp. 533-44. Tübingen: Francke, 1992.

————. "The Religions from the Perspective of Christian Theology and the Self-Interpretation of Christianity in Relation to the Non-Christian Religions." *Modern Theology* 9, no. 3 (July, 1993): 285-97.

————. "Religious Pluralism and Conflicting Truth Claims." In *Christian Uniqueness Reconsidered: The Myth of a Pluralistic Theology of Religions,* edited by G. D'Costa, pp. 96-106. Maryknoll, N.Y.: Orbis, 1990.

————. "A Response to My American Friends." In *The Theology of Wolfhart Pannenberg,* edited by Carl E. Braaten and Philip Clayton, pp. 313-36. Minneapolis: Augsburg, 1988.

————. "A Response to the Discussion." In *Theology as History,* edited by J. Robinson and J. Cobb, Jr., pp. 221-76. New York: Harper, 1967.

————. "The Resurrection of Jesus and the Future of Mankind." Translated by M. B. Jackson in *The Cumberland Seminarian* 19 (1981): 41-51.

————. ed. *Sind wir von Natur aus religiös?* Düsseldorf: Patmos, 1986.

————. "Sünde, Freiheit, Identität: Eine Antwort an Thomas Pröpper." *Theologische Quartalschrift* 170 (1990): 289-98.

————. *Systematic Theology,* vols. 1-3. Translated by G. Bromiley. Grand Rapids: Eerdmans, 1991-98. German: *Systematische Theologie, I-III.* Göttingen: Vandenhoeck & Ruprecht, 1988-93.

————. "Theological Appropriation of Scientific Understandings." In *Beginning with the End: God, Science, and Wolfhart Pannenberg,* edited by C. R. Albright and J. Haugen, pp. 427-43. Chicago: Open Court, 1997.

————. "A Theological Conversation with Wolfhart Pannenberg." *Dialog* 11 (Autumn 1972): 286-95.

————. "Die Theologie und die neue Frage nach der Subjektivität." *Stimmen der Zeit* 202 (1984): 805-16.

————. *Theologie und Philosophie: Ihr Verhältnis im Licht ihrer gemeinsamen Geschichte.* Göttingen: Vandenhoeck & Ruprecht, 1996.

————. *Theology and the Kingdom of God.* Philadelphia: Westminster, 1969.

————. *Theology and the Philosophy of Science.* Translated by F. McDonagh.

Philadelphia: Westminster Press, 1976. German: *Wissenschaftstheorie und Theologie*. Frankfurt am Main: Suhrkamp, 1973.

————. "Theology and Science." *The Princeton Seminary Bulletin* (1992): 299-310.

————. "A Theology of the Cross." *Word and World* 8, no. 2 (Spring 1988): 162-72.

————. "Theta Phi Talkback Session." *The Asbury Theological Journal* 46, no. 2 (1991): 37-41.

————. *Toward a Theology of Nature: Essays on Science and Faith*. Louisville: Westminster/John Knox, 1993.

————. *What Is Man?* Translated by Duane Priebe. Philadelphia: Fortress, 1970. German: *Was ist der Mensch? Die Anthropologie der Gegenwart in Lichte der Theologie*. Göttingen: Vandenhoeck & Ruprecht, 1962.

————. "Wie von Gott reden? Ein Gespräch mit Professor Wolfhart Pannenberg." *Herder Korrespondenz* 35, no. 4 (April 1981): 182-89.

————. "Zur Bedeutung des Analogiegedankens bei Karl Barth: Eine Auseinandersetzung mit Hans Urs von Balthasar." *Theologische Literaturzeitung* 78 (1953): 18-24.

Pannenberg, W., Avery Dulles, and Carl E. Braaten. *Spirit, Faith and Church*. Philadelphia: Westminster Press, 1970.

Pannenberg, W., Rolf Rendtorff, Trutz Rendtorff, and Ulrich Wilkens. *Revelation as History*. Translated by David Granskou. New York: Macmillan, 1968. German: *Offenbarung als Geschichte*. Göttingen: Vandenhoeck & Ruprecht, 1961.

Pannenberg, W., G. Sauter, S. M. Daecke, and H. N. Janowski. *Grundlagen der Theologie — Ein Diskurs*. Stuttgart: W. Kohlhammer, 1974.

Works on Wolfhart Pannenberg and Related Subjects

Albright, Carol R., and Joel Haugen, eds. *Beginning with the End: God, Science, and Wolfhart Pannenberg*. Chicago: Open Court, 1997.

Allen, Diogenes. *Philosophy for Understanding Theology*. Atlanta: John Knox, 1985.

Anshen, Ruth Nanda. "The Möbius Strip," preface to the books in the series *Convergence*, which she edits (see, e.g., Noam Chomsky, *Knowledge and Language*. London: Praeger, 1986, xxiiff.).

Apczynski, J. "Truth in Religion: A Polanyian Appraisal of Wolfhart Pannenberg's Theological Program." *Zygon* 17, no. 1 (1982): 49-79.

Augustin, George. *Gott eint-trennt Christus? Die Einmaligkeit und Universalität*

Jesu Christi als Grundlage einer christlichen Theologie der Religionen: ausgehend von Ansatz Wolfhart Pannenbergs. Paderborn: Bonifatius, 1993.

Barth, Karl. *Church Dogmatics*. Translated and edited by G. W. Bromiley and T. F. Torrance. Edinburgh: T. & T. Clark, 1936-69.

Beilby, James. "Proper Basicality, Warrant and Religious Diversity: An Appraisal of Plantinga's *Warranted Christian Belief*." Paper presented at the Midwest Meeting of the American Academy of Religion, April 17, 1998, St. Paul, Minnesota.

Bell, Catherine. "Modernism and Postmodernism in the Study of Religion." *Religious Studies Review* 22, no. 3 (July 1996): 179-90.

Berten, Ignace. *Geschichte, Offenbarung, Glaube. Eine Einführung in die Theologie Wolfhart Pannenbergs*. Translated from the French *Histoire, Revelation et Foi* by Sigrid Martin. Munich: Claudius Verlag, 1970.

Bloesch, Donald G. Review of *Systematic Theology, III*, by W. Pannenberg. *Christianity Today* (August 10, 1998): 69-70.

Braaten, Carl E. "The Current Controversy in Revelation: Pannenberg and His Critics." *Journal of Religion* 45 (1965): 225-37.

Braaten, Carl E., and Philip Clayton, eds. *The Theology of Wolfhart Pannenberg: Twelve American Critiques, with an Autobiographical Essay and Response*. Minneapolis: Augsburg, 1988.

Bridges, James T. *Human Destiny and Resurrection in Pannenberg and Rahner*. New York: Peter Lang, 1987.

Brinkman, M. E. *Het Gods- en Mensbegrip in de Theologie van Wolfhart Pannenberg*. Kampen: J. H. Kok, 1979.

Brown, Delwin. *Boundaries of Our Habitations*. Albany: State University of New York Press, 1994.

Brown, Harold. *Rationality*. London: Routledge, 1990.

Buller, Cornelius. *The Unity of Nature and History in Pannenberg's Theology*. Lanham, Md.: Littlefield Adams Books, 1996.

Burrell, David. *Freedom and Creation in Three Traditions*. Notre Dame: University of Notre Dame Press, 1993.

Clayton, Philip. "Anticipation and Theological Method." In Braaten and Clayton, eds. *The Theology of Wolfhart Pannenberg*, pp. 122-51. Minneapolis: Augsburg, 1988.

———. "Being and One Theologian." *The Thomist* 50 (October 1988): 645-71.

———. *Explanation from Physics to Theology*. New Haven: Yale University Press, 1989.

———. *God and Contemporary Science*. Grand Rapids: Eerdmans, 1997.

————. "The God of History and the Presence of the Future." *The Journal of Religion* 65, no. 1 (June 1985): 98-108.

Clayton, Philip, and Steven Knapp. "Ethics and Rationality." *American Philosophical Quarterly* 30, no. 2 (April 1993): 151-61.

Cobb, John, Jr. "Pannenberg and Process Theology." In *The Theology of Wolfhart Pannenberg*, edited by Braaten and Clayton, pp. 54-74. Minneapolis: Augsburg, 1988.

Corcoran, Kevin. Review of *Systematic Theology, II*, by W. Pannenberg. In *Perspectives* 11 (May 1996): 21-22.

Culpepper, Gary. "Wolfhart Pannenberg's Proleptic Christology in Light of His Trinitarian Theology and Metaphysics." Ph.D. diss., Catholic University of America, 1994.

Devitt, Michael. *Realism and Truth*. 2nd ed. Oxford: Basil Blackwell, 1991.

Dieckmann, Elisabeth. *Personalität Gottes — Personalität des Menschen: Ihre Deutung im theologischen Denken Wolfhart Pannenbergs*. Altenberge: Oros Verlag, 1995.

Ehrenreich, Barbara, and Janet McIntosh. "The New Creationism: Biology under Attack." *The Nation* (June 9, 1997): 11-16.

Fackre, Gabriel. Review of *Systematic Theology, I*, by W. Pannenberg. In *Interpretation* 47 (July 1993): 304-6.

Farley, Wendy. *Eros for the Other: Retaining Truth in a Pluralistic World*. University Park: The University of Pennsylvania Press, 1996.

Farrer, Austin. *Finite and Infinite*. 2nd edition. Westminster: Dacre Press, 1959.

Fauvel, J., et al., eds. *Möbius and His Band: Mathematics and Astronomy in Nineteenth-Century Germany*. Oxford: Oxford University Press, 1993.

Fraijó, Manuel. *Das Sprechen von Gott bei W. Pannenberg*. Tübingen: B. V. Spangenberg, 1976.

Galloway, Allan D. *Wolfhart Pannenberg*. London: George Allen and Unwin Ltd., 1973.

Gózdz, Krzysztof. *Jesus Christus als Sinn der Geschichte bei Wolfhart Pannenberg*. Regensburg: Pustet, 1988.

Greiner, Sebastian. *Die Theologie Wolfhart Pannenbergs*. Würzburg: Echter, 1988.

Grenz, Stanley J. "The Irrelevancy of Theology: Pannenberg and the Quest for Truth." *Calvin Theological Journal* 27 (1992): 307-11.

————. "Pannenberg and Evangelical Theology: Sympathy and Caution." *Christian Scholar's Review* 20, no. 3 (1991): 272-85.

————. *Reason for Hope: The Systematic Theology of Wolfhart Pannenberg*. Oxford: Oxford University Press, 1990.

—————. "Wolfhart Pannenberg: Reason, Hope and Transcendence." *The Asbury Theological Journal* 46, no. 2 (Fall 1991): 73-90.

Gunton, Colin. *The One, The Three and The Many.* Cambridge: Cambridge University Press, 1993.

—————. *Yesterday and Today: A Study in Continuities in Christology.* Grand Rapids, Eerdmans, 1983.

Haack, Susan. *Evidence and Inquiry: Towards Reconstruction in Epistemology.* Oxford: Basil Blackwell, 1993.

Hackman, D. W. "Validation and Truth: Wolfhart Pannenberg and the Scientific Status of Theology." Ph.D. diss., University of Iowa, 1989.

Halsey, Jim S. "History, Language, and Hermeneutic: The Synthesis of Wolfhart Pannenberg." *Westminster Theological Journal* 41 (Spring 1979): 269-90.

Hauerwas, S., Murphy, N., and M. Nation, eds. *Theology without Foundations.* Nashville: Abingdon Press, 1994.

Hinton, Rory A. A. "Pannenberg on the Truth of Christian Discourse: A Logical Response." *Calvin Theological Journal* 27 (1992): 312-18.

Hodge, Charles. *Systematic Theology,* vol. 1. Grand Rapids: Eerdmans, 1981.

Hofstadter, Douglas R. *Gödel, Escher, Bach.* New York: Vintage, 1980.

Holwerda, David. "Faith, Reason and the Resurrection in the Theology of Wolfhart Pannenberg." In *Faith and Rationality,* edited by Alvin Plantinga and Nicholas Wolterstorff, pp. 265-316. Notre Dame: University of Notre Dame Press, 1983.

Hütter, Reinhold. Review of *Systematic Theology, I,* by W. Pannenberg. In *Modern Theology* 9 (January 1993): 90-93.

Ipe, J. "The Hermeneutics of Human Openness." Ph.D. diss., Lutheran Theological School at Chicago, 1988.

Jackson, Gregory D. "Creation and Reconciliation in the Theology of Wolfhart Pannenberg." Ph.D. diss., Southern Baptist Theological Seminary, 1993.

Jansen, Henry. *Relationality and the Concept of God.* Amsterdam: Rodopi, 1995.

Jenson, Robert. Review of *Systematic Theology, II,* by W. Pannenberg. In *First Things* 53 (May 1995): 60-62.

Johnson, Elizabeth. "Analogy/Doxology and Their Connection with Christology in the Thought of Wolfhart Pannenberg." Ph.D. diss., Catholic University of America, 1981.

—————. "The Ongoing Christology of Wolfhart Pannenberg." *Horizons* 9, no. 2 (1982): 251-70.

————. "The Right Way to Speak about God? Pannenberg on Analogy." *Theological Studies* 43 (1982): 673-92.

Jüngel, Eberhard. *God as the Mystery of the World*. Translated by Darrell L. Guder. Grand Rapids: Eerdmans, 1983.

————. "Nihil divinitatis, ubi non fides." *Zeitschrift für Theologie und Kirche* 86, no. 2 (1989): 204-35.

Kegan, Robert. *In over Our Heads: The Mental Demands of Modern Life*. Cambridge, Mass.: Harvard University Press, 1994.

Klein, Günther. *Theologie des Wortes Gottes und die Hypothese der Universalgeschichte. Zur Auseinandersetzung mit W. Pannenberg*. Munich: Chr. Kaiser, 1964.

Koch, Kurt. *Der Gott der Geschichte: Theologie der Geschichte bei Wolfhart Pannenberg als Paradigma einer Philosophischen Theologie in ökumenischer Perspektive*. Mainz: Matthias-Grünewald Verlag, 1988.

LaCugna, Catherine M. *God for Us*. San Francisco: HarperCollins, 1991.

Lakeland, Paul. *Postmodernity: Christian Identity in a Fragmented Age*. Minneapolis: Fortress, 1997.

Lewis, G. R. Review of *Anthropology in Theological Perspective*, by W. Pannenberg. In *Journal of Psychology and Theology* 14, no. 1 (Spring 1986): 64-65.

Lindbeck, George. *The Nature of Doctrine*. Philadelphia: Westminster Press, 1984.

Loder, James E., and W. Jim Neidhardt. *The Knight's Move: The Relational Logic of Spirit in Theology and Science*. Colorado Springs: Helmers and Howard, 1992.

Madison, Gary B. *The Hermeneutics of Postmodernity*. Bloomington: Indiana University Press, 1988.

McGrath, Alister. "Christology and Soteriology: A Response to Wolfhart Pannenberg's Critique of the Sociological Approach to Christology." *Theologische Zeitschrift* 42, no. 3 (May-June 1986): 222-36.

McKenzie, David. "The Rational Theology of Wolfhart Pannenberg: A Philosophic Critique." Ph.D. diss., University of Texas at Austin, 1979.

————. *Wolfhart Pannenberg and Religious Philosophy*. Lanham, Md.: University Press of America, 1980.

Molnar, Paul. "Some Problems with Pannenberg's Solution to Barth's 'Faith Subjectivism'." *Scottish Journal of Theology* 48, no. 3 (1995): 315-39.

Müller, Denis. *Parole et Histoire: Dialogue avec W. Pannenberg*. Geneva: Labor et Fides, 1983.

Murphy, Nancey. *Anglo-American Postmodernity*. Boulder, Colo.: Westview, 1997.

————. "A Lakatosian Reconstruction of Pannenberg's Program." In *Begin-*

ning with the End: God, Science and Wolfhart Pannenberg, edited by C. R. Albright and J. Haugen, pp. 409-21. Chicago: Open Court, 1997.

————. *Reasoning and Rhetoric in Religion.* Valley Forge, Penn.: Trinity Press International, 1994.

————. "Textual Relativism, Philosophy of Language and the Baptist Vision." In *Theology without Foundations,* edited by Stanley Hauerwas et al., pp. 245-70. Nashville: Abingdon, 1994.

————. *Theology in the Age of Scientific Reasoning.* Ithaca, N.Y.: Cornell University Press, 1990.

Murphy, Nancey, and James McClendon, Jr. "Distinguishing Modern and Postmodern Theologies." *Modern Theology* 5, no. 3 (April 1989): 191-213.

Neuhaus, Richard John. "Profile of a Theologian." Introduction to English edition of *Theology and the Kingdom of God,* by W. Pannenberg. Philadelphia: Westminster, 1969.

Nnamdi, Reginald. *Offenbarung und Geschichte: Zur hermeneutischen Bestimmung der Theologie Wolfhart Pannenbergs.* Frankfurt am Main: Peter Lang, 1993.

Olive, Don H. *Wolfhart Pannenberg.* Waco: Word Books, 1973.

Olson, Roger E. "Pannenberg's Theological Anthropology." *Perspectives in Religious Studies* 13, no. 2 (Summer 1986): 161-69.

Olthuis, James H. "God as True Infinite: Concerns about Wolfhart Pannenberg's *Systematic Theology,* Vol. 1." *Calvin Theological Journal* 27 (1992): 318-25.

Pailin, David. *The Anthropological Character of Theology: Conditioning Theological Understanding.* New York: Cambridge University Press, 1990.

Pasquariello, Ronald D. "Pannenberg's Philosophical Foundations." *Journal of Religion* 56 (1976): 338-47.

Peters, Ted. *God as Trinity: Relationality and Temporality in Divine Life.* Louisville: Westminster/John Knox Press, 1993.

————. "Truth in History: Gadamer's Hermeneutics and Pannenberg's Apologetic Method." *Journal of Religion* 55 (1975): 36-56.

Phillips, D. Z. *Faith after Foundationalism.* San Francisco: Westview, 1995.

Phillips, Timothy R., and Dennis L. Ockholm, editors. *The Nature of Confession: Evangelicals & Postliberals in Conversation.* Downers Grove, Ill.: InterVarsity Press, 1996.

Placher, William. "History and Faith in the Theology of Wolfhart Pannenberg." Ph.D. diss., Yale, 1975.

————. "Revealed to Reason: Theology as 'Normal Science.'" *The Christian Century* 109 (1992): 192-95.

Plantinga, Alvin. "Reason and Belief in God." In *Faith and Rationality*, edited by Alvin Plantinga and Nicholas Wolterstorff, pp. 16-93. Notre Dame: University of Notre Dame Press, 1983.

Polk, David P. "The All-Determining God and the Peril of Determinism." In *The Theology of Wolfhart Pannenberg*, edited by Carl E. Braaten and Philip Clayton, pp. 152-68. Minneapolis: Augsburg, 1988.

———. *On the Way to God: An Exploration into the Theology of Wolfhart Pannenberg*. Lanham, Md.: University Press of America, 1989.

Rescher, Nicholas. *Objectivity: The Obligations of Impersonal Reason*. Notre Dame: University of Notre Dame Press, 1997.

———. *Pluralism: Against the Demand for Consensus*. Oxford: Clarendon Press, 1993.

———. *A System of Pragmatic Idealism*, vol. 1. Princeton: Princeton University Press, 1992.

Robinson, James M. "Revelation as Word and as History." In *Theology as History*, edited by James M. Robinson and John B. Cobb, Jr., pp. 1-100. New York: Harper and Row, 1967.

Rorty, Richard. *Philosophy and the Mirror of Nature*. Princeton: Princeton University Press, 1979.

Russell, John M. "Pannenberg on Verification in Theology: An Epistemic Response." *The Iliff Review* (Winter 1986): 37-55.

Sanders, Andy. "Criticism, Contact with Reality and Truth." *Tradition and Discovery* 23, no. 3 (1996-97): 24-37.

———. *Michael Polanyi's Post-Critical Epistemology*. Amsterdam: Rodopi, 1988.

———. "Traditionalism, Fallibilism and Theological Relativism." *Nederlands Theologisch Tijdschrift* 49 (1995): 194-214.

Schott, Faye. "Comparing Eberhard Jüngel and Wolfhart Pannenberg on Theological Method and Religious Pluralism." *Dialog* (1992): 129-35.

———. "God Is Love: The Contemporary Theological Movement of Interpreting the Trinity as God's Relational Being." Ph.D. diss., Lutheran School of Theology at Chicago, 1990.

Schrag, Calvin. *The Resources of Rationality: A Response to the Postmodern Challenge*. Bloomington: Indiana University Press, 1992.

———. *The Self after Postmodernity*. New Haven: Yale University Press, 1997.

Schüssler Fiorenza, Francis. "Review Essay: Wolfhart Pannenberg's *Systematic Theology*, Volume One." *Pro Ecclesia* 2 (1993): 231-39.

Schweitzer, Don. Review of *Systematic Theology, II*, by W. Pannenberg. In *Journal of the American Academy of Religion* (Fall 1996): 685-88.

Schwöbel, Christoph. "Rational Theology in Trinitarian Perspective:

Wolfhart Pannenberg's *Systematic Theology.*" *Journal of Theological Studies* 47, no. 2 (October 1996): 498-527.

———. "Wolfhart Pannenberg." In *The Modern Theologians,* 2nd edition, edited by David F. Ford, pp. 180-208. Oxford: Blackwell, 1997.

Shults, F. LeRon. "Constitutive Relationality in Anthropology and Trinity: The Shaping of the *Imago Dei* Doctrine in Barth and Pannenberg." *Neue Zeitschrift für systematische Theologie und Religionsphilosophie* 39 (1997): 304-22.

———. "A Dubious Christological Formula: From Leontius of Byzantium to Karl Barth." *Theological Studies* 57 (1996): 431-46.

———. "*Holding On* to the Theology-Psychology Relationship: The Underlying Fiduciary Structures of Interdisciplinary Method." *Journal of Psychology and Theology* 25, no. 3 (1997): 329-39.

———. "Integrative Epistemology and the Search for Meaning." *Journal of Interdisciplinary Studies* 5, no. 1 (1993): 125-40.

———. "Schleiermacher's 'Reciprocal Relationality': The Underlying Regulative Principle of His Theological Method." In *Schleiermacher on Workings of the Knowing Mind,* edited by Ruth Drucilla Richardson, pp. 177-95. Lampeter, Wales: Edwin Mellen, 1998.

———. "Structures of Rationality in Science and Theology: Overcoming the Postmodern Dilemma." *Perspectives on Science and Christian Faith* 49, no. 4 (December 1997): 228-36.

———. "Truth Happens? The Pragmatic Conception of Truth and the Postliberal Research Program." *The Princeton Theological Review* 4, no. 1 (February 1997): 26-36.

Sokolowski, Robert. *The God of Faith and Reason: Foundations of Christian Theology.* Washington, D.C.: The Catholic University of America Press, 1995.

Sosa, Ernest. "The Raft and the Pyramid: Coherence versus Foundations in the Theory of Knowledge." In *Midwest Studies in Philosophy,* vol. 5: *Studies in Epistemology.* Minneapolis: University of Minnesota Press, 1980.

Sponheim, Paul. "To Expand and Deepen the Provisional." In *Beginning with the End: God, Science and Wolfhart Pannenberg,* edited by C. R. Albright and J. Haugen, pp. 378-95. Chicago: Open Court, 1997.

Stenmark, Mikael. *Rationality in Science, Religion and Everyday Life.* Notre Dame: University of Notre Dame Press, 1995.

Stone, Jerome. *The Minimalist Vision of Transcendence.* Albany: State University of New York Press, 1992.

Stroble, Paul. Review of *Systematic Theology, I,* by W. Pannenberg. In *Journal of the American Academy of Religion* 61 (Summer 1993): 375-77.

Sumner, George. "Pannenberg and the Religions: Conflictuality and the Demonstration of Power in a Christian Theology of the Religions." Ph.D. diss., Yale, 1994.

Thiel, John. *Nonfoundationalism*. Minneapolis: Fortress Press, 1994.

Thiemann, Ronald F. *Revelation and Theology: The Gospel as Narrated Promise*. Notre Dame: University of Notre Dame Press, 1987.

Thiselton, Anthony. *New Horizons in Hermeneutics*. Glasgow: HarperCollins, 1992.

Thomas Aquinas. *Summa Theologiae*. Blackfriars edition. New York: McGraw-Hill, 1964.

Tracy, David. "Lindbeck's New Program." *The Thomist* 49 (1985): 467-75.

Trigg, Roger. *Rationality and Science: Can Science Explain Everything?* Oxford: Blackwell, 1993.

Troeltsch, Ernst. *The Social Teaching of the Christian Churches*. Translated by O. Wyon. London: George Allen & Unwin, 1931.

Tupper, E. Frank. *The Theology of Wolfhart Pannenberg*. Philadelphia: Westminster, 1973.

van Huyssteen, J. Wentzel. *Essays in Postfoundationalist Theology*. Grand Rapids: Eerdmans, 1997.

―――. "Postfoundationalism in Theology and Science: Beyond Conflict and Consonance." In *Rethinking Theology and Science: Six Models for the Current Dialogue*, edited by Niels Henrik Gregersen and J. W. van Huyssteen, pp. 13-49. Grand Rapids: Eerdmans, 1998.

―――. *The Shaping of Rationality*. Grand Rapids: Eerdmans, 1999.

―――. *Theologie van die Rede: Die funksie van die rasionele in die denke van Wolfhart Pannenberg*. Kampen: J. H. Kok, 1970.

―――. *Theology and the Justification of Faith: Constructing Theories in Systematic Theology*. Translated by H. F. Snijders. Grand Rapids: Eerdmans, 1989.

―――. "Tradition and the Task of Theology." *Theology Today* 55, no. 2 (July 1998): 213-28.

Viladesau, Richard. Review of *Systematic Theology, I*, by W. Pannenberg. In *Theological Studies* 54 (March 1993): 171-73.

Walsh, Brian. "A Critical Review of Pannenberg's *Anthropology in Theological Perspective*." *Christian Scholar's Review* 15, no. 3 (1986): 247-59.

―――. "Introduction" to "Pannenberg's 'Systematic Theology, Vol. I': A Symposium." *Calvin Theological Journal* 27 (1992): 304-6.

―――. "Pannenberg's Eschatological Ontology." *Christian Scholar's Review* 11, no. 3 (1982): 229-49.

Warin, Pierre. *Le Chemin de la Théologie chez Wolfhart Pannenberg*. Rome: Gregorian University, 1981.

Wolterstorff, Nicholas. "Introduction." In *Faith and Rationality,* edited by Alvin Plantinga and Nicholas Wolterstorff, pp. 1-15. Notre Dame: University of Notre Dame Press, 1983.

Wood, Laurence W. "Above, Within or Ahead of? Pannenberg's Eschatologicalism as a Replacement for Supernaturalism." *The Asbury Theological Journal* 46, no. 2 (Fall 1991): 43-72.

Worthing, M. W. *Foundations and Functions of Theology as Universal Science: Theological Method and Apologetic Praxis in Wolfhart Pannenberg and Karl Rahner.* Frankfurt am Main: Peter Lang, 1996.

Yu, Carver T. *Being and Relation.* Edinburgh: Scottish Academic Press, 1987.

Index

268